A Pragmatist's Guide
to Leveraged Finance

A Pragmatist's Guide to Leveraged Finance

Credit Analysis for
Below-Investment-Grade
Bonds and Loans

Second Edition

Robert S. Kricheff

Harriman
House

HARRIMAN HOUSE LTD
3 Viceroy Court
Bedford Road
Petersfield
Hampshire
GU32 3LJ
GREAT BRITAIN
Tel: +44 (0)1730 233870

Email: enquiries@harriman-house.com
Website: harriman.house

First published in 2013. This second edition published in Great Britain in 2021.
Copyright © Robert S. Kricheff

The right of Robert S. Kricheff to be identified as the Author has been asserted in accordance with the
Copyright, Design and Patents Act 1988.

Hardback ISBN: 978-0-85719-849-5
eBook ISBN: 978-0-85719-850-1

British Library Cataloguing in Publication Data
A CIP catalogue record for this book can be obtained from the British Library.

To my parents, Marge and Irv Kricheff, whom I love. They are wonderful people—great parents, grandparents and role models.

Contents

About the Author

Robert S. Kricheff is the global strategist and a principal and portfolio manager at Shenkman Capital, a $27 billion investment firm focused on credit. Prior to this he was a managing director at Credit Suisse for over twenty years, working in leveraged finance analysis on bonds, bank debt, and credit default swaps, and ran the Leveraged Finance Sector Strategy Group. At various times he oversaw emerging market and European bond research.

Robert has lectured at New York University, University of London, and Columbia University, and at industry events such as the Milken Institute conferences. He has a BA in Economics and Journalism from New York University and an MSc in Financial Economics from SOAS University of London.

He has published three books and two ebooks on investment analysis, including *Data Analytics for Corporate Debt Markets*, *A Pragmatist's Guide to Leveraged Finance*, and *That Doesn't Work Anymore*.

Acknowledgments

I would like to thank everyone I have worked with in my career thus far, including all the clients, issuers and counterparties I have been fortunate to interact with—I have learned from all of them.

I would specifically like to acknowledge John T. Lutz of McDermott Will & Emery LLP in New York City for his advice on this project and others, his exceptional legal guidance, friendship and great sense of humor (yes, in a lawyer). I would also like to thank his partner Nathan Coco at McDermott Will & Emery LLP in Houston for taking the time to review the section on bankruptcy and restructuring; his expertise added considerable value to this section.

A thank you to Mark R. Shenkman, President & Founder of Shenkman Capital, and Justin Slatky, Chief Investment Officer of Shenkman Capital, for the opportunity to work at a dynamic firm and for all the time spent sharing ideas. Another thanks to our partner David Lerner for reviewing the section on CLOs and adding many insights that I used in the sections on bank loans.

I am grateful for so many things my Mom has done for me, and that exceptionally long list includes reviewing the earlier edition of this book and preparing notes on how to improve the editorial content.

Finally, I want to acknowledge John Kolmer, a great person and boss, whom I still tell stories about.

Introduction

What's in this chapter:

- defining the market
- how companies enter the market
- unique aspects of leveraged finance credit analysis
- the book

T HE GLOBAL HIGH yield leveraged bond and loan market is several trillion dollars. The market includes financings issued by corporations across a huge swath of industries and issuers from North America, Europe, Asia, and South America, as well as both developed and emerging markets. Debt is issued in multiple currencies and includes both public and private debt markets. It is one of the most unique and vibrant investment segments in the world.

There are numerous careers that interact with these markets, including managing money, selling, or trading at a broker-dealer, investment banking, private equity (PE), research analysis, and capital markets, or advisory roles such as investment consultant or lawyer. For all of these roles that interact with the leveraged debt markets, the basic skills of credit analysis are key to operating effectively and understanding these markets. The skills are also applicable to direct/private lending and exceptionally valuable for those operating in the equity markets.

Defining the Market

The leveraged finance market is generally defined by credit quality. The companies that issue debt in these markets are typically rated by the major credit agencies[1] as below investment grade. Below investment grade is typically defined as below a BBB or Baa3 rating. The market encompasses a wide spectrum of credit risk, from fairly stable BB-rated securities that are close to investment grade all the way down to those in bankruptcy.

Although leveraged loans and bonds have been issued in several currencies, including US dollars, Canadian dollars, British sterling, and Euros, the issuers are still predominantly based in the USA. But the Eurozone and emerging markets are growing quickly. This book primarily uses examples from the US dollar markets.

How Companies Enter the Market

Many companies issue debt that is initially rated below investment grade by the major agencies. In many cases, the funding was raised for expansion or acquisition that added leverage to a company. In some cases, the debt was part of start-up funding. Leveraged buyouts are another common way in which an issuer comes to the leveraged debt market. Usually, this is where PE firms, or individual investors, add debt to buy out a company.

Sometimes, developmental companies issue in the debt markets. These are fairly early-stage companies and because of limited cash flow generation, their debt is rated below investment grade. This type of funding was key for the development of the cable and satellite television industries and the mobile telephone industry. Many of these companies got most of their early funding through the leveraged finance market and probably would not have developed as quickly without financial innovations in this market. New casinos and energy facilities have also come to this market to be financed as start-ups, as well as new economy companies in the arena of ride sharing and electric cars.

There are also companies that originally issued debt in another market that become part of the leveraged debt markets. These are known as fallen angels.

---

1 Generally, the major credit rating agencies are considered to be Moody's, Standard & Poor's (S&P) and Fitch.

These companies were investment-grade debt issuers, but as operations weakened or some specific event occurred, they were downgraded and became part of the leveraged market. This happened to General Motors for a period of time, and during the Covid-19 pandemic, to Ford. The existence of the leveraged finance market allows these fallen angels to still have access to public and private financing and gives first-time issuers the flexibility to finance growth projects.

Companies' ability to access funding in the leveraged finance markets can be a key to survival and can lead to great cash flow growth and job creation. Many companies that have grown dramatically were greatly helped in this process by access to this source of debt financing.

Unique Aspects of Leveraged Finance Credit Analysis

Ever since Michael Milken and his team at Drexel Burnham Lambert helped the modern high yield market evolve, it has been driven by innovation and events. Few companies in the high yield market are stagnant or stable. Some produce steady improvements as they evolve toward investment grade, and others go through transitions, evolving through new ventures or acquisitions. Still others may be for sale or are looking to refinance to return capital to shareholders. Some companies are struggling and may be slipping toward default and bankruptcy. It is unlikely that any below-investment-grade companies are in a state of equilibrium.

The leveraged debt market has many of the features of traditional investment-grade fixed income, and also has the event-driven volatility typically associated with equities. Furthermore, there are structural features within the securities and among the participants that are only seen in the leveraged debt market. For these reasons, the analysis involved in evaluating these investments is unique.

Credit analysis can be very rewarding, and in some ways, the conclusion is more concrete than in stock analysis. It can be said that for analysis to be proven right when buying a bond, an investor just needs to wait to maturity; but for analysis to be proven right when buying a stock, others have to be convinced to buy the stock too. This is true. Correct credit analysis in buying a bond will eventually reap the yield at which the bonds were bought, or sometimes greater if an early takeout occurs. When an investor buys a stock, the only way the price goes up is when more people become convinced that they should pay more for it than the first investor just paid.

In leveraged finance, if an investor buys a bond or loan, and it goes along just fine and pays off at maturity, the return often outperforms many other assets due to the high coupon. Because of this investment's ability to outperform just by fulfilling its obligations, a credit analyst in this market always looks to protect the downside in an investment and considers how things could go wrong. Therefore, when analyzing scenarios for a credit, good analysts must take a cynical approach and constantly ask themselves how they could get hurt. In the interim between a bond's or loan's purchase and its retirement, the prices can move fairly wildly. Analysts must keep in mind the investment time frame within which they are working.

Analyzing these companies and their credit quality is a dynamic process. The tools described in this book are just that: tools. No quantitative model can give a complete answer of whether a debt security for a company will default, or whether one loan will outperform another. The skills covered in this book are used every day and are valuable in determining a security's value. However, making a decision about a credit involves numerous subjective aspects, which could include trying to understand the motivations of management or the impact of new legislation. That's what makes it much more of an art than a science.

Leveraged finance credit analysis borrows tools that are generally associated with many other fields. Some of them come from traditional fixed-income markets, as well as equity markets, but also from probability and game theory. The skills necessary to analyze leveraged finance credits come from both fixed-income and equity markets.

The basic foundation of credit analysis is focused on two concepts:

1. **Financial liquidity**: The goal is to analyze whether the company has liquidity from cash generated by operations, or elsewhere, to pay the investors interest and principal over the life of the loan.
2. **Asset protection**: If the liquidity is not there to repay the debt, the holder of the loan or bond must look to the value of the underlying asset from which it can be repaid. Almost all the other aspects of credit analysis derive from these two fairly basic ideas.

The Book

This book covers the major practical aspects of doing credit analysis. It does not delve into theory. Instead, it focuses on how people in these markets work as they prepare and utilize leveraged finance credit analysis.

A considerable amount of space is devoted to the concepts of financial liquidity and asset protection. The chapters on financial ratios and metrics offer valuable tools for analyzing the quality of these two concepts. A significant amount of space is also devoted to structural issues and the basics of bankruptcy analysis. Understanding them can be key to understanding asset protection, protecting an investment's downside, and explaining how various investments in the same capital structure should be valued relative to each other. One chapter gives examples of how to use these tools to react to breaking news events, as analysts must do every day. Some concepts, such as spreads, floating-rate notes, and deferred pay coupons, are repeated in a few places in different ways because new market participants often ask about them.

Keep in mind that nothing is a constant in the analysis of leveraged finance securities. Many examples in this book are followed by a whole series of exceptions and caveats. When doing credit analysis, nothing is always true, and nothing is ever certain.

Closing Comment

Companies that are in the below-investment-grade market are usually in transition and this can cause volatility in operational results and the prices of the debt instruments. Almost every issue of debt in these markets has certain unique features or structural nuances to it. These factors make leveraged finance credit analysis frustrating, but also challenging and fun. It is not a market in which complacency does well. The words of Oscar Wilde are a good creed for anyone who wants to do leveraged finance credit analysis: "To believe is very dull. To doubt is intensely engrossing. To be on the alert is to live; to be lulled into security is to die."[2]

---

2 Quoted in the *The Portable Curmudgeon* by Jon Winokur, Plume Publishing, 1992.

:

Chapter 1

Common Leveraged Finance Terms and Trading Parlance

What's in this chapter:

- definitions of general terms
- duration, spread, and yield definitions
- a pragmatic comment on yields, prices, and trading terminology

J UST AS SPECIALTIES from firefighting to neurosurgery have their own lingo, so does the leveraged finance market. Understanding the terminology that is common to this marketplace will help analysts to operate effectively.

This chapter outlines commonly used key terms. Some definitions are fairly generic to the securities business; others tend to be specific to the leveraged finance market. In many cases, there are several different words that describe the same thing. Even the market itself goes by several names: leveraged finance, high yield, and the junk market. There are also cases where the same word is used to describe a number of different things. Throughout the book, we will repeat some of these definitions and concepts with examples.

Definitions of General Terms

- *Amortization*: Generally refers to spreading some type of payment over time. When it is used in reference to a bond or loan, it usually refers to the required paydown of a debt instrument. On company financial statements, it refers to the depletion in the value of intangible assets on the balance sheet, whereas the term *depreciation* refers to depletion of tangible assets.
- *Basis points*: There are 100 basis points (often abbreviated as *bp* or *bps*) in 1 percentage point. As an example, 0.5% = 50 basis points, 2% = 200 basis points.
- *Bullet bond*: A bond that is not callable, meaning the company that issues it cannot require the holder to sell the bond back to the company. These are also sometimes labeled NCL, an acronym for the term *noncallable for life*.
- *Call*: The right to purchase a bond or loan at a set price for a set period of time. When leveraged finance debt is issued, the company that issues it will often have the right, for certain periods of time, to call the bonds at a price above where they were sold.
- *Collateralized loan obligation (CLO)*: A securitized structure (typically below investment grade), in which loans are packaged together and used to secure a series of bonds that the collateralized loan obligation issues. There are numerous structural rules around the securitization collateral. The bonds issued by the collateral pool are tiered in seniority.
- *Corporate bank loan*: A loan to a company that, legally, is not a security but a financing. It usually takes the form of a term loan (typically, not reborrowable), or a revolver (can be repaid and then reborrowed). Loans have a coupon and a stated maturity. The coupon is usually a floating rate. Other terms often used to describe a bank loan include leveraged loan, bank debt, and syndicated loan. Traditional bank loans are held by banks. Loans sold to the institutional investment community are sometimes called an institutional tranche or a term loan B.
- *Corporate bond*: A loan to a company in the form of a security. Bonds are also called debentures or notes.
- *Covenant*: A rule laid out in the bond indentures and/or loan documents by which the company agrees to operate as part of the terms of the loan or the bond. Affirmative covenants (typically more of these are in loans than in bonds) are something the company must do. This can include items such as a requirement to report financials or maintain a minimum level of cash flow. Another term for an affirmative covenant is a maintenance covenant. Negative covenants typically prevent or restrict what a company can do.

They may include requirements that must be met before a dividend is paid or more money is borrowed.

- *Credit*: Typically refers to the issuer of the bond or loan, not a specific issue of debt. It can be used to refer to the overall credit quality of an issuer of debt, too, such as, "That is a good credit," or "That credit is in decline."
- *Default*: When the company that issues a bond or loan fails to make a required payment on time. A technical default occurs when a maintenance/affirmative covenant is violated. Most bond and loan agreements allow the company a grace period in which it can try to cure the default.
- *Direct lending*: Usually refers to a loan made privately with an investor and not syndicated among buyers. Typically, this means there is no market to buy or sell this debt. Direct lending is also sometimes called private debt.
- *Equity*: The accounting value of the company, shown on a balance sheet, after debt and other obligations are subtracted from the total value. It is also referred to as book value and can refer to a company's common stock as well. The term *equity value* can refer to the balance sheet equity value or the value of a company's stock. In leveraged finance, it can refer to new money being invested in a company that is not debt, or the excess value that the company has above the value of the debt.
- *Grace period*: Most loan agreements and bond indentures have a set period of time in which they are allowed to cure a nonprincipal default before the borrowers can accelerate and force a bankruptcy. This grace period is usually thirty days.
- *Indenture*: A legal document containing all the terms that the issuer of a bond agrees to.
- *Interest rate*: Interest required to be paid on the bond or loan. This is sometimes called a coupon or referred to as the rate when discussing a new financing.
- *Issuer:* The company that issues the loan or bond; often referred to as the credit.
- *Leverage*: A company's level of debt. In some countries this is referred to as gearing. To be clearer when referring to the amount of debt, the full term is *financial leverage* (*gearing*). Leverage can indicate the total amount of debt or some ratio of a company's debt. In business analysis there is also *operational leverage*, which measures how much an improvement in a company's revenue will increase its profits.
- *LIBOR*: London interbank offering rate—an interest rate based on the cost that banks pay to borrow money overnight. It is often used as the base rate for floating-rate notes and is similar to the US prime rate. If the

floating rate is +1% and LIBOR is at 2%, the borrower would have to pay 3%. If LIBOR were 1%, the borrower would pay 2%. In this case, LIBOR is the base rate. LIBOR is expected to be phased out and various rates are expected to replace it around the globe. In the USA, the main contender is SOFR (secured overnight financing rate).

- *Loan book or bank book*: A summary of a new loan offering that can be given to a potential investor. Sometimes it is private, sometimes public, and sometimes there is both a private and a public version. Generally, it is a bank loan version of the bond prospectus.

- *Maturity*: The date on which the bond or loan must be repaid. Another term for this is *due date*.

- *Money terms*: Refers to the principal due, maturity, and interest rate due on a bond or loan. These terms usually cannot be changed during the life of the loan or bond without the agreement of all the borrowers.

- *Par*: A bond or a loan has an amount that is due at maturity (e.g., $1,000). Bond and loan prices are quoted as a percentage of that amount due at maturity (e.g., 96%). In common parlance, the percentage sign is dropped (e.g., 96). The amount that is due at maturity is referred to as par value, face value, and also as 100. In this example, the buyer would pay $960 for the debt and get $1000 at maturity.

- *Pari passu*: A Latin term meaning "without partiality." The term generally refers to two debt instruments being ranked equally in priority of payment.

- *Principal*: A typical bond or loan has two components of what the borrower owes: the principal amount and the interest payments. The principal refers to the amount of money the borrower owes. The interest payments are a contracted fee that is paid for borrowing that money. If a buyer pays 96 for a loan that pays an interest rate of 5% and it matures in a year at par, an investor will make four percentage points on the principal plus the interest payments.

- *Pro forma*: A Latin term meaning "as a matter of form." It refers to financial statements that have been adjusted for certain assumptions such as a merger or new debt offering.

- *Pro rata*: A Latin term meaning "according to the rate." It refers to a method of allocating something equally and proportionally. If a company has to pay a fee to all of the lenders in a bank loan, the fee will be distributed proportionally, or pro rata, depending on how much of the loan each investor owns.

- *Prospectus*: New bonds are issued along with a summary document of the company's business, recent results, and proposed bond indenture. This is one of the best documents to use to quickly get familiar with a company.

- *Put*: The right to sell a bond or loan at a set price for a set period of time. In some cases, debt holders have the right to force the company to buy back a bond prior to maturity. This is a put.
- *Technical default*: When the company that issues a bond or loan fails to follow one of the rules under its covenants; this usually involves the violation of an affirmative covenant in the bank loans, not a payment.
- *Tranche*: From the French for "cut" or "slice," a tranche refers to a portion of an investment issue. Typically, it is used to reference the different tiers of debt in a capital structure. For example, within one company's capitalization, a bank loan and a senior subordinated bond would each be referred to as a separate tranche.

Duration, Spread, and Yield Definitions

- *Duration*: This is a measure of a bond's price sensitivity to changes in interest rates or spreads. It is quoted in years. The simple way of thinking about it is that if a bond were to have a duration of two years and interest rates were to move up by 1% (or 100 bps), the price of the bond would go down by two points. Usually, lower coupons and longer maturities lead to greater duration. There are many ways to calculate duration, but for high yield bonds, option adjusted duration (OAD) is common. Duration becomes less accurate for large interest rate changes.
- *Spread*: Commonly used as a measure of relative value, a spread employs the yield-to-maturity (see below) minus some interest rate benchmark. In the US dollar market, the yield is usually spread against a Treasury security with an equivalent maturity of the bond. In the European market, it is typically measured off a UK gilt or German bund. Historically, bank loans are usually spread off LIBOR. Spread is a good tool to compare the relative value of bonds (or loans) of different maturities as that value normalizes for the curve in interest rates. Spreads are usually stated in bps. If a bond with a five-year maturity is yielding 5% and the five-year US Treasury note is yielding 1.5%, the spread to maturity on the bond is 350 bps.
- *Spread-to-worst (STW)*: The same as a spread in the prior definition but using the yield-to-worst (see below) date instead of the maturity date. STW is usually the best tool to compare the relative value of different bonds or loans with varying maturities.
- *Yield-to-call (YTC)*: The yield, assuming that the bonds are taken out at the next call date. Note that bank loans typically have little to no call protection, so

they can often be retired almost at any time (which also makes duration a less valuable tool to use in leveraged loans). Yields are typically stated as a percent.

- *Yield-to-maturity (YTM)*: A calculation that takes into consideration the price that is paid for the bond or loan, as well as the interest payments and principal payments expected to be made over the life of the bond and the amount of time to maturity. It calculates an annualized return on the investment. It assumes that cash payments are reinvested at the same rate that the bond or loan is paying.
- *Yield-to-worst (YTW)*: A more commonly used variation of YTM, it assumes the retirement is based on the call schedule and uses the call date or maturity that results in the worst return. It applies only when a bond or loan is being bought at a premium (a price above par), and it calculates the lowest return to any possible call date.

A Pragmatic Comment on Yields, Prices, and Trading Terminology

Here are some simple and logical things to remember about bond prices and yields:

- Bonds trading below par are referred to as trading at a *discount*. Bonds trading above par are referred to as trading at a *premium*.
- When bonds are at par, the yield is equal to the coupon.
- When bonds are at par or at a discount, the YTW and YTM are the same. When they are at a premium, the two will usually differ.

A bond is bought with a coupon of 10% at 102 and is due to mature in one year. One year from now, the investor will get back principal of 100. So why is the YTM less than the coupon? Because the investor will get paid ten points in the coupon during that year but will lose the two points that were paid above the par value. Therefore, the total return or yield will be lower than 10%. If, instead, the buyer only paid 98 for the bond, the yield would be greater than 10%.

Leveraged loans have different structures from those of bonds, and therefore yields and spreads are often looked at, and calculated, differently for loans than they are for bonds. Generally, the stream of payments for loans is less predictable than it is for bonds. First, bank loans typically have a floating-rate coupon; some bonds do too, but it is less common. An assumption has to be made on what that coupon will be over the life of the investment. One option is to assume that the coupon will be constant at the rate at which the loan is bought. Another option is to make some assumption as to how the base rate will move over the life of the investment. This is often done by looking at the levels of futures contracts on the base rate, which show market expectations of where the base rate will be over time. Bank loans are often callable at any time by the company, or sometimes they offer a short period of call protection when the loans are not callable, perhaps a year or less. Therefore, it is harder to estimate when the loan will likely be retired. Convention dictates that yields and spreads are run to the maturity date of the loan and also to a yield, assuming it is retired in three years. To compare these calculations to a bond's yield or STW, it is most realistic to use whichever is the lower of the two calculations for the loan and compare it to a bond's YTW or STW. Loan maturities are typically shorter than bond maturities.

Trading Parlance

When a trader gives a market, it usually is given with a bid and an ask (an ask is also sometimes called an offer). This is common for most security and loan markets. The bid is where the trader is willing to buy, and the ask is where the trader is willing to sell. If the market bid is 98 and the market offer is 99, it might be written like this: 98=99. If the trader is willing only to bid on the bonds, it might be written like this: 98=. If someone accepts the bid price and sells the bonds to the trader, the trader may say he/she has been hit. If someone buys the bonds from the trader, the trader may say he/she has been lifted.

Typically, the minimum size at which a corporate bond can be traded is $1,000. However, in practice, the minimum round lot trade is $1,000,000. The same is true for loans. (This is one reason why it tends to be an institutional investor market and not an individual investor market.)

When prices are given for bonds and loans, they are typically given as a percentage of face value. For example, if a bond were trading at 100% of face value, a trader would quote the price as par, or 100. If it were trading at a discount to face value—for example, at 98 or 99—this would mean for a round lot of a million dollars' worth of bonds, the buyer would pay $980,000 or $990,000. Although a percentage sign actually should be placed after these prices, in practice this is rarely done. More commonly, people mistakenly use a dollar sign.

Sometimes a price is given in yield instead. Yields are usually given as a percentage, so a 10% bond at par may be referred to as trading at par, or at 100, or at a yield of 10%. It is the same price quoted in different terms. Unless otherwise stated, this usually refers to the YTW.

Bank loans and bonds trading at very low spreads (said to be trading tight) are frequently quoted by their STW rather than a percentage of par or a yield. When spreads are used, they are typically quoted in bps. If a US dollar bond is trading at 10% and the equivalent maturity Treasury is trading at 6%, the spread between the two would be 4 percentage points. But this would typically be quoted in bps as a spread of 400 bps.

Interest payments are made on specific dates, generally monthly on bank loans and semi-annually on bonds. But the bonds continue to accrue interest between the payment dates. In a typical transaction, when a bond is bought, the full amount that is paid is the agreed-upon price plus accrued interest. For example, if a bond has a 10% coupon and pays semi-annually, it pays 5% on each interest payment date. If someone bought the bond halfway between the interest payment dates (ninety days after the last coupon payment), that investor would pay the price set for the bond plus 2.5% of accrued interest. If a bond is trading without accrued interest because it is in default, it is said to be trading flat.

Closing Comment

Terminology can sometimes be confusing, especially on pricing and when several words mean the same thing. This is true in any specialty field. Some of the concepts that can be a bit more difficult to grasp will be repeated in various sections of the book, with examples.

Chapter 2

Defining the Market: Ratings Agencies and Indexes

What's in this chapter:

- the credit rating agencies
- the indexes

THE LEVERAGED FINANCE market is generally defined to include bonds and loans issued by corporations to which the major credit rating agencies (Moody's, S&P, and sometimes Fitch) have assigned ratings that are below investment grade, or speculative grade. Many nonrated loans and bonds are also considered part of the leveraged finance market. There are various indexes that track the below-investment-grade bond and loan market, and they each tend to define the market slightly differently.

The Credit Rating Agencies

Many pools of investment money have strict limits on investing in bonds and loans rated below investment grade. For example, in most countries around the world, regulators will require regulated entities, such as banks and insurance companies, to hold a higher level of reserves against investments that are below investment grade. This is done to establish a cushion against potential losses, but it also cuts into the return of those investments.

Exhibit 2.1 lists the major categories for Moody's and S&P, which also add qualifiers to the ratings. While it is not shown in the exhibit, each letter rating will usually have a qualifier attached to it. Moody's uses a range of numerals 1–3 and S&P uses plus and minus signs. If a bond is assigned an A1 rating and then moves down to an A2 rating, a bond investor may in industry parlance say, "it was notched down." If a rating is moved from an A3 to a Baa1 and the "letter rating" changed the investor would say it was "downgraded." The latter will have a bigger impact on how the bond trades.

Exhibit 2.1: Major Ratings Categories of the Major Agencies

Moody's	S&P
Aaa	AAA
Aa	AA
A	A
Baa	BBB
Ba	BB
B	B
Caa	CCC
Ca	CC
C	D
D	

Bonds that are rated BBB-/Baa3 and above are considered investment grade or nonspeculative. In Moody's ratings descriptions, the Ba bonds are the first to have the qualifier that they are "judged to be speculative and are subject to substantial credit risk."[3] S&P includes a paragraph describing all the bonds rated BB and below, stating that they are "regarded as having significant speculative characteristics. 'BB' indicates the least degree of speculation and 'C' the highest. While such obligations will likely have some quality and protective

---

3 "Ratings Symbols and Definitions," Moody's Investors Service Inc., September 2020, www.moodys.com/sites/products/AboutMoodysRatingsAttachments/MoodysRatingSymbolsandDefinitions.pdf.

characteristics, these may be outweighed by large uncertainties or major exposure to adverse conditions."[4]

Criticism of the ratings agencies has been laid out in great detail since the Great Financial Crisis (GFC), but the agencies can add value and play an important role in the market. These agencies are typically shown projections from the companies. Analysts can glean insights from agency write-ups, particularly on new issues. The agencies also highlight short-term and long-term concerns and what might trigger a rating change. However, their value to analysts or investors trying to determine relative value and the future direction of a credit is very limited.

The agencies are typically backward-looking in their analysis. More importantly, in a market such as the leveraged finance market, which is heavily event driven, the agencies have historically responded slowly to news events that can impact the credit quality of an issuer. They also give little to no insight into how the debt will trade and which prices represent value.

How bonds and loans trade is one of the most important factors for market participants, and the ratings often do not help much. At any given time, an investor can typically find two identically rated single B issues trading at yields that are 1,000 bps apart or more, a significant variance. The variance within the CCC-rated category can be even greater. This shows how little the markets sometimes value the agencies' ratings when they try to determine the actual value and risks of below-investment-grade debt.

Some trigger points in ratings can have a meaningful impact on the trading levels, but it often takes a while after the facts are in place for the agencies to react. For example, many bond and loan buyers are limited or restricted from buying investments rated CCC- or lower. Similarly, many funds have limits on buying issues rated less than investment grade, so an upgrade to BBB- can add to the universe of potential buyers and cause prices to rally. These crossover points can influence trading levels, although much of the price movement often occurs well before the ratings agencies get around to actually upgrading or downgrading the debt. One of the most valuable sections of an agency write-up can be where it outlines which targets would have to be met to cause an upgrade or downgrade. It is a good idea to monitor credits that are

4 "S&P Global Ratings Definitions," Standard & Poor's Financial Services LLC, August 2020, www.standardandpoors.com/en_US/web/guest/article/-/view/sourceId/504352.

barely clinging to an investment-grade rating and may be on the watch for a downgrade. These credits may be the next opportunities in high yield.

Nonrated Debt

Some bonds and loans in the below-investment-grade market are nonrated. This is very common in the convertible bond market, but not as common in the nonconvertible bond and loan markets. The ratings agencies charge to rate a company, and some companies therefore choose to forgo this service. The general view is that, in the nonconvertible market, not having a rating may cause the company issuing the debt to pay a higher coupon because this lack of rating will limit the number of buyers. Sometimes a company that expects a CCC rating or lower may decide that the agency rating won't help it and therefore chooses to not hire an agency's services. However, agencies may choose to rate a company even if they are not hired to do so. Sometimes analysts will prepare a shadow rating for a nonrated debt instrument. Private debt is usually not rated.

Convertible bonds are typically not included when describing the below-investment-grade universe, but they are an important hybrid market to watch. Sometimes convertible bonds trade at such low levels, or the stock price has moved so much, that they are a *busted convert*, meaning that the feature to convert the bond to equity is perceived to have no value. In these cases, the convertible is trading as a regular bond would and may attract traditional fixed-income buyers, but many leveraged finance investors have restrictions on owning convertible bonds.

Indexes

The idea of an index to measure how an investment or asset class is performing is not new, as the Dow Jones stock market indexes go back to the 1880s. Over the last few decades, investors have increasingly focused on indexes and used these indexes to define a market. Several indexes track the high yield bond and leveraged loan markets in both the USA and globally.

The indexes have very specific inclusion rules with the result that not all bonds are included in them. These rules may define a minimum issue size, a specific maturity range, or currencies that are either included or excluded from the index. From time to time, the index companies change these rules, which can sometimes make the indexes change more than the actual market does. Many investors have their performance measured against an index (often referred to as a benchmark). Changes in an index may be driven more by business reasons than by logic. It is important to remember that these indexes are not altruistic or academic; they are big for-profit businesses. While those who run indexes are likely to be sensitive to maintaining the integrity of their products, they also want more firms to use their products more frequently, which can add a bias to decisions on how an index is run.

Closing Comment

The rating agencies and the indexes tend to be the organizations that define the market in leveraged finance. Ratings do not determine the trading level of bonds and loans, but can influence them. Since many investors are measured relative to an index, the inclusion or exclusion of a debt investment in a major index can impact buying and selling of that investment. It is important to remember that these are businesses run for profit, and as such, they may evolve in ways that benefit their business model but not the markets. Both the rating agencies and the indexes have numerous flaws and shortcomings, but are important to the markets and widely followed, so they need to be understood.

Chapter 3
The Participants

What's in this chapter:

- the issuers
- private equity
- the sell side
- the buy side
- the major types of investors in the market
- how each participant operates in the market

THE LEVERAGED FINANCE market has three major groups of participants. The first is that of the issuers, which in this case are corporations that choose to borrow money in these markets; PE firms are a specific type of issuer. The second group is that of the sell side, which, for the purposes of this discussion, involves all aspects of structuring, advising, and placing the debt instruments that make up the market. They also usually are involved in helping to facilitate trading and therefore, to a certain extent, are investors as well. Third is the buy side. This is a diverse group of investors in these financial instruments, which, for the purposes of this discussion, includes allocators of capital. This simplified discussion excludes major subsets of market participants, such as lawyers, electronic trading platforms, and street brokers.

The Issuers

In the leveraged finance market, debt issuers are corporations or corporation-like entities. The reasons for their issue of debt can be very diverse. They may simply be looking for more capital to expand. They may be growing companies that utilize various forms of less permanent capital to expand and are looking to put in place a more permanent debt structure (maybe a construction loan for a new project). They may be looking to fund an acquisition or may be facing an unusual obligation, such as a lawsuit or tax settlement.

Alternatively, a company may be issuing debt for purely financial reasons. It may want to replace older maturing debt or return some capital to shareholders through a special dividend or stock buybacks, and is willing to use debt to finance these activities—or it may be going private, and the debt will finance this transaction (effectively, another way of returning capital to shareholders).

Some companies are quite comfortable staying rated below investment grade for their lifetime. Management teams in certain industries may believe that their company has an optimal capital structure that keeps it below investment grade, based on its growth characteristics and tax structure, and this is the best way for it to maximize long-term returns for its owners. Other entities may believe that the lower leverage and lower cost of capital that an investment-grade rating brings are the best route to take for a company's capital structure. Some companies strive to be upgraded and leave the market; others are more comfortable with increased leverage; others are struggling to improve operations, deleverage, and avoid bankruptcy.

Private Equity

Private equity firms are an important participant in the market. They fall into the issuer category, but as a special type of issuer. PE firms generally raise funds from investors in partnerships that are designed to buy companies, increase the value of the enterprises they buy, and, over time, monetize these gains. They typically do this by selling the company, going public, paying themselves dividends, or using some other means to return value to themselves and their investors.

PE firms often use leverage in their acquisitions to enhance their returns. Financings to fund PE transactions make up a large part of the leveraged finance market. By their nature, the companies owned by PE firms tend to be event driven as the sponsors (another term for PE buyers) look to enhance value and eventually monetize their investment. More rapid monetization can increase their returns. Given the PE firms' goal to enhance the return on the equity and the debt investors' goal to, typically, see a credit improve or have their debt retired at a premium, there can be a conflict between the goals of the two groups.

The Sell Side

The sell side is primarily made up of investment banks, which play several major roles in the market. They advise corporations on financial issues and help them structure financings, which could take any number of forms: bonds, loans, convertible bonds, stock (equity), and asset-backed structures.

Investment banks also have a capital markets function in which they market and sell to appropriate investors the securities they helped structure. After the debt is placed, most investment banks act as a broker-dealer and participate in making markets in the securities and loans that they placed (and that other banks placed as well).

When structuring debt funding for a company, the investment bank will advise the company that is issuing the financing on the structure, size, and covenants of the borrowing, as well as the likely interest rate that investors will require for them to buy the issue. Then they undertake due diligence on the company, help educate potential investors about the loans, and decide what the final terms on the debt offering will be, based on investor feedback.

The process is similar when bond or loan issuance is involved. However, when the funding is in the form of a loan, the bank loan arranger (or agent bank) historically has held or retained a reasonable amount of the loan on its books. If there is a revolving facility, the banks usually have held this obligation as well. Additionally, bank loan agreements usually require the approval of the agent bank to trade (or transfer) a loan from one investor to another, which, theoretically, can limit the liquidity. In the bond market, the investment bank is required to fully distribute the issue before it can start market making in the bonds. This is an interesting juxtaposition between the two markets. Once a bond is distributed and can trade freely, the banks can hold positions on their balance sheet; these are typically trading positions.

Sometimes an investment bank will commit to financing a transaction with its own balance sheet, in case it cannot place the financing in the marketplace. Issuers can find this beneficial because they have a backstop, knowing they will have the financing in place. This type of backstopped financing is usually more costly than what it would be in a regular best-efforts placement in the market. The bank will make this type of commitment to win the business and would likely only commit to it in a competitive situation. This type of transaction is viewed as a bridge to a public financing and is typically called a bridge loan, which is most common in transactions involving an acquisition, especially those involving a PE firm as the buyer. This committed financing is often important to the company that is being bought because it does not want its shareholders taking the financing risk.

An important role of the investment bank, or commercial bank, is that it can use its balance sheet to provide liquidity to the investors who bought the initial debt. The initial investors may want to buy more or sell some, or all, of the position they own over time. The bank also looks to keep investment professionals abreast of developments at the corporation that issued the debt. Secondary trading has changed significantly since the GFC. There were significant restrictions put in place on the size and type of positions that investment banks could hold. While many of these rules have been rolled back, as the investor base has grown and the number of investment banks is less than it was pre-GFC, the amount of capital that these banks have relative to the market's size appears to be much smaller than it was. Additionally, electronic trading has increased dramatically as a method of transacting for investors and its popularity will likely grow over time.

The sell side includes a plethora of different types of personnel. As a sampling, these include bankers, salesmen, traders, analysts, liability management teams, and capital markets personnel. The sell-side universe can also include law firms, accountants, and middle market employees who help settle transactions.

The Buy Side

The buy side encompasses a broad range of buyers and investors of leveraged finance instruments. These asset managers get the funds they invest from individuals, pensions and other retirement funds, insurance accounts, endowments, and similar sources. Individual investors rarely invest directly in high yield corporate debt.

Individual investors may put money into mutual funds or exchange traded funds (ETFs) that are dedicated to the leveraged debt markets. These investment vehicles are called commingled because an investor's money is pooled with that of other investors. There are also commingled funds that might invest across a number of different assets, and part of the fund may be allocated to buy leveraged debt securities. These funds could be diversified fixed-income funds or even equity funds with a broad mandate.

The Major Types of Investors in the Market

A significant number of assets that are managed by money managers are not in mutual funds. These may be separately managed accounts that are segregated pools of money from pension funds, endowments, or wealthy individuals. Individuals may also have life insurance policies. Part of the large pool of investments that insurance companies invest in can encompass high yield loans and bonds. Sometimes large organizations such as insurance companies will manage the money in-house, while others will allocate the money to money managers.

Many large companies that allocate money to outside money managers will have a team that analyzes and chooses what portion of their capital they want to allocate to which asset classes, which strategies, and which managers. There are also large, professional, independent organizations that can be hired to help allocate to third-party managers. These professional allocators may only carry out due diligence, research, and approval of managers, but they also might handle decisions on diversification and asset class weighting. The allocators are a very important part of the buy side.

Institutional managers as well as wealthy individuals and others can choose to invest in alternative investment vehicles, such as hedge funds or distressed investment funds. Hedge funds and distressed investment funds can short securities as well as go long. Many hedge funds and other more opportunistic investors are not dedicated to investing in the leveraged debt markets and may opportunistically increase or decrease their overall exposure to the asset class. Sometimes a hedge fund may want to strategically get broad market exposure. One way to do this is by buying into an ETF. These funds offer trading liquidity throughout the trading day. Most of the leveraged finance ETFs are designed to copy some broad index that, theoretically, mimics the market.

These ETFs are often referred to as passive investments because they are designed to invest along a set of rules and not differentiate between good or bad holdings. This differs from active managers who make specific allocations within a portfolio to individual investments, industries, credit quality, durations, and other specific portfolio features. Active managers do not want to own everything in an index. This passive versus active debate has been a major discussion across the investment world for several years.

How Each Participant Operates in the Market

Structured products are also buyers of leveraged finance debt. These structures are usually collateralized debt obligations (CDOs) or CLOs. In the current market, CLOs are much more popular and are estimated to account for about 60% of the buying of leveraged loans. These products have a set of rating and diversity rules that they have to follow when buying debt. The loans that the CLO buys are the collateral and then bonds are issued, backed by the collateral. These loans have different seniority levels, which dictate their payment priority. Typically, the loans making up the collateral and the notes that are issued by the CLO have floating-rate coupons, and the managers of the CLOs will look to match assets (the collateral) and liabilities (the bonds issued by the CLO) to make sure they can service interest expenses. There is also a market in trading these CLO bond tranches. Investors from around the globe have bought CLO bonds.

Direct lending and private debt markets are sometimes included as part of the leveraged debt markets. Private placements have been a longtime feature of the debt markets. In the last decade there has been a boom in the USA, and to some extent in Europe, in direct lending. Private debt can take many forms, but much of the issuance is used to fund midsized and smaller, PE leveraged buyouts. These transactions are placed directly between the investment firm and the issuing company and do not usually use a sell-side firm. In addition, these investments are generally not syndicated, so there is only one owner of the debt and no market on which these direct loans are traded. The skill used in assessing whether a loan should be made in these direct private market transactions is the same credit skill used in public markets.

Different investment vehicles on the buy side also often offer different types of liquidity to the investors. In mutual funds, investors can usually buy and sell daily. In ETFs, they can do so throughout the trading day. Other vehicles may have only monthly subscriptions and withdrawals. Some specialized funds, such as direct lending, special situation, distressed, or hedge funds, may have several years of lock-up.

Different Fee Structures Abound on the Buy Side

Fee structures on the buy side vary greatly from those on the sell side. On the sell side, most firms get paid fairly comparable fees for advising a company, placing a new issue, and trading issues in the secondary market. On the buy side, the fee structures can vary much more widely. ETF managers tend to charge very low fees as they are typically not making active investment decisions. Many asset managers will charge a flat fee based on a percentage of the assets under management. Hedge funds and some specialized investment vehicles may charge a performance fee. The fee structures can impact investment styles.

Closing Comment

There are many different roles at PE firms, issuing companies, the sell side, and the buy side. Almost all of these jobs require some understanding of credit analysis. Depending on the job and the firm, the ultimate goal of how credit analysis is used may vary. The design, organization, and prioritization of goals within credit analysis can be tapered to meet different needs and different organizations.

Chapter 4

Features of Bank Loans

What's in this chapter:

- basic types of bank loan
- bank loan structures
- covenants, waivers, and amendments

L EVERAGED BANK LOANS have features similar to bonds but also many unique characteristics. Leveraged bank loans can be referred to as bank loans, syndicated loans, term loans, or just loans. Despite being referred to as bank loans, in the leveraged loan market they are often not held by banks. They are usually structured by commercial banks and then syndicated to buyers that form a diverse group of institutional investors, such as mutual funds, CLOs, and insurance and pension funds. This nonbank loan market is often called the institutional loan market, or the syndicated loan market, and tranches of term loans sold to nonbank institutions are also often referred to as term loan B (TL B). Term loan A tranches are typically held by commercial banks. These A tranches may have better terms, perhaps a slightly shorter maturity, and often will have more debt amortization. Term loan B tranches rarely have meaningful amortization. Typical institutional bank loans differ from typical bonds in that the loans tend to have security (e.g., a more senior ranking), a shorter maturity, a floating-rate coupon versus a fixed rate, and less call protection.

Basic Types of Bank Loan

Bank loans broadly can be divided into revolving credit lines and term loans. The revolving credit lines, or revolvers, are generally for temporary funding of a business. They can be borrowed and repaid and reborrowed over the life of the loan. Revolvers are not normally meant to be long-term financing and tend to have shorter maturities than term loans. Some asset-backed loans are structured similarly to revolvers. They may include a revolver in which the amount that can be borrowed (borrowing base) is based on and secured by the value of an asset, such as customer receivables. Revolvers can be an attractive way for companies with short-term funding needs to get temporary capital, especially if the cash needs are a regular seasonal occurrence.

Revolvers are commonly held by banks rather than institutional investors. This is partly because the borrower pays a small fee on the undrawn portion of the revolver until that money is actually borrowed, after which the borrower pays a more regular interest rate on the borrowed portion of the revolver. The institutional investors need to hold money in reserve in case the company draws the revolver, and while the money remains undrawn, the investors earn only a *de minimis* rate. Because of the reserve banking system, it is easier for banks to provide these types of loan than it is for institutions, which often do not have the ability to call capital from their investors.

Usually, term loans are more permanent, and it is not atypical for them to have five-year maturities. Generally, if the principal is repaid on a term loan, it cannot be reborrowed. Term loans may also have principal amortization, in which a certain amount is required to be repaid each year, though this is a more common feature in the traditional bank loan market than in the institutional market.

Bank Loan Structures

Loans are not securities as bonds and stocks are. They are not traded on an exchange, and their documentation can vary greatly compared to that of bonds. The documents drawn up between the issuing company (borrower) and the investor (lender) constitute a loan contract and there is much less standardization than in bond documents, although standardization has increased over time. One of the nuances of contract management is that a contract cannot be subjected to a traditional type of short sale as a security can be.

As with bonds, a lead bank usually underwrites the loans, and the bank is the arranger and, usually, the administrative agent (agent bank), which has certain obligations regarding documentation, due diligence, and information flow. However, an important difference is that in the sale of a new-issue bond, the underwriter generally has to have the issue fully distributed and off its own balance sheet to begin making markets and providing liquidity for the issue. In the bank market, the agent and, to a lesser extent, others involved in distributing the bank loan, had traditionally been expected to hold onto part of the loan. It is increasingly common for underwriting banks to own little or none of the leveraged loan after it is syndicated.

Trading loans can take more documentation than bonds because they are contracts and do not have central clearing for trades as securities do. There are two different ways to trade bank loans: by assignment (more common) or through participation. With assignment, the purchaser of the bank debt ends up owning the piece of bank debt and has voting rights, and so on. Assignments typically need to get approval from the agent bank and the company. This can limit the number of market makers in a loan. The other way of trading bank debt is through participation. Here a buyer gets a legal claim to the economics of owning the bank debt, but the debt actually remains held by the seller. Voting rights and such are retained by the seller.

Loans usually have floating-rate coupons, meaning that they are priced as a spread off some index (e.g., base rate) that measures short-term borrowing costs in the economy. Traditionally this was LIBOR, but other short-term lending rates are being developed to use as the base rate. The coupon moves up and down over time if the base rate moves. If a loan were to have a spread of +300 bps and the base rate were 200 bps, the loan would be paying investors an interest rate of 5%. If the base rate were to move to 250 bps, the interest rate that the loan would pay would be 5.5%. Sometimes a minimum floor is put on the base rate, so if the loan were to be priced at +300 bps with a floor of +100 bps, even if the base rate were to drop to +50 bps, the loan would still pay a coupon of 4%, not 3.5%. The coupon usually resets every three months and the base rate is a three-month rate. Some agreements give the borrower the option to choose between one and three months. The base rate would typically also shift from a one-month borrowing rate to a three-month rate, as would the timing of coupon payments.

There are nuances that can impact the issuer of a bank loan's cost of capital. Sometimes an issuer or investor pays a fee to swap their loan for a fixed-rate coupon for part or all of the life of the loan. Sometimes, in more traditional bank loans, there is a grid that lowers or increases the spread the issuer has to pay, depending on how strong a certain ratio or other metric may be.

Loans may have principal amortization during the life of the security. This is exceptionally rare in bonds. However, these amortizing loans are significantly less common in the leveraged loan institutional market than in the traditional bank loan market and when there is amortization it is usually minimal.

Loans sometimes will have a required cash flow sweep. This is a special type of amortization: a defined portion of excess cash flow from operations may be required to pay down bank debt each year. This is not that common for loans, but it is rare to see for bonds.

Ordinarily, bank loans are callable by the company either immediately or very soon after they are issued; and if they have call protection, the premium that the company has to pay is usually very low and goes away quickly. However, it is not uncommon for bank loans to be issued below par, effectively giving the initial buyers of the loans a premium if the loans are repaid early. Bondholders usually want some call protection to reap benefits from credit improvements.

Any bank loan repayments, even open market repurchases, mostly need to be made pro rata across all tranches and to all holders of bank debt. This is not true for bonds. However, there are some exceptions in bank structures. Sometimes there are first-out tranches of debt that are required to be paid out ahead of other tranches of bank debt, especially from proceeds from an event, such as a public stock offering or asset sale.

Bank loans are usually senior or at least pari passu with bonds. Normally, they have security in all or substantially all of the company's assets, or at least subsidiary guarantees.

Covenants, Waivers, and Amendments

Bank loans are more likely to have affirmative covenants that require certain financial metrics be maintained (e.g., a certain maximum leverage ratio). These are often called maintenance covenants; bonds typically do not have such covenants. Maintenance covenants have become less common in the institutional market. Loans without these affirmative covenants are sometimes referred to as covi-lite loans.

It is generally considered easier to get amendments and waivers from loan holders than from bondholders. A waiver is for temporary relief and an amendment is for permanent relief of some loan terms. For example, if the issuer of a loan begins to experience an operational rough patch and cannot meet its maintenance covenants, it goes to its loan group and offers to pay a fee for a change or temporary waiver on the covenant test. When a company is troubled and violating some of the covenants in its loan agreement, lenders often continue to give waivers and work with the company. This is due to a number of reasons:

- *Bank safeguards*: Banks typically rank senior and usually have security in the assets. Thus, they are more confident than more subordinated lenders that they will be repaid principal and interest in any restructuring.
- *Agent bank control*: As all transactions need to be approved by the agent bank, it has a better sense than the bond market of who the holders of the loans are, and the agent may even exert control in the transaction of the debt to try to prevent the loan from getting into the hands of investors that may be less likely to grant waivers.
- *Lender liability*: The concept of lender liability may dissuade lenders from forcing a company to default on a technical matter.
- *Amendment and waiver fees*: These are a way of getting at least some repayment from a troubled or potentially troubled loan.

Information on Bank Loans

Information flow can be more stilted in the loan market than in the bond market. Investors who are not holders of a loan may have more difficulty getting information on the company, such as financial statements. An investor in the loan may have to decide whether to be on the public or private side of information. This may restrict ability to transact in the loans and in other public securities issued by the same company. Investors on the private side can get monthly financials and regular projections prepared by the company, which are not available on the public side. As a rule, in the USA on the public side, investors and noninvestors can get quarterly and annual results; in Europe, semiannual and annual are common. The detailed terms of bank agreements are sometimes made available in the exhibits to a public financial statement, but not always. Even companies with public stock do not always make their bank agreements public. Sometimes the agreement is filed on a special gated website where investors have to get permission from the company to gain access. When analyzing a bank document, remember to check for any amendments or waivers that may have changed the terms of the agreement over time.

Closing Comment

Differences in the terms and structures of bank loans are even more varied than in the leveraged bond market. Pricing information can also be more difficult to obtain in the bank loan market than in the bond market, as many loans trade infrequently and the flow of financial information may be more restricted. Bank debt is usually at the top of the capital structure, but do not be lulled into thinking that all bank debt ranks the same. Just because bank debt is secured does not mean it is secured by all the assets; it may share its security with other debt. Whenever possible, read the terms of a bank agreement carefully to fully understand ranking, guarantees, and security.

Chapter 5

Why Is Leveraged Finance Investment Analysis Unique?

What's in this chapter:

- similarities to equity
- similarities to debt
- structural issues
- the three parts of leveraged finance investment analysis

L EVERAGED FINANCE INVESTMENT analysis encompasses key components from equities and traditional fixed-income markets, and requires 1) analysis that is specific to below-investment-grade debt; 2) developing an opinion on the quality of the issuer, which involves many tools common to the equity markets; 3) an understanding of the structure of the individual investment instruments, an analysis that is relatively unique to leveraged credit; and 4) analysis of relative value that utilizes traditional fixed-income measures such as yield, spread, and duration.

Similarities to Equity

Companies with more debt leverage (gearing) have less margin for error. Therefore, the security prices of these companies react more dramatically to relatively small changes in operating results or news headlines than prices of companies with less leverage (such as investment-grade companies). This more volatile reaction in price is more like the way stocks behave than traditional investment-grade corporate or government-issued bonds behave. Numerous studies have shown that returns in the leveraged finance market are more highly correlated to equities than to fixed-income markets.

Investors in investment-grade bonds fully expect to get their principal and interest serviced from cash flows or other liquidity sources. The speculative nature of, and higher debt levels in, the high yield market increase an investor's risk of not getting repaid. This leads leveraged debt investors to analyze a company's asset value, which is important in case cash flows cannot service the debt. The process of assessing the asset value of a company is akin to the way in which traditional equity research is done. Credit analysts will also often compare ratios that measure the level of debt of the company to ratios that equity analysts use to arrive at a company's asset value.

Because of the level of leverage, operational results are very important to leveraged debt investors. Disappointing results or operating trends can cause significant price movements in leveraged bonds and loans compared to investment-grade bonds. This heightened focus on operational trends is similar to equity analysis methodology, as opposed to traditional fixed-income research, which is often more focused on interest rate risk. While an equity analyst may be biased toward analyzing the impact of operational trends on earnings, leveraged debt market analysts will focus on how the trends are likely to impact leverage or free cash flow (FCF) generation.

Financially meaningful mergers, acquisitions, and asset sales are significantly more common in the leveraged finance markets than in the investment-grade market. These frequent event-driven changes to the credit quality of a company also align more with the type of analysis that equity analysts do than the type of work investment-grade analysts do.

Similarities to Debt

Leveraged finance bonds and loans are not equities. Despite the similarities, they are still debt instruments. Key ratios used to analyze a credit, capital structure considerations, sensitivity to interest rates, and the key tools for determining value for leveraged finance investments are all more similar to traditional debt markets than they are to equity market analytical methods.

Key ratios used in leveraged finance credit analysis are focused on how well protected the investor is in the debt. A ratio of cash flow/interest expense can give an investor an idea how well the company can service the interest expense on the debt. A ratio of debt/asset value can help an investor determine how well protected the principal of the debt is if the company defaults.

The terms used to compare relative value in the leveraged debt markets are similar to those used throughout most debt markets. They include various calculations of yield and spread, as well as duration and maturity schedules. When debt instruments become distressed, they are often analyzed using estimated recovery values, and these methodologies tend to be more similar to equity valuation methodologies.

Structural Issues

Below-investment-grade credit analysis requires more time to be spent on understanding the nuances of the debt structure. It also involves analyzing and trying to anticipate structural changes to the capital structures in the market.

When one company has more debt and higher interest expense than another company, a larger portion of its cash flow has to go to service debt. This can lead management to spend more time on the capital structure of the company than it would if the company were unleveraged. Management will regularly look at ways to improve the cost of borrowing and increase liquidity. Therefore, when analyzing leveraged companies, think as a corporate finance officer would. Analyze the capital market transactions the company might undertake to improve its capital structure and consider whether the existing debt would be helped or hurt by such a transaction.

Corporate structural issues can occasionally become a factor in equity and investment-grade analysis. But in the below-investment-grade-debt markets, focusing on structural issues within the capitalization and within the specific debt instrument is a way of life. Covenant and structural analysis are part of the job in leveraged finance analysis. This can also involve analysis of how different tranches of debt would be treated in a bankruptcy.

The Three Parts of Leveraged Finance Investment Analysis

There are many components to the task of analyzing a leveraged finance investment, but they all fall broadly into three categories:

1. *Credit analysis*: This is an analysis of the operational and financial prospects of the company that issued the debt and includes how well the expected cash flow can service the debt, the company's liquidity, the value of its assets, how it has performed operationally, how it is likely to perform in the future, and its competitive position. This analysis is used to determine whether the company has the cash-flow-generating ability to meet its interest and debt repayment obligations, and should it fall short, how well its asset value compares to its debt obligations.

2. *Bond and loan structural analysis*: This is an analysis of the terms and structure of the debt issue and requires an understanding of the interest and maturity terms and the conditions under which the company can call the bonds or loans. It also involves analyzing the investment's priority ranking. For example, are there prioritized loans that would be paid off in a bankruptcy sooner than the issue that is being analyzed? There is a myriad of covenants that can be meaningful to the performance of the potential investment. If there are multiple tranches of debt outstanding in a company's capital structure, there must be an understanding of how all of the terms of these other issues could affect the specific investment that is being analyzed.

3. *Relative value analysis*: Investment decisions always have to be made within the context of relative value. For example, would an investor be better off buying the stock of company A, or company B, buying a five-year government bond, or sitting in cash? In leveraged finance, the analysis can examine the relative value of various tranches of debt issued by one company, or the benefits of buying a debt instrument in company A versus one issued

by company B. This type of analysis often involves comparing credit quality and structural issues. It also involves making calculated assumptions about a company's future and may incorporate scenario analysis.

To be successful in the leveraged finance field, there must an understanding of all of these aspects of analysis.

Closing Comment

A mix of skills is needed in leveraged finance, and at times, all these skills must be utilized. There are situations where one aspect of the analysis outweighs others and knowing which items to prioritize is a developed and critical skill. No analysis is complete unless all of these aspects are considered.

Chapter 6

A Primer on Prices, Yields, and Spreads

What's in this chapter:

- the basics
- a few points on yields
- a few points on spreads
- duration
- total return event analysis
- a pragmatic point on terminology
- a pragmatic point on trading bonds: accrued interest
- deferred payment bonds: understanding accretion

THIS CHAPTER COVERS how prices, yields, and spreads are used in the leveraged finance market. All are measures of value. Yields are a proxy for expected returns and spreads are a measure of these returns, net of the "risk-free" interest rate yield curve component. There are several different measures of yields and spreads, and they are used when trading bonds and loans and when discussing the relative value of potential investments. In different situations and for different types of analysis, some of these measures will be more valuable than others.

The Basics

The market quotes the price of bonds and loans in reference to the dollar price, the yield, or the spread. The price (as opposed to the yield or spread) is not actually the dollar price that is paid for the investment, but a percentage of the face value of the investment.

The practice of placing a dollar (or other currency) sign in front of a bond price is wrong. The bond price is quoted as a percentage of face value. For example, if the price at which an investor is buying a bond is 90 for a bond that, at maturity, will pay $1,000 (face value, or par value), the investor would pay $900 for that bond, not $90 (1,000 × 0.90, or 90%). Similarly, if the price of a bond paying €2,000,000 at maturity were quoted at 85, the buyer would not pay €85, but €1,700,000.

Bonds have different coupon terms and maturity dates, both of which play an important part in calculating the expected total return of the investment. Therefore, comparing two bonds by price doesn't tell an analyst which bond represents better value. In discussions of relative value, it is more common to discuss yield or spread.

Yield is a rate of return based on an investment bought at a certain price and held to a certain date, at which point it is retired at a certain price. A yield is the combination of the interest income received and any change in the price that was paid for the principal on the debt and the price it is sold at. Since no one can predict the price and the date on which it will be sold, the yield calculations assume that the investment is either held to maturity or until it is called.

Spread is the yield less some risk-free rate. The risk-free rate is usually a government bond that matures on the same date that is being used for the yield calculation. If a US dollar-based bond matures in five years and the investor is running a YTM, the spread will be that yield minus the yield on the five-year US Treasury bond. If the bond were issued in Euros, it would be logical to use the five-year German government bund. The spread over the government bond can be thought of as the extra payment investors need for taking the risk of not being repaid. Theoretically, a higher spread should equate with more credit risk. The spread calculation also helps to normalize relative value for different maturities and removes the natural tendency of the yield curve. In the government bond market, yields of longer maturity will typically trade higher. When a line of all the yields is plotted by maturity, it is known as a yield curve. If two bonds of different maturities are being compared, the yield may not give good insight into the differences in credit quality, because the longer-dated bond may trade at a higher yield due to the interest rate curve. Using spread helps normalize the relative value discussion in relation to the yield curve.

Generally, loans are floating-rate debt. This means that the coupon moves as general interest rates in the economy move. The terms of the loan will state which index or measure is used as a proxy for the general interest rates. Traditionally this rate was an estimate of the overnight borrowing rate for banks, known as LIBOR, which was regularly published and also available in different currencies. LIBOR is in the process of being phased out, and different countries are developing new measures, all of which use a short-term borrowing rate to act as a proxy for general market interest rates. In the USA, SOFR is the most popular replacement for LIBOR. This proxy for interest rates is referred to as the base rate. Each loan has a spread over this base rate, and if the two are added together, the combination equates with the interest rate or coupon on the loan. For example, using LIBOR as the base rate, if LIBOR is 1% and the loan's coupon is +350 bps, the company will pay 4.5%, or 450 bps interest rate on its loan until the next reset date. The bank loans are generally priced off one-month or three-month rates.

Bank loans also usually only have one or two years of call protection, or sometimes none. It is convention to run the yield either to maturity or to a three-year maturity. When comparing the yield to a bond, the lowest yielding methodology should be used for both the bond and the loan. However, the yield calculation on the loan is hypothetical. The loan can be called well before three years, which can happen at any time. An investor does not know what the coupon will be over the life of the loan because it resets. This can be an advantage to the loan holder when interest rates are rising, but a disadvantage when they are declining. In countries with developed financial markets, there is a futures market in interest rate instruments. This is where investors can buy and sell contracts based on where they believe interest rates will be in the future. Bank loan investors can use the data from this futures market to estimate where yields on the loan will be over time and use that to calculate the yield; or more simply, can just assume the current rate does not move.

The floating-rate structure can be very helpful if an investor is buying the leveraged finance instruments to offset floating-rate obligations such as floating-rate annuities or bank deposits. However, if an investor is not as concerned about matching floating-rate liabilities and will be holding the investment long term, or to maturity, the floating-rate instrument can add more uncertainty to the investment's total return because the income component will vary depending on the long-term interest rate environment. Additionally, the base rate for floating-rate instruments is usually predicated on short-term rates, so changes in relationships between short-, intermediate-, and long-term rates can also impact the relative value of floating-rate notes.

A Few Points on Yields

- The YTM and YTW are measures of rates of return. The actual calculations are fairly time-consuming. But many programs can calculate these yields rapidly, such as systems from Bloomberg. Systems can be built using programs such as Microsoft Excel and even financial calculators can run the calculations. The YTM takes the price paid for the debt and calculates the present value of its cash flows from its interest payments and the amount paid back at maturity and determines the return, or yield, using present value calculations and a rate of reinvestment of the cash flows.

- When the bonds are at par (100% of face value), the YTM and the coupon on the bond are the same. When the price is higher, the yield goes down and is below the coupon. The inverse is true when the price is below par. This is because even if investors pay 101 for a bond, at maturity, they will only be paid 100, so the paid premium of 1% of face value will reduce the total stream of cash flows they will get from holding the bond to maturity.

- A bond is callable when the terms of the bond or the loan allow the company to buy back the bonds at a set price, at the company's option. The debt is usually not callable right away and, in the case of bonds, there is usually a call schedule that starts at a premium price to the par value and reduces to par over time. When a bond is callable, the YTW comes into play, but only if it is trading above par at a premium. If the bonds were trading at a price above the call price, the YTC would be lower than the YTM. Whichever yield is lower is usually the one that is used to quote the bond price, run the initial analysis, and be conservative. When there is a bond and a schedule of call prices and call dates, yield calculation systems will run a yield to each call price and choose the one with the lowest yield to use as the YTW.

The YTW is what is used throughout the rest of this book, unless noted. In Exhibit 6.1 there is an example of a call schedule and the yield for each call date. In this case, year 8 is the YTW.

Exhibit 6.1: Sample Call Schedule and Yields

Issuer: Corporation X; Coupon: 4.875%; Maturity: 10 years; Price: 103.5

	Date	Call Price	Yield-to-Call
Call Date	Year 5	102.4375	4.50%
Call Date	Year 6	101.6250	4.41%
Call Date	Year 7	100.8125	4.36%
Call Date	Year 8	100.000	4.32%
Maturity	Year 10	100.000	4.42%

- In Exhibit 6.1, notice that the first call date is not for five years after the bond is issued. Notice also that the first call price is half of the coupon, which is common for bonds. In this case, the price is at a premium price, so the yield to the first call date is below the coupon: 4.5% versus 4.875%. The YTW is not the first call date, however. It is actually the yield to the call price in year 8. If the bond is called earlier than the YTW date, or left outstanding longer, the yield (the return) on the bond will be greater than the YTW. This is important to analyze when doing relative value between bonds and loans, and requires scenario analysis to consider what the probability is for each call date. For example, if corporation X in Exhibit 6.1 is bought by an investment-grade company in year 5, and the acquirer can borrow money at 1%, it would probably be worth calling the bonds at the first call date rather than waiting. In this case, the bondholder would get a return over the YTW, but if another company were to become the acquirer and could issue debt at 4%, it might not be worth calling the bonds until year 8. The differences in the YTC are not great in this example, but in many situations the differences can be meaningful. This is especially true as bonds get closer to their call dates and maturities, and small price movements make a big difference.
- Over time, the bulk of the return from leveraged debt markets and most individual nonconvertible bonds and loans issued in these markets comes from the coupon. However, any premium, or discount, in the price of the security when it is bought impacts the returns and the yield calculations. Yield calculations will take a premium over par and amortize it against the

coupon payment until the debt retirement date. As a simplified example, an investor buys a bond at 105. When it matures in five years, the issuer owes 100. That extra five points of premium gets subtracted from the coupon over each period using a discounted accrual method to calculate the expected return of investment. The opposite occurs if the investor buys the bond, or loan, at a discount. Early call dates accelerate this premium or discount amortization against the coupon. That is the major reason why, in Exhibit 6.1, the bond bought with a 3.5 point premium (i.e., for a total price of 103.5) has a lower yield if retired in year 8 than in year 10, because in the 10-year yield, there are two more years of coupon to offset the premium price.

A Few Points on Spreads

- Considering all the different yields, such as YTM, YTW, and YTC, how should an analyst look at the spread? The way to do it is to use corresponding spreads and yields. If the lowest yield corresponds to a call date that is five years out, use a Treasury bond with a five-year maturity to run the spread. The STW is simply the YTW minus the yield on the risk-free government bond of a similar maturity. Spread is quoted in bps.
- Using Exhibit 6.1 and a YTM of 4.42%, and assuming this is a US dollar-denominated bond, if the ten-year US Treasury bond were yielding 1%, the STM on this bond would be 342 bps. For STW, one would use the lowest yield. In this case it would be the year 8 call, where the yield was 4.32%. If the eight-year Treasury bond were yielding 82 bps, or 0.82%, then the STW would be 360 bps. If the bond were issued in British sterling (pounds), the spread typically would be calculated based on the British government equivalent. With bank loan spreads, the base rate would be used to calculate the spread.

Duration

Duration is an important concept that must be understood in order to understand relative value analysis. Duration is a measure of the estimated change in price for a change in the yield or spread.

As a rule, duration is thought of as how a bond responds to a move in interest rates and it is assumed that those interest rate moves lead to a change in the price of the bonds because the yield has to adjust to the new interest rate environment.

For example, if the yield on a ten-year Treasury note is at 1%, a typical high yield bond is yielding 5%, and the yield on the Treasury note suddenly moves to 2%, investors will demand a higher yield on the high yield note as well.

Duration is important when comparing bonds as it can be used to determine which bond would see a greater price move if interest rates were to move up or down. Duration can be thought of as the potential for price volatility. Duration is quoted in terms of years. There are several different duration calculations, but all use, as part of the calculation, a present value of the stream of payments compared to the price of the debt instrument. Duration measures the potential for price volatility, not return volatility. Analyzing returns in terms of bonds' price movement is only part of the equation; the price movement as well as the return from the coupon payments must both be included.

A longer duration means the price of the bond is more sensitive to a change in yield. A longer maturity and a lower coupon will lengthen the duration because it will take longer to get all the cash flows associated with the investment.

The rule of thumb is that the duration is equal to the price movement in the bond for a 100 bps movement in interest rates. If a bond has a duration of four years and the yield on the bond increases by 100 bps, the price should drop by approximately four points. This is an approximation, and when changes in yields become very large, duration becomes less accurate.

Exhibit 6.2 shows two bonds that were each trading at a price of 101 and what happens to the price when the yield on both bonds increases by 100 bps. Bond Beta has a lower coupon and drops to 94.69, while Bond Psi has a higher coupon and a shorter maturity, and the price only drops to 96.88.

Exhibit 6.2: Comparison or Price Sensitivity of Two Bonds of Different Duration

Bond	Coupon	Maturity	Yield	Price	Duration	Yield +1%	New Price
Bond Beta	5.0%	8 years	4.84%	101.00	6.4 years	5.84%	94.69
Bond Psi	7.0%	5 years	6.76%	101.00	4.1 years	7.76%	96.88

It is quite common in bonds to use duration-to-worst (DTW). This measure uses the YTC schedule as shown in Exhibit 6.1, establishes what the worst return would be, and then uses the modified duration method to calculate the duration to that date. This can be misleading, as we pointed out above, as the bonds may actually not get retired on that to-worst date; they may come out earlier or be left outstanding longer. Therefore, the bond's price sensitivity to interest rate movements may not be fairly reflected by using DTW, just as duration of yields and spreads changes as the price of the bonds changes and the outcomes become more varied when the bond is trading at a premium.

One method for calculating duration that is more effective for investments with embedded call options is known as OAD. These calculations take into account the probability of a bond with embedded call options being called at various prices. This only becomes a factor when the bond price is above par, and usually at or above the call prices.

Convexity is a concept that is related to duration. Duration assumes a relatively linear relationship between a bond's yield and price. This is fairly accurate for smaller changes in yields. Over larger changes, the relationship becomes more curved and, typically, is convex. The basics of convexity are that when a debt instrument has positive convexity, if yields go down, duration increases, so prices go up more for each decline in yield. If yields go up, a debt instrument with positive convexity would see duration decline. In this case, a bond with positive convexity would see its price decline by less when yields go up than the increase in price when yields go down by an equivalent amount. The more convexity, the greater this would be. There are times when a debt instrument has negative convexity: the bond's duration increases as yields rise and prices decline by more than prices would rise for an equivalent decline in yields.

Because bank debt structures usually have very limited call protection and floating-rate interest payment structures, duration is much less of a factor in the loan market. If a loan is callable and its coupon resets quarterly, it is often viewed to have a three-month duration. A loan trading at a discount implies that the issuing company is unlikely to call it, as this would cost the company a higher interest rate to refinance the loan than it is currently paying. (The same is true for bonds.) Because of these features, loans are viewed to have very little, if any, duration. Floating-rate instruments do have price sensitivity to changes in spreads, and in the floating-rate market, it is common to use spread duration.

In terms of spread duration, assume that the term *duration* means "modified duration," and assume that spread is a measure of credit risk. Prices of bonds can be impacted by interest rate movements, but prices also can move based on how the market perceives credit risk in the bond.

For example, assume interest rates are staying constant and a bond is trading at a spread of 300 bps. If the equivalent maturity in US Treasury bonds is yielding 2.0%, then this bond would be priced at a yield of 5%. If the company had a terrible earnings release, the market is likely to demand a higher yield because it now perceives a higher risk that the company may not be able to pay back its debt. A buyer of these bonds may now demand a 450 bps spread, equal to a yield of 6.5%, to buy the bonds.

In this case, the yield on the bond has gone up not because of a change in interest rates, but because of a change in spread, due to a change in perceived credit risk. The price sensitivity to this change in the spread for a fixed coupon instrument can be estimated by using duration. In this example, if the bond had a duration of four years, then an increase of 150 bps (1.5%) in yield can be expected to cause about a six-point move in the price of the bond.

The concept for a fixed-rate bond is similar to interest rate duration, but the driver is different. A floating-rate loan may have almost no interest rate duration because the interest rate can adjust to a move in rates every quarter. However, a floating-rate note can have material spread duration, which can move the price of the loan, as an investor may demand a larger spread over its base rate, or if the credit quality gets better, sellers may require a tighter spread.

If a loan has a coupon that is base rate +500 bps, and there is bad news on the credit, and investors demand a spread of +700 bps, that loan will have to move down in price so that the yield equates to the new required spread. The spread duration gives an estimate of how much that price would move for a 100 bps move in spread.

Total Return Event Analysis

The information about yields, spreads, and prices is fairly universal with bonds. In leveraged finance, analysts also often need to look at total return in the case of a major news event that reprices risk, an early debt retirement, or a bankruptcy. An easy way to address this quickly is to use a bond calculation system and customize a YTW calculation. Instead of using the call price in the calculation, put in whatever the expected exit price would be, such as the price at which the bonds will likely be trading in a year, or where a tender price might occur. Then change the call date to the date when the event is going to occur. This calculation should be equivalent to the expected return for the scenario.

For example, assume that high yield company Zeta is bought by investment-grade company Alpha. If Alpha has a much lower cost of borrowing, it might not even wait for the bonds to be callable. Alpha may decide to try to offer a price to buy the bonds early. This is called a tender offer. The bondholders are not required to sell into the tender, but it is an option for them. Analysts would want to calculate the yield on their bonds if they tendered them. So, using the yield calculator, there is usually a custom option, and the analysts can adjust the date the bond would come out and the price, and the calculator can give the yield into this tender, which will be equivalent to the total return.

A different example of using yield calculations is to see where a bond might be sold a year ahead. Assume investors are confident that the credit quality of a bond will improve over the next year, and that the bond will be trading at a spread 100 bps tighter one year ahead. They could use a bond calculator to reset the date forward a year, input the spread they expect the bond to be trading at on that date, and see what the expected price would be. Then, using the current date and price, they could run a custom yield for a take-out one year ahead, at the expected price, as an estimate of the total return on the bond for the next year.[5]

In a bankruptcy analysis, investors might want to see what the return is if a bond is bought at a certain price today and the bankruptcy does not settle for two years. Then they would estimate the different types of values they might get at the end of the bankruptcy. Similarly, in a stressed situation, they might

---

5 To see the price of a given yield and spread a year out, it is important to change the settlement date on the bond calculator for one year out, because in almost all cases, the relationship between the price, yield, and spread will change over the next year, due to the bonds being one year closer to maturity.

want to assume that a bond pays interest for one year and then goes through a one-year bankruptcy. In these cases, it is typical to run an internal rate of return of the stream of payments, starting with the price paid for the bond (including accrued interest), to see the total return.

A Pragmatic Point on Terminology

In practice, the prices of bonds and loans are quoted in several different ways: on a price basis, a yield basis, and a spread basis. The yield and spreads are YTW and STW unless otherwise stated.

Bonds and loans that trade at relatively low yields are more likely to be quoted using spread. Bonds and loans that trade at higher yields tend to be quoted in price and/or yield. Distressed bonds and loans are usually quoted in price. Bankrupt instruments are always quoted in price because they usually don't pay in interest.

When bonds and loans trade at lower yields and spreads, closer to the risk-free rate, they are often said to be trading tighter. If they trade at yields further from the benchmark, they are said to be wider. Also, if two bonds of similar quality trade at different yields, the one with the lower yield may be referred to as trading rich. The other might be said to be trading cheap. This *tighter/wider* and *rich/cheap* terminology is used for any number of relative value conversations.

A Pragmatic Point on Trading Bonds: Accrued Interest

Typical corporate bonds pay interest every six months. If a bond is bought between the interest payments, it is understood that the buyer will pay the seller any of the unpaid interest that accrued since the last interest payment. This accrued interest is not included in the quoted price but will be included in the amount that is paid for the bond. At the next interest payment date, the debt holder will be paid all of the interest; the bond seller will not receive any. The price only refers to the principal of the bond. As an example, assume a bond has a 12% coupon that pays interest on February 1 and August 1. If a buyer purchases $1,000,000 par amount of the bonds on September 1 at a quoted price of 101,[6] the buyer will pay the seller $1,010,000 (1,000,000 × 1.01)

---

6 The price is actually quoted as a percentage of par. Par is the same as 100. Par is also sometimes called face value. In this case par is equal to $1,000,000.

plus one month of accrued interest equal to 1% of par value, or $10,000. So even though the price quoted was 101, the cash paid is $1,020,000. Then, on February 1, the buyer will be paid interest of half the coupon, or 6% of the par value of the bonds (which is $1,000,000). In this case, the interest payment will be $60,000.

Deferred Payment Bonds: Understanding Accretion

One type of bond that has been prevalent during certain cycles in the high yield market is a deferred pay security, which includes discount notes and pay-in-kind (PIK) notes. To understand these notes, the differences between face value and accreted value must be understood. Changes in tax laws that have eliminated some of the tax deductibility of noncash interest and market changes have made these structures less popular, but they remain important concepts and structures to be aware of.

Zero coupon bonds are usually issued below par and pay par at maturity. Remember, par is equal to 100% of the lender's claim. So, as an example, assume a new bond is issued with a coupon rate of 0%. When it is issued, it is sold for 65, but at maturity, it will pay off 100 in five years. Although the value of this note on the day it is issued is only 65, and the claim in a bankruptcy is only 65 on the day it is issued, the value increases each day it moves closer to maturity. This is called accretion. It is important to note that the note's value and its claim in bankruptcy are based on the accreted value, not the face value (par, 100) that would be due at maturity.

For example, if a five-year note were issued at a discount price of 61.4% of face value, the YTM would be 10%. Assume that at maturity the amount due on this bond is $500 million.

- The price of the bond, when it was issued, would be 61.4 (quoted as a percentage of face value), the same as its accreted value.
- The amount of debt on the company's balance sheet would be $307 million ($500 million × 0.614).

After one year from issuance, the note should have accreted to 67.68% of face value.

- If, on that date a year after it was issued, an investor still wanted to buy the bond with a yield of 10% (the yield that it was issued at), that investor would pay the accreted value price of 67.8. If the investor believed the bond's risk required a higher yield, the price would be below accreted value.
- The $500 million face amount obligation that was on the balance sheet the previous year at $307 million has now accreted to $338.5 million ($500 million × 0.678). The increase in the accreted value is booked as interest expense on the income statement.

In the high yield market, there have been some twists on this typical zero coupon note structure. One structure that has been seen is a zero/step coupon: the coupon is zero for a period of time and then starts paying cash interest. For example, a discount can be issued that matures in ten years. It is issued at a discount, and for the first five years the coupon is 0%. Its principal amount accretes for the first five years until it reaches par. After the fifth year, the bond starts paying cash interest until maturity.

PIK notes are another form of deferred pay debt. Instead of being issued at a discount, these bonds are issued at par. PIK notes will have a stated coupon, but the company can pay the interest on these notes by issuing additional bonds, valued at par, instead of cash. This PIK structure causes the debt on the balance sheet to increase in a pattern similar to a zero coupon note. Typically, these bonds PIK for three or five years and then are required to start paying cash interest. After each PIK payment, the next interest payment is calculated based on the new amount of bonds outstanding—that is, the original amount plus the amount of bonds that have previously been issued from the PIK payments. Twists known as toggle bonds have evolved on the PIK structure: the company issuing the notes has an option for five years to either PIK the notes or pay in cash. Frequently it can do both.

A few points on PIK and toggle notes:

- Unless the company has announced that it will pay in cash, the notes do not trade with accrued interest. (The price in the market will usually increase, commensurate with the implied interest accrual, and drop on the payment date.)
- Once the interest is paid in additional bonds, the next interest payment is made on the original bonds plus those issued for the PIK payment.

- If the bonds are trading at a significant discount (or premium) to par value, the traders usually adjust the yield because the PIK interest payment has a market value of less than (or greater) than par.

Closing Comment

Price, yields, spreads, and duration are tools that are constantly used to describe the price of a loan or a bond, and are the major tools used in determining both relative value between investment options and the cost to the issuer of the debt. Yields, spreads, and duration are affected by many factors including price, coupon, and maturity of the debt instrument, and whether the bonds are callable or not.

Chapter 7

Financial Issues: A Primer on Financial Statement Analysis

What's in this chapter:

- financial statements
- EBITDA and adjusted EBITDA
- capital expenditures
- interest expense
- taxes
- changes in working capital
- free cash flow
- balance sheet
- a pragmatic point on financial statements

U NDERSTANDING FINANCIAL STATEMENTS is the first step in credit analysis and understanding how a company works. Credit analysis derives key data from these documents along with other important information. Although accounting standards differ slightly around the globe, resulting in differences in formulating financial statements country by country, the formulation of financial statements is becoming increasingly standardized with the use of international accounting standards. The examples in this book use the generally accepted accounting principles (GAAP) of the USA.

The Financial Statements

A company's financial statements include more than just key numbers. Material amounts of descriptive information are included that help add insight to any analysis. Whenever possible, read through all the information in the financial statements, especially the footnotes. When time is limited, try to focus on these sections:

- a description of the business (if you're looking at a new company)
- management's discussion of recent results
- recent events (which often include events that happened after the reporting period)
- the section describing liquidity
- the footnotes regarding the debt structure

Most companies make quarterly financial results available. Some European and other non-US companies report only semi-annually. Sometimes a company puts out an earnings release as a press release that may contain different or additional information from what is included in its formal financial filings. For companies that file with the US Securities and Exchange Commission (SEC), the press release will be filed on Form 8-K; quarterly financials will be filed on Form 10-Q; and the annual financials will be filed on Form 10-K.

The key parts of the financial statement used in credit analysis are the income statement, balance sheet, and consolidated statement of cash flows. All three of these sections need to be utilized for even the most basic credit analysis. The income statement shows the flow of the company's operational results on an accounting basis during the periods covered in the statements. The balance sheet is a snapshot of the company's assets and liabilities (including debt) at the end of the period. The statement of cash flows is very valuable and shows the most detail on where cash has come into the company and where it has gone out during the period covered by the financial statements. This will cover everything from operations to capitalized expenses, debt issuance or repayments, and equity infusions, all on a cash basis. Significant amounts of information and understanding of the business will be derived from spending more time studying the numbers. Initially, four key items should be the focus:

- key measures of cash flow, most commonly using adjusted earnings before interest, taxes, depreciation and amortization (EBITDA) and free cash flow
- the amount of debt obligations
- the cost to service the debt obligations, such as interest expense and near-term maturities
- other potential sources of liquidity to help service debt

EBITDA

The most widely used figure as a measure of cash flow from operations is EBITDA. (Some people use operating income before depreciation and amortization (OIBDA), but the two measures are relatively close.)

EBITDA is not a GAAP figure but is derived using GAAP numbers. It is looked upon as a measure of cash from operations available to service interest expense and other obligations, which is why interest and taxes are added back. The depreciation and amortization are added back because they are the most common noncash charges that are part of the income statement. EBITDA is also often viewed as the key unleveraged cash flow figure on which people value companies or, at least, it is a reasonable proxy.

EBITDA is often faulted in textbooks. Typical reasoning is that depreciation is a proxy for capital spending, so it is unrealistic to add it back. Another argument is that there are truer measures of cash flow. For this reason, some prefer EBIT (excluding depreciation and amortization). However, the bottom line is that the relatively easy-to-derive EBITDA figure is the one that is most widely used when looking at leveraged finance credit analysis, so it cannot be ignored. We will construct almost all these other measures of cash flow starting with EBITDA.

EBITDA can usually be derived from the income statement. The income statement shown in Exhibit 7.1 is a typical example. Start with the net income on line 11 and add back taxes, interest expense, depreciation, and amortization from lines 10, 8, 4, and 5, respectively. From this, an analyst can derive a simple EBITDA.

Exhibit 7.1: Income Statement Sample in $000,000s

		A	B	C
		Year 1	Year 2	Year 3
1	Revenue	3,659	3,666	3,870
	Costs			
2	Operating costs	1,544	1,539	1,575
3	Selling, general, and administrative	770	790	810
4	Depreciation	900	955	995
5	Amortization	150	240	260
6	Total expenses	3,364	3,524	3,640
7	Operating income	295	142	230
8	Interest expense	500	479	485
9	Earnings before taxes	(205)	(337)	(255)
10	Taxes (tax benefit)	(6)	(7)	(12)
11	Net income	(199)	(330)	(243)
	EBITDA (11 + 10 + 8 + 5 + 4)	1,345	1,337	1,485

Sometimes, however, depreciation and amortization are not broken out on the income statement and they are included in other expense lines, as shown in Exhibit 7.2. When this is the case, go to the statement of cash flows. An example of a statement of cash flows is shown in Exhibit 7.3. The first section focuses on cash related to operating activities, as opposed to investing or financing. This section derives a figure called net cash, provided by operating activities. Within the line items in this section, depreciation and amortization are shown on line 2. Use this data to add back these noncash items to net income on the income statement in Exhibit 7.2. The statement of cash flows contains numerous other helpful items, several of which we will come back to later. For credit analysis, this statement is one of the most useful financial pages on any company.

Exhibit 7.2: Income Statement Sample 2 in $000,000s

		A	B	C
		Year 1	Year 2	Year 3
1	Revenue	3,659	3,666	3,870
	Costs			
2	Operating costs	2,594	2,734	2,830
3	Selling, general, and administrative	770	790	810
4	Total expenses	3,364	3,524	3,640
5	Operating income	295	142	230
6	Interest expense	500	479	485
7	Earnings before taxes	(205)	(337)	(255)
8	Taxes (tax benefit)	(6)	(7)	(12)
9	Net income	(199)	(330)	(243)
10	Adjusted EBITDA	1,357	1,356	1,505

Exhibit 7.3: Statement of Cash Flows in $000,000s

		A	B	C
		Year 1	Year 2	Year 3
1	Net income (loss)	(199)	(330)	(243)
	Adjustments to Reconcile Net Cash Provided by Operating Activities			
2	Depreciation and amortization	1,050	1,195	1,255
3	Noncash compensation	12	19	20
4	Noncash interest expense	40	10	10
5	Income taxes (benefit)	(6)	(7)	(12)
	Changes in Operating Assets and Liabilities			
6	Accounts receivable	(29)	28	(9)
7	Inventories	(5)	0	(14)
8	Accounts payable	(11)	5	8
9	Deferred revenue	15	16	17
10	Net cash provided by operations	867	936	1,032
	Investing Activity			
11	Purchases of fixed assets	(1,000)	(860)	(700)
12	Proceeds from sale of assets	20	50	35
13	Net investing activity	(980)	(810)	(665)
	Funding Activities			
14	New borrowings	200	0	(50)
15	Distributions to shareholders	0	0	(100)
16	Net cash from funding activities	200	0	(150)
17	Cash at beginning of year	100	142	268
18	Cash at end of year	142	268	485

Adjusted EBITDA

Just as EBITDA is a commonly used measure, so is adjusted EBITDA. This generally adds back other types of noncash items. A very common add-back is noncash or stock compensation, which appears on line 3 in Exhibit 7.3. Sometimes an analyst will choose to add back other noncash items, such as noncash charges or write-downs of asset values. When using adjusted EBITDA on a spreadsheet or report, it is strongly recommended that a footnote be used for the adjusted EBITDA showing exactly which items are being added back to EBITDA to avoid any confusion and to facilitate the recreation of adjustments for other periods.

Many times, when a new issue of a bond or a loan is coming to market, the issuer and underwriter will try to use their own definition of adjusted EBITDA. This has become increasingly common when an acquisition is involved and particularly when it is a leveraged buyout (LBO) done by a PE firm. In these cases, they will often include synergies that the buyer expects to get from combining the acquired company with other operations or expected cost savings that the new ownership expects to be able to accomplish after taking over the company. These are often referred to as add-backs. Sometimes these cost savings may already be completed, or they may take a few years to accomplish and involve cash payments to achieve these savings (such as severance pay if lay-offs are involved). However, the company usually includes all these cost savings as add-backs in their current calculation of adjusted EBITDA even if they have not been completed. There are several reasons why they do this: 1) to show better cash flow numbers when marketing their bonds and loans to investors; 2) to give guidance to investors on what they believe they can accomplish with the acquisition so that 3) the banks can show the transaction to be less leveraged, especially if they are committing capital to the fund the transaction; and 4) because the company often gets to use the adjusted EBITDA figure in its covenants, which provides more freedom but weakens the covenants.

Analysts have to look at these add-backs and decide how much credit they want to give for these anticipated cost savings. They also have to determine if there are offsetting cash expenses that are needed to accomplish these cost savings that are not being included in the figures, and then derive an adjusted EBITDA figure. However, that is just a first step. Analysts have to try to determine what others in the market are giving the company credit for in the add-backs. For example, in a new loan offering, analysts may believe the company should get credit for only 75% of the add-backs and this is what they base their analysis on. However, if everyone else buying the loan is giving the company 100% credit for the add-backs, and one year later, the company has accomplished only 75%, the analysis may have been right, but the loans will likely trade down as other buyers are disappointed with the results.

Another problem with add-backs is that they need to be utilized to determine if the company is meeting its covenants. Often the company can use its adjusted EBITDA calculation for the covenants, but it does not have to disclose all the details publicly, which can make the analysis of these expected cost savings more difficult. In many cases, the bank covenants don't just allow these add-backs one time; they can be used in the future, too, if the company chooses to make more acquisitions or believes it can get more cost savings, which means it could make an acquisition with more leverage and use add-backs that show an inflated EBITDA.

Overall, adjusted EBITDA by itself is not a problem. Concerns arise if the adjustments are not fully disclosed and if they are abused.

OIBDA as an EBITDA Substitute

OIBDA is operating income before depreciation and amortization. Operating income is calculated before taxes and interest expenses are deducted, so they do not need to be added back for the calculation. OIBDA is similar to EBITDA, but because it uses operating income instead of earnings as its starting point, it excludes nonoperational items such as income from discontinued operation, gains, or losses from subsidiaries, and other nonoperating items. For these reasons, one could argue that OIBDA is a significantly better figure to use, and in many cases it is. However, realistically, EBITDA is still the standard. People tend to start with EBITDA and then make the adjustments to get to an adjusted EBITDA they believe is realistic. It also matters what the cash flow measures are being used for. Are they being used to analyze the cash available to service debt, or are they being used to analyze the asset value of the operations?

Capital Expenditures

Capital expenditures are the amount that a firm invests in longer-term assets. These are not considered regular operating expenses for accounting purposes but are considered longer-term investments. Since they are not considered part of operations, capital expenditures do not appear on the income statement. Instead, they appear on the statement of cash flows under investing activities. This investment is also recorded on the balance sheet as an asset, and the income statement includes a depreciation expense related to the expenditures but spread out over the useful life of the asset, not when the cash is actually spent for accounting purposes.

Depreciation is not a cash item but represents the decline in value of a capital investment, or a proxy for how much would need to be saved each year over the useful life of the investment to be able to replace it. In reality, this does not always match up, especially when considering how much rapidly evolving technology is changing industries and could be increasing or lowering investment costs. Analysts will want to use adjusted EBITDA and then subtract capital expenditures to help derive real cash that is available from operations. Sometimes this is called unleveraged free cash flow, but there are more detailed free cash flow measures. Capital expenditures are shown in the statement of cash flows. The label may vary. Sometimes they are called capital expenditures, and at other times they may be called purchases of fixed assets (or a similar phrase), as shown on line 11 of Exhibit 8.3.

Here is a simple example that details capital expenditures and depreciation: A manufacturing company decides to invest $100 million in a new plant for a new product. That is recorded as a use of cash in the investment section of the statement of cash flows, with a label of "investment in fixed assets," and as the money is spent, it is also recorded as a new asset on the balance sheet. Using a simple straight-line method to depreciate this investment, if the plant is supposed to last ten years, the company would record $10 million of depreciation expense per year for each of the next ten years on its income statement. The asset on the balance sheet would be reduced each year by that same amount. However, the plant may actually last much longer, or it may become obsolete sooner, or technology could cause the cost of the plant to come down, so ten years from now the plant may cost less to replace. Importantly, when looking at cash flow generation, the company is not spending the $10 million a year of depreciation that appears on the income statement and therefore can use it for other items. Tax laws often allow for more creative depreciation than just using a straight-line method and may allow companies to depreciate the investments faster.

Analysts often want to determine how much capital expenditure is necessary to maintain the business and how much is discretionary. This helps determine the true cash needs to keep the business running if liquidity is tight. This is not shown in the financial statements. Some maintenance expenditures are recorded as capital spending but are really necessary to operate the business. Perhaps some of them can be deferred for a bit of time, but eventually, that is likely to impact the business. For example, a restaurant company has to replace serving utensils because of daily wear and tear, but its decision to install a new billing and order system is discretionary. Insights into the level necessary for maintenance capital expenditures can sometimes be gleaned from management's earnings releases or management comments. Sometimes it has to be estimated by looking at the historical patterns or learning from what competitors are doing.

Developments such as globalization and technology are changing how companies spend their capital. A company may produce a physical product but use complex supply chains where third parties produce much of the product. In these cases, the company may not be investing in a physical plant but may be investing significantly in intellectual property of the product designs and the logistics related to the supply chain. This can make for efficient use of capital but could represent risks for the firm if it does not have as much control over these extended and unowned production facilities if disruptions occur.

Interest Expense

Interest is critical to understand. Not all of the interest expense that is recorded on the income statement is an actual cash item. The income statement records a total interest expense figure, as shown on line 6 of Exhibit 7.2. However, several debt structures (such as the deferred pay structure mentioned in the preceding chapter) and other factors may result in a difference between the cash interest expense paid and the amount recorded on the income statement. To see what the true cash interest is, start with the total cash interest from the income statement and then look at the statement of cash flows to see what noncash interest expenses need to be adjusted.

On line 4 of the statement of cash flows, the noncash interest expense is broken out. An analyst could record both the cash and noncash interest expense. Note that on this statement, the noncash interest in column A, line 4, is much larger than the next two years in columns B and C. This implies that perhaps a deferred pay bond was outstanding in year 1 that was either retired or perhaps began paying cash interest afterward.

In situations where liquidity is extremely tight, it is worth noting that interest expense can accrue on the balance sheet before it is actually paid. For example, a $100 million bond may have a 12% coupon. Therefore, every month, $1 million of interest expense would accrue and be recorded on the balance sheet, but the bond only pays interest to the bondholders two times a year. In this case, we can assume that it pays in June and December. Therefore, if the company is close to running out of liquidity in the first quarter of the year, it is important to note that the $3 million of accrued interest is just on the financial statements. From January through March it did not actually get paid out and will not be paid to bondholders until June.

Financial statements are historical. At the start of forward-looking analysis, it needs to be remembered that the interest rate a company has to pay on its debt can change over time. As a rule, there are three ways the interest expense will change:

1. All, or a portion, of the debt might have a floating-rate coupon and this rate could go up or down.
2. The company has to retire some existing debt due to a maturity or decides to retire the debt for some other reason and uses new debt to refinance the existing debt. That new debt may come with a higher or lower interest rate.
3. The company retires debt with some funding source other than issuing new debt, which will reduce the debt and the interest expense for the company.

Some companies may use interest rate hedges. These can be used to effectively make a floating-rate debt instrument act like fixed coupon debt or can be used to do the opposite. There is a cost for these interest rate hedges, and if they are not matched exactly with the maturity of the debt, they can create an additional liability for the company. This type of hedge is usually described in the footnotes of the financial statements.

Taxes

Because of the leverage and the nature of below-investment-grade companies, they are often not major taxpayers. But taxes can be another cash obligation that must be accounted for. As in the case of interest expense, very often the taxes listed on the income statement are not the same as the actual cash payments due to deferrals or other tax strategies.

Be careful to properly account for reported taxes versus actual cash taxes. Taxes may be recorded on the income statement, but because of items such as net loss tax carryforwards, they may not actually be a cash item. In Exhibit 8.1, in the income statements, the tax benefits are not actually cash inflows to the company. Tax items from the income statement should be used and adjusted for items in the statement of cash flows to determine if they are truly cash or noncash items. In the financial statements above, the tax adjustments occur on line 5 in the statement of cash flows.

Changes in Working Capital

Working capital is defined using two figures from the balance sheet: current assets (line 6) and current liabilities (line 15). The changes in working capital can often be a meaningful source or use of short-term cash that is not shown on the income statement but can be derived from the statement of cash flows. On the statement of cash flows, the changes in the components of working capital can be seen on lines 6 through 9. Working capital items are balance sheet items related to operations.

To explain this, we'll go over a simple example of how this might work for one line item. Accounts payable is money that the company owes to others—for example, suppliers of raw materials or delivery companies. When that figure on the balance sheet goes down, this means that the company used cash to pay its obligations due to others. This would appear as a use of cash on the statement of cash flows, as it was in year 1 (column A, line 8).

To calculate the changes in working capital during a given time period, add up the line items from the statement of cash flows from lines 6 through 9, remembering that the numbers in parentheses are negative.

Changes in working capital should always be calculated, and material changes to historical patterns or large items in changes in working capital should always be looked into to understand what caused them.

In some free cash flow calculations, analysts will want to include changes in working capital. This can be especially important for companies with significant seasonality in their business, such as a retailer that builds up inventory ahead of holiday shopping. Depending on the business, working capital may increase or decrease as the business is expanding or contracting. In some industries, working capital swings are more intense.

An analyst must try to understand how to look at working capital appropriately for each business and each cycle. Most businesses go through periods where changes in working capital are a use of cash and some where it provides a source of cash. These cycles can be due to seasonality in a business, changes in customers or types of contract, and new product timing, as a few examples.

One of the important considerations when using changes in working capital is to make sure the data covers a long enough period of time to be meaningful. Looking at changes in working capital for just one quarter or even half a year can be misleading. Even looking at changes in working capital over a one-year period can be misleading for some businesses, depending on what changes or delivery cycles they go through. When a company is in a tight liquidity position, changes in working capital can be a vital item that can force the company to default or that might supply critical liquidity for a period of time.

Statements Vary

Keep in mind that not all financial statements are laid out in the same way. The amount of detail and the breakout of various line items can vary greatly from company to company. This can be particularly true in the statement of cash flows, especially in the line items encompassed in working capital.

Free Cash Flow

Free cash flow (FCF) is a derived figure that, like adjusted EBITDA, is not shown on the financial statements. FCF uses information from both the income statement and the statement of cash flows. It is a good measure of cash liquidity generated from operations. This figure is useful in credit analysis for bondholders to see what is available to pay down debt obligations each year and analyze how the company chooses to use its cash.

It is generally preferred to use an FCF figure that nets out interest expense, cash taxes, and capital expenditures, and adjusts for changes in working capital as well (see Exhibit 7.4). Capital expenditures are an investment item on the statement of cash flows, but a large component of them can be an ongoing and vital business expense and often a large use of cash.

Exhibit 7.4: FCF in $000,000s

		Year 1	Year 2	Year 3
1	Adjusted EBITDA	1,357	1,356	1,505
2	Purchases of fixed assets	(1,000)	(860)	(700)
3	Interest expense	(500)	(479)	(485)
4	Noncash interest expense	40	10	10
	Adjustments to working capital:			
5	Accounts receivable	(29)	28	(9)
6	Inventories	(5)	0	(14)
7	Accounts payable	(11)	5	8
8	Deferred revenue	15	16	17
9	Free cash flow	(133)	76	332

The importance of capital expenditures and working capital can vary by industry. Companies in certain industries, such as manufacturing and retailing, can be big capital spenders and see significant changes in working capital. Companies in other industries, such as media, are not big users of either. When there are exceptional items in capital expenditures or working capital that appear to be one-time in nature, analysts will have to decide if they want to include them or exclude them from the FCF calculation. This may vary depending on the objective of the analysis. For example, if the financial statements are being analyzed for near-term liquidity, it would make sense to include these one-time expenditures; but if the analysis is to ascertain the long-term ability of the company to grow its cash flow, it may make sense to exclude them (but be sure to footnote this in models).

Analysts may wish to deduct cash spent on dividends to shareholders and stock buybacks. These payments theoretically do not directly impact debt levels or the ability to pay interest. Insights can be gleaned from knowing where management wants to deploy capital and their desire to pay down debt, which can affect how the debt of the company will trade.

The Balance Sheet

The balance sheet is a snapshot in time of a company's assets and liabilities. The most important items for credit analysis are the cash and debt, as well as the related footnotes.

Cash and equivalent sources of liquidity will appear on the Assets portion of the balance sheet. In Exhibit 8.5, line 1 shows the cash on hand. Line 2 has an item for marketable securities. This often includes other highly liquid stocks or bonds that can be quickly monetized. These items are usually accounted for, along with cash, as a form of liquidity.

Sometimes there is a line item for restricted cash. Typically, this is not counted as cash for liquidity, as it is not generally available for the company to use to meet liquidity needs. But the footnotes to the financial statements should be read to find out what this cash is, because sometimes it is reserved to meet debt obligations.

Exhibit 7.5: Sample Balance Sheet in $000,000s

	Assets	Year 2	Year 3
	Current assets		
1	Cash and equivalents	268	485
2	Marketable securities	50	55
3	Accounts receivable	200	231
4	Inventory	180	190
5	Prepaid expenses	50	70
6	Total current assets	748	1,031
7	Net value of fixed assets	3,000	3,200
8	Goodwill and intangibles	1,000	1,000
9	Other assets	75	80
10	**Total assets**	5,571	6,342
	Liabilities and Shareholder Equity		
	Current liabilities		
11	Accounts payable	290	300
12	Accrued expenses	250	375
13	Deferred revenue	190	190
14	Current portion long-term debt	0	50
15	Total current liabilities	730	915
16	Long-term debt	5,100	5,000
17	Capitalized leases	100	100
18	Shareholders' equity	(359)	327
19	**Total liabilities & Equity**	5,571	6,342

On the liability side of the balance sheet, the first item to go to is the current portion of debt, which is line 14 of the balance sheet in Exhibit 7.5. This is the debt that is due within one year. It must be analyzed to see if it is manageable relative to the company's liquidity, including the FCF the company can generate and its ability to refinance the debt in the public or private markets.

Then note the total debt number, which is on line 16 in Exhibit 7.5. There may be a more detailed breakout of the debt items, which might include several lines of the balance sheet. Another item to consider on the liability side of the balance sheet is capitalized leases, on line 17, which are like a debt obligation.

Typically, it is conservative to count debt due within one year, long-term debt, and capitalized leases all as part of total debt.

To look at net debt, subtract cash and equivalents from the total debt figure.

These items give a basic understanding of how much debt a company has, but there are other items to consider to get a fuller picture of a company's debt. If time permits, it is recommended to read all the footnotes to the financial statements. If time is limited, read the footnote covering the debt. This footnote will give details about each part of the debt structure. It may also give insights into other short-term sources of capital, such as revolving credit lines, and will show how much debt comes due each year. Debt maturities represent possible downside event risks for a company, as they are liquidity events.

A Pragmatic Point on Financial Statements

Many books on financial analysis focus on the income statement. This is often the first place an analyst looks when examining a company. However, when analyzing a leveraged company, spending more time with the statement of cash flows is strongly recommended. Never believe that an analysis is complete if you do not understand what is going on with the various items on this part of the financial statements.

The statement of cash flows is usually divided into three sections: operating activities, investing activities, and financing activities. This is a good layout to understand where cash is being generated and where it is being used.

The statement of cash flows shows a more realistic picture than the income statement of where the cash is coming from and going to, and can give a very quick picture of liquidity. In particular, always look at the line in the statement of cash flows labeled "cash flow from operating activities" and compare the absolute figure and relative changes in this figure to the various measures of EBITDA and FCF. This is the one figure from the financial statements that analyzes corporate cash flow quickly. It is net of interest expenses and taxes but adds back noncash items, so it is a relatively clean figure of FCF before any deduction for capital expenditures.

Closing Comment

An understanding of where to find key items on the financial statements is one of the first steps in developing credit analysis skills. When exploring the financial statements and the textual parts of the financial statements as well, look for changes in any trends. Particularly, look for trend changes in revenue, cash flow, and debt, as well as how the company is choosing to deploy its FCF. Notably, is it choosing to deleverage or return capital to shareholders or to balance the two?

Chapter 8

Financial Issues: Credit Ratios

What's in this chapter:

- ratio analysis
- the base ratios: EBITDA/interest and debt/EBITDA
- a pragmatic point on valuations
- FCF ratios

AN ENDLESS NUMBER of credit ratios can be constructed. The analysis of a few key ratios is the most widely used credit analysis tool in the leveraged finance market. These ratios focus on how strong or weak a credit is in relation to its ability to service its debt, and also tend to focus on financial liquidity and asset value relative to the level of debt service and total debt outstanding. In fact, they are the base on which credit analysis is built. They can be used in many ways including, most commonly, 1) to show how these trends have changed over time for a company, and 2) to compare the ratios of different companies to understand the relative value of investing in their debt.

Ratio Analysis

Ratio analysis does not offer a complete answer about the credit quality of a debt issuer. Common complaints about ratio analysis include that it can be too simple, that it only gives a partial idea of a company's credit profile for just one point in time, and that it can become a reason not to do more in-depth work. Although ratio analysis on its own does not define a company's credit quality, ratio analysis is a valuable tool and is the most widely used quality reference point in credit analysis.

When discussing a bond or loan, the key credit ratios are usually among the first items discussed because they make comparisons easy. Ratio analysis can be used to compare changes in a company's credit quality over time, even if it has undergone major changes. As an example, a company has completed a series of acquisitions over several years, and an analyst wants to see whether this has improved or weakened the company's credit profile. Looking at a few ratios over time can give some quick insights. More importantly, ratio analysis makes it relatively easy to compare companies of different sizes, even in different industries, and averages in the market.

The usefulness of ratio analysis depends on the quality of the inputs used, which include items such as the calculations of adjustments to EBITDA, interest expense, and debt outstanding. When creating a ratio, keep in mind that the ratio does not capture a trend but is typically a static snapshot of a period of time. Be sure to understand what the ratio is being used to analyze and if it is the best ratio to answer the questions. For example, is the focus on how well a company can handle total interest, its ability to meet short-term maturities, or how well asset value can cover the debt obligations?

The Base Ratios

The two most basic ratios to understand are EBITDA/interest and debt/EBITDA. From these two basic ratios, more detailed and specialized ratios can be built.

The EBITDA/interest ratio gives a snapshot of the ability to service interest expense payments and is the most basic of the liquidity ratios. But EBITDA does not always tell the full story of operational cash flow available to service interest. Often people will look at the following:

1. *(EBITDA-capital expenditures)/interest expense*: There are many variations on this ratio. However, generally, they all answer how well the cash generated from a company's operations, including capital spending, can service its near-term debt obligations.

2. *Debt/EBITDA*: This is the most basic ratio to determine how much asset protection is offered to the bonds. The debt/EBITDA ratio is usually the ratio used to ascertain how leveraged a credit is. In Europe and elsewhere outside of the USA, leverage is often referred to as gearing. Later, this chapter links this ratio to ratios used to calculate a company's asset value and how these concepts can be used together.

These two ratios are frequently shouted across trading desks when two credits are compared and are generally the first metrics that salespeople, analysts, traders, bankers, and portfolio managers refer to when discussing a credit.

While there are definite benefits and shortcomings of ratio analysis, it is the most widely used technique in analyzing leveraged finance credits because it is a great tool for comparisons.

EBITDA/Interest Ratio

The most basic item a lender to a company wants to see is if the company can pay the interest on the bond or loan. The quickest way to look at that is the adjusted EBITDA/total interest ratio.

A ratio of 1× shows that the company's cash generated from its business operations can just cover the interest expense for any given period. The bigger the ratio, the better the company can service its interest. If the ratio is below 1×, the company will need other sources of liquidity to pay its interest expense.

An analyst will also want to look at the EBITDA/cash interest ratio. The preceding chapter explains how to derive cash interest versus total interest using the statement of cash flows. Exhibit 8.1 shows the adjusted EBITDA/total interest ratio and the adjusted interest/cash interest ratio using the income statements and the statement of cash flows from the preceding chapter.

Exhibit 8.1: Adjusted EBITDA/Interest Ratios

	A	B	C
	Year 1	Year 2	Year 3
Adjusted EBITDA/total interest	2.7×	2.8×	3.1×
Adjusted EBITDA/cash interest	3.0×	2.9×	3.2×

If the difference between the two ratios is not large, it is typically ignored, and the total interest ratio is used. However, if the difference between the two is large, the ratios should be run both ways.

For example, if the goal of analysts is to discover how well the company met its cash obligations for the past year, they could use the ratio with cash interest. However, assuming that the company has a large, deferred pay debt obligation that starts paying cash over the next year, or in common parlance, goes cash pay, analysts might want to look at the ratio for total interest. That is closer to the amount that needs to be serviced in the very near future and may be the more realistic level of cash obligations they should worry about.

Note that in both of these cases, we used adjusted EBITDA as the numerator. In this case, it was simply adjusted for the noncash compensation and is the more realistic ratio to use than pure EBITDA. However, there may be more adjustments that need to be made to the EBITDA figure and that could be more complex. To keep track of these, always footnote which adjustments are being made and try to be as consistent as possible in using these adjustments. Mergers and acquisitions as well as large cost savings or expansion plans can all often lead to material adjustments that an analyst might want to make.

The other common ratio is (adjusted EBITDA-capital expenditures)/interest expense. Capital expenditures are counted as long-term investments for accounting purposes but can actually be an ongoing operating cost of many businesses. Think of a hotel chain that regularly has to replace carpeting and contrast it with a packaging company that may be building a new plant for canned goods. The carpet expenditures can be capitalized, but they are likely to be ongoing every few years, while the canning plant would appear to be more one-time in nature.

As mentioned in the preceding chapter, it is sometimes difficult to determine what portion of capital spending is a regular ongoing cost and what portion may be a one-time, or exceptional, expenditure. If there are a large number of one-time expenditures that are not easy to break out from the general capital expenditures figure, this ratio can become less meaningful.

When an analyst wants to discern what portion of capital expenditures is used for regular ongoing maintenance and what portion is more of a one-time, or special project, expenditure, the text in the financial reporting or the footnotes might help. If the discussion of a special one-time project appears in the text of a company's financial statements, it would typically appear under "Management's Discussion of Results" in the Liquidity section and might read like this:

> Our capital expenditures for the year totaled $200 million. The expenditures included approximately $75 million related to our new computer center that was completed this year.

This implies, but doesn't state, that about $125 million of the expenditures were regular ongoing expenditures. For a snapshot of the company's typical ability to cover interest expense with EBITDA-capital expenditures, analysts might want to use the $125 million figure rather than the reported $200 million. This is especially true if this $125 million figure aligns more closely with historic levels of capital spending. If the analysts make this further adjustment in a presentation or report, they should clearly label and footnote how the capital expenditures are being adjusted.

When using this ratio and comparing companies in different industries, you need to remember that industries can have very different levels of capital expenditures. Adjusting for capital expenditures can help to normalize the true cash flow available to service debt for credits in varied businesses. Exhibit 8.2 shows these ratios for the company outlined in the preceding chapter.

Exhibit 8.2: Adjusted EBITDA-Capital Expenditures/Interest Ratios

	A	B	C
	Year 1	Year 2	Year 3
Adjusted EBITDA-capital expenditures/ total interest	0.7×	1.0×	1.7×
Adjusted EBITDA-capital expenditures/ cash interest	0.8×	1.1×	1.7×

These ratios give a snapshot in time that can be compared to other time periods for the same company to see if these ratios have been improving or declining. Looking at our example, it appears that in column A, year 1, the company was spending more on capital expenditures, relative to its EBITDA generation, than in later years. Furthermore, adjusted EBITDA net of capital spending was not enough to cover interest expenditures, so the company likely had to use another source of funding to help cover its costs in column A, year 1. However, by year 3, EBITDA increased, or capital expenditures or interest expense decreased, so that the interest coverage ratios net of capital expenditures are now reasonably above 1×. The ratio can show a direction of the credit quality and the liquidity, but you should do more detailed work to see what is actually causing the improvement.

These ratios by themselves do not capture the company's other cash obligations, such as debt maturities or uses of working capital. They also do not show what other resources the company may have to meet these various obligations, such as cash or borrowing capacity.

They are a tool to quickly get a sense of a company's ability to service debt and compare companies. They do not provide a complete picture of the company's liquidity and credit risk and analysts should never think that these simple ratios can do that. Analysts will want to dig further into the ability of cash flow from operations to meet all obligations and other sources of liquidity. They will also want to examine discretionary spending by the company for items such as dividends or stock-buybacks.

Debt/EBITDA

The debt/EBITDA ratio may be the most widely used ratio when comparing different companies. It is fairly simple to calculate. Do not become overly dependent on it, because by itself it has shortcomings.

It is commonly called the leverage ratio. This refers to how much debt is being leveraged on the cash flow generation of the company. Do not confuse this with operating leverage, which is often discussed in financial analysis. (Operating leverage refers to how much of an increase in revenue flows through to cash flow.) But in this book, and in the leveraged debt markets, leverage ratio means the debt/EBITDA ratio or some related ratio.

In the simplest form of this ratio, the numerator is the total long-term debt figure, and the denominator is the EBITDA. However, there are various ways of adjusting this ratio in both the numerator and the denominator, depending on the circumstances. The most common adjustment is to calculate this ratio as net debt/adjusted EBITDA, which is sometimes called a net leverage ratio. In this case, simply subtract the cash on hand from the numerator. This is commonly used if the company has a large cash position that is not earmarked for some special use. For example, suppose a company has a large stockpile of cash but has said it may shortly invest it in a developmental project. An analyst might want to subtract that cash from the debt ratio when calculating leverage. However, if the company states it is simply holding onto the cash for general liquidity, and it has no history of being acquisitive, it will likely make sense to subtract it and use a net debt figure.

Another numerator adjustment to consider is using total debt rather than long-term debt. The ratio normally excludes short-term maturities (debt maturing under one year), but this could be added back. If this debt is primarily related to short-term seasonal working capital needs, or cash is in place to retire the debt, it makes sense to exclude this debt from the calculation. If the debt is likely to be refinanced with new longer-term debt, it would seem logical to include this short-term debt in the leverage ratio calculation.

If this ratio is used to compare companies with very similar businesses, it can give a quick picture of which company is likely to have better asset protection (the less leveraged one). However, this does not give a sense of how much of an asset value cushion there is. To do that, there needs to be an estimate of how the company would be valued. Companies are often valued based on a multiple of cash flow: if the company generates EBITDA of $100 million, someone might be willing to pay $500 million for the company, which would imply it was worth 5× its EBITDA. If the same company had a debt/EBITDA ratio of 2.5× ($250 million of debt) it would imply that the $500 million asset value of the company covered the $250 million of debt 2×. The 5× figure that is being used to value the company in this example is often called the valuation multiple.

Many factors can impact what a company's valuation multiple is. Company A may have a higher multiple than company B because it has a higher cash flow growth rate, more consistent cash flow, lower capital expenditure requirements, or any number of other factors.

If a company being analyzed has public stock outstanding or comparable companies with public equities can be found, look at the total market enterprise value (EV) of these companies and see what this EV divided by adjusted EBITDA equals. This valuation multiple can be compared to the leverage ratio to get a sense of the market's view of the asset value relative to the debt level.

The total market enterprise value would be the public value of the company's stock plus all its debt, net of any cash on hand. There are other nuances that can be considered in developing this ratio. However, for our example, we can assume that if we were to look at three comparable publicly traded companies, they would trade at an average valuation multiple of 5×.

Exhibit 8.3 shows the calculation for an EV multiple. Take the total number of shares outstanding and multiply by the share price. Then add total debt and subtract the cash on hand, because the cash is not part of the value of the operating business. This market value of the equity plus the debt is a company's market enterprise value and is the numerator in the ratio. The denominator is the adjusted EBITDA. Note that the total number of shares is usually shown on the balance sheet, or more details can be included in the footnotes to the financial statements. Remember to use the same calculation for EBITDA in deriving both the valuation multiple and the leverage ratio.

Exhibit 8.3: Comparable Company Enterprise Value Calculation

	Comparable Company 1	Comparable Company 2	Comparable Company 3
Number of shares outstanding (in 000,000s)	175	330	345
Recent stock price (in dollars)	25	5	45
Total market equity value (in $000,000s)	4,375	1,650	15,525
Total debt (in $000,000s)	2,000	1,000	4,000
Minus cash on hand (in $000,000s)	100	300	200
Total enterprise value (EV) (in $000,000s)	6,275	2,350	19,325
Adjusted EBITDA (in $000,000s)	1,200	490	3,875
EV/adjusted EBITDA (valuation multiple)	5.2×	4.8×	5.0×

Another way that the size of the equity cushion can be estimated is if acquisitions of comparable companies have occurred within the industry. These acquisition transactions can be a great validation of what the value could be for the company. For example, suppose a comparable company were recently sold to a larger entity, and the buyer paid $1 billion for the company. Prior to being bought, the company generated $200 million of adjusted EBITDA; then the price it was sold for was equal to a valuation multiple of 5×.

If comparing different types of company in very different industries, what does the leverage ratio say? Well, in a vacuum, not much. The ratio is valuable if the ratios are examined on a relative basis, comparing the leverage ratios of each credit to the valuation multiples that are applicable to each industry, and then comparing the asset value cushions over the debt. When using public market equity multiples, an assumption has to be made that the stock market is valuing the company on trailing EBITDA, not on expectations of future EBITDA or some other metric.

Usually, companies in the same industry tend to be valued at fairly similar multiples. The valuations between industries can vary due to longer-term business trends, the level of competitiveness, the size of companies in that sector, and similar factors. Therefore, what are considered reasonable multiples for companies in one industry may be very different from what are considered reasonable in another industry. For example, a highly cyclical manufacturing company may trade at 5× to 6× adjusted EBITDA, and investors may feel more comfortable giving this type of company a leverage ratio between 3× and 4×. Meanwhile, investors may feel much more comfortable with a higher leverage ratio for a satellite communications company that has shown more stability and growth in its adjusted EBITDA and may see comparable equities trade at a multiple of adjusted EBITDA closer to 9×. Just as the valuations for different types of companies vary, so does the amount of leverage, or gearing, that investors find reasonable for a company.

There are two other debt ratios that are often used to look at leverage. They are less commonly used as they have less practical value, but analysts should be familiar with them: debt/equity and market-adjusted debt/EBITDA.

Debt/equity is a ratio that often appeared in older textbooks on financial analysis. In this case, equity is an accounting-derived value for the company when all liabilities are subtracted from all assets. This figure appears on the balance sheet and is shown in Exhibit 7.5 on line 18. The problem is that this is an accounting-derived number that can be adjusted by mergers and acquisitions, write-ups, and write-downs of assets, as net income losses (not cash flow losses). This accounting equity value rarely reflects a company's true value in the marketplace or for potential buyers of the company. The accounting measure of equity is sometimes referred to as book value, so this ratio is also sometimes referred to as debt/book value.

One of the common adjustments to the debt/equity ratio is using the market value of the equity instead of the book value. The implication is that the marketplace is properly valuing the company. The debt/equity market value is not dissimilar to comparing the leverage ratio to the market valuation multiple.

Market-adjusted debt (MAD)/EBITDA factors in the market value at which a company's bank loans and bonds are trading. This implies that securities bought at a discount are the real leverage risk that is being taken. For example, assume that a company has $1 billion of bank debt, $500 million of senior notes, and $200 million of subordinated notes outstanding. Also assume that an investor can buy each one at 95, 80, and 75 of face value. The market-adjusted debt would be $1.5 billion, as shown in Exhibit 8.4.

Exhibit 8.4: Market-Adjusted Debt (MAD) in $000,000s (Except Price)

	Amount	Price	MAD
Bank debt	1,000	95	950
Senior notes	500	80	400
Subordinated notes	200	75	150
Total	1,700		1,500

If the company's EBITDA were $400 million, its debt/EBITDA ratio would 4.25×, but its market-adjusted ratio would be 3.75×. To some extent, this ratio is unrealistic. If investing at the subordinated debt and a restructuring occurred, the bank loan and the senior notes would, conceivably, be paid their full face value before the subordinated notes would get anything. An investor would not really be buying the debt at 3.75×. It could be argued that this ratio is realistic for the most senior piece of the debt structure, the bank debt in this case, but not for the more junior tranches of debt.

When using any ratio based on market values, try not to just use the most recent price, especially if the price has been volatile. It can be helpful to use an average of the price over time. It is tempting to use the most recent, easily accessible data, but markets are fickle and can change rapidly. Some analysts like to average peak and trough market value ranges over a period of time, which is also reasonable in many cases.

EBITDA/total interest and debt/EBITDA, and their close derivatives, are the most widely used ratios. There follows a section on FCF/debt ratio. This is a valuable quick and comparative measure of financial strength but not as widely used.

Some Pragmatic Points on the Leverage Ratio

It is helpful to think of ratios in different ways.

What does the reciprocal of the debt/EBITDA ratio show? The reciprocal of this ratio is EBITDA/debt. This shows the maximum interest rate that the company could have on the debt and equals 1× interest coverage. For example, if the debt/ EBITDA ratio is 1,500/250 = 6×, the reciprocal is 0.167. If this company had a 16.7% interest rate, its interest expense would equal its EBITDA, so its interest coverage ratio would be 1×.

To quickly look at how high an interest rate this company could handle and still have enough to pay off $50 million of debt a year and service $50 million of capital expenditures a year, do the following: subtract $100 million from the EBITDA to service these two obligations and rerun the reciprocal. This would equal 150/1,500, which equals 0.10, or 10%. This type of analysis can give a quick snapshot when looking at restructuring or refinancing scenarios.

Something else to keep in mind is what it means if two companies have identical leverage ratios but very different EBITDA/interest expense ratios. It probably means one has much higher borrowing costs than the other, so why that is the case should be examined.

Another way to use the leverage ratio is that it can be run at various levels of seniority in the debt structure. If a company had €1 billion in secured bank debt, €500 million in senior subordinated debt, and €250 million of adjusted EBITDA, it could be said that its bank leverage was 4× (1 billion/250 million) and its total leverage was 6× (1.5 billion/250 million). The size of the increase in leverage between the two tranches has a big impact on how the two pieces of debt might trade relative to each other. If the difference in the leverage ratio between the bonds and loans were 1× rather than 2×, the yields on the secured and unsecured debt should be closer than if the differential were 2×.

A Pragmatic Point on Valuations

The preceding section highlighted EBITDA multiples for valuing a company. Using EBITDA multiples is a quick and fairly efficient way to derive enterprise values. Ratios such as EV/EBITDA are frequently used as a valuation measure. Another common multiple used in the equity market is the price/earnings ratio. Ultimately, these methods are shorthand versions for discounted cash flow (DCF) analysis, which is the best way to measure cash-flow-producing assets. The valuation of stock, theoretically, should represent the aggregate of what the universe of investors thinks is the right DCF value for a company.

This is true even for assets that are not producing cash flow. As an example, think of a company that has unused real estate. Buyers, consciously or unconsciously, will factor in what all the costs will be to develop the land and net that against the cash flow they believe they can get for the developed property. They may think of this in a value-per-square-foot format, but ultimately, that value per square foot is a proxy for how much cash flow can be generated from the asset.

Of course, don't assume that the DCF calculations are pure science that will result in everyone reaching the same number; numerous subjective factors are involved:

- What measure of cash flow will be used: FCF, EBITDA, or some other measure?
- What types of assumption are being used for the rate of growth or decline in the cash flow?
- Over what time period will the analysis be run?
- What terminal value will be applied to the calculation?
- What discount rate will be used (a proxy for the rate of return)?

Being pragmatic, it would not be practical to run a DCF on every company and respond in a timely manner to the typical daily pressures of analytical work. Using comparable EBITDA multiples is a great proxy for this longer analysis. However, it is worthwhile remembering that cash flow, or potential cash flow, over time, is the ultimate driver of value in most investment decisions.

It is a good exercise to periodically pick a company and run a DCF analysis to try to solve the market valuation. The analytical process will show what expectations need to be applied to the DCF to achieve the valuation and whether the assumptions that the market appears to be using make sense. This is a great way to spend a weekend or some vacation time.[7]

FCF Ratios

FCF ratios are another way to measure credit quality. These ratios can be used to show, hypothetically, how long it would take a company to pay off all its debt using cash generated by the company.

To determine the FCF that will be used, start with adjusted EBITDA and net out capital expenditures, cash interest expense, cash taxes, and changes in working capital. This FCF before capital expenditures should approximate the "net cash provided by operations" on the statement of cash flows. If it doesn't, the analyst should have a good explanation for the discrepancies.

Exhibit 8.5 shows a basic calculation for this FCF. It utilizes information from the prior chapter's Exhibit 7.2: Income Statement Sample 2, and Exhibit 7.3: Statement of Cash Flows.

---

7 DCF uses a measure of cash flow (CF) over a period of time, an interest rate or discount rate (DR), which is used to adjust each period of cash flow to an estimated present value, and a certain number of periods. The simple formula is DCF=$\Sigma((CF/1+dr)^n)$ for n periods. It could look like this: If the cash flow is $100 every year and the discount rate that was chosen is 5% (maybe based on the Treasury rates) and the time horizon of five years is chosen:

DCF = ($100/1+0.05)^1)+ ($100/1+0.05)^2) + ($100/1+0.05)^3) + ($100/1+0.05)^4) + ($100/1+0.05)^5).

Usually, a terminal value is added as well. This is an estimate of what the asset could be sold for at the end of the period and it is discounted using the same discount rate. This value is added to the discounted cash flow stream. If the asset valuation is estimated to be 5× cash flow at the end of year five, the formula is 5×100=500, (500/1+0.05)^5).

Exhibit 8.5: Sample of FCF in $000,000s

	All Using Column C from Exhibit 7.2 and 7.3	
Adjusted EBITDA	1,505	(Line 10 from Exhibit 7.2)
Less:		
Cash taxes	0	(Line 8, Exhibit 7.2; line 5, Exhibit 7.3)
Cash interest expense	475	(Line 6, Exhibit 7.2; line 4, Exhibit 7.3)
Capital expenditures	700	(Line 11, Exhibit 7.3)
Working capital (benefit)	(2)	(Sum of lines 6 through 9, Exhibit 7.3)
FCF	328	

Below are some considerations on each of the key components used in calculating FCF.

Changes in Working Capital

In some businesses, changes in working capital are so minimal that they may not even be worth including. If looking at quarterly numbers, be careful not to extrapolate or annualize swings in changes in working capital from one quarter. For many companies, they are highly seasonal. For some companies, changes in working capital may look extreme in one quarter but are relatively neutral over longer time periods.

Dividends

Dividends are discretionary and usually regular payments to the equity holders. In the USA, quarterly dividends are typical; in Europe, annual dividends are more common. If a company has been paying a regular dividend, it is often reluctant to stop or even reduce these payments for fear of how this may be perceived by shareholders. Some companies occasionally pay a special dividend rather than a regular one. Because of the discretionary nature of dividends, many analysts do not deduct them when arriving at FCF. However, if the FCF/debt ratio is used to determine how much cash is available to pay down debt, and the company is a regular dividend payer, it is not likely to cut that dividend to pay down debt unless it absolutely has to. If the company is a regular dividend payer, subtracting that payment from FCF is prudent too.

Acquisitions

An acquisition is usually an occasional or one-time event for a company. However, some companies are constantly buying assets, and doing so is an ongoing part of their business plan. An analyst must decide whether to include these acquisitions in the calculations for FCF. Typically, they are not included because of their discretionary nature. Acquisitions and divestitures are usually shown in the investment section of the statement of cash flows.

One-Time Charges

One-time charges typically appear on the income statement as an expense item. This type of charge often has both a cash component and a noncash component.

A noncash portion of this charge would appear in the statement of cash flows as an addition to cash from operations. Net the noncash portion of the charge from the total portion on the income statement to determine the actual cash spent on these charges. An example would be a company undertaking a number of layoffs. The charge may include payments to be made to the laid-off workers over a period of years. The total charge on the income statement may be the present value of these payments, but only a portion of this was actually paid out in the year of the layoffs, and that would be the cash portion.

You must decide whether the cash portion of these irregular expenses should be included or excluded in the FCF calculation. For example, suppose an analyst is trying to determine the ability of a credit to pay down debt over time. Over the last several years, the company has only had a cash restructuring charge appear once. In this case, it is probably best to ignore it. However, if the goal is to see how much cash flow is generated to meet a maturity this year, it might be important to include. If this type of charge seems to have occurred with great frequency over recent years, it would be best to charge it against the company's cash flow in the FCF calculation.

The FCF/Debt Ratio

Once it has been determined which method of FCF calculation is being used, an analyst will probably want to compare it to different time periods and other companies. The easiest way to do this is by using it in a ratio. One ratio that can be used is FCF/debt. Using the FCF from Exhibit 8.5, and previous examples of FCF of $377 million and debt of $1.7 billion from Exhibit 8.4, this ratio would be 22% for our sample company.

In this example, the ratio tells us that in the past twelve months, the company generated enough FCF to retire 22% of the debt structure per year. The higher the number, the more quickly the company can deleverage and deal with maturities. This is not to say that the company will necessarily choose to pay down debt with the cash it generates, but it can. This is a useful tool to see a company's relative strength in generating true cash from operations and its ability to meet its obligations. The FCF level can also be compared to the amount of upcoming debt maturities. Calculations with FCF show a truer cash generation picture of the company than EBITDA.

A Pragmatic Point on FCF

When FCF is not very high, carefully examine the maturity schedule and other required uses of liquidity as well as other sources of liquidity. Liquidity sources obviously include cash and equivalents and undrawn bank borrowings. Read the terms of the bank borrowing agreement to make sure the proceeds would actually be available to draw; covenants usually have to be met before the borrowing is available. Also look at assets that could be sold and try to assess whether the company would be able to raise money in the public or PE or debt markets.

Closing Comment

Ratio analysis is the basis of a significant part of the investment decision-making process, as it allows an investor to easily make comparisons to historical performance and among various credits and investment opportunities. The two most basic ratios in leveraged finance credit analysis are linked to the two most critical questions of credit analysis: 1) is there enough liquidity to service the debt and all other cash obligations, and 2) in case there is not enough liquidity, is there enough asset value to repay the lenders? The two key ratios in their most basic form are very simple. The ratios become more nuanced as adjustments are made to the numerator and denominator to gain a more realistic assessment and meet analytical needs.

Chapter 9

Financial Issues: Business Trend Analysis and Operational Ratios

What's in this chapter:

- revenue and EBITDA trends
- volatility of operating results
- margins and expenses
- capital expenditures

INTEREST COVERAGE AND leverage ratios are financial or credit metrics. They measure how well the company can service aspects of its debt structure. It is also critical to look at how well the underlying business is doing to understand trends that will lead to cash flow increases or declines and impact the credit ratios going forward. This will involve examining trends in the business's performance metrics and operational ratios.

It is also important to examine risks in the business that may not be easily captured with numbers in the financial statements. Sometimes data on these topics is easy to track, but other times, it can take considerable work and creativity to find sources to monitor some of these items. Checklists or rankings can be good tools to monitor subjective issues such as the following:

- the competitive environment in which the company operates
- the barriers to entry in the industry
- sensitivity to the macro economy or to event risks
- dependence on a few key customers
- how capital-intensive the business is
- whether the company is a price taker or a price setter

Revenue and EBITDA Trends

Presenting the financial data in different ways can often help an analyst look at operational trends in a credit. It is best to focus on basic trends in a company's revenue and EBITDA over the last three to five years, as shown in Exhibit 9.1. When possible, it is also good to analyze this by quarter for at least the latest two years, comparing year-over-year results for each quarter (see Exhibit 9.2). It can also prove helpful to show all or some of the data in a graphic format as shown in Exhibit 9.3. Experiment with different graphic display formats; the same format does not always work for every data series. In Exhibit 9.3, it is easy to see movements and trends in several of the financial items, but because of the scale and the smaller changes in EBITDA, it is hard to visually decipher trends. Therefore, showing it graphically, by itself, or without the revenue line, may provide a better visual for EBITDA.

Exhibit 9.1: Simple Trend Analysis Annually in $000,000s

	Year 1	Year 2	Year 3	Year 4	Year 5
Revenue	1,300	1,250	1,325	1,355	1,395
% change		(3.8%)	6.0%	2.3%	3.0%
EBITDA	273	253	282	294	315
% change		(7.5%)	11.8%	4.3%	7.1%
Margin	21.0%	20.2%	21.3%	22.0%	22.6%

Exhibit 9.2: Simple Trend Analysis Quarterly in $000,000s

	Year 2 Q1	Year 3 Q1	Year 2 Q2	Year 3 Q2
Revenue	300	305	310	325
% change		1.7%		4.8%
EBITDA	60	61	64	68
% change		1.9%		7.4%
Margin	20.0%	20.1%	20.5%	21.0%

Exhibit 9.3: Annual Trend Analysis Graphic

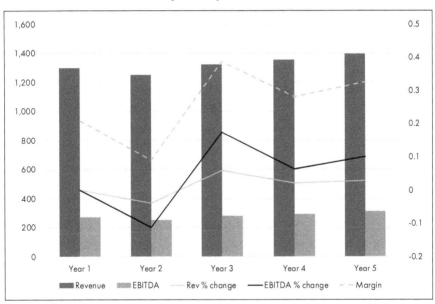

This analysis is designed to look for trends and relationships in the patterns of a company's operating data. One common comparison is looking at how well the company has grown revenue relative to broad economic measures, such as the gross domestic product (GDP) in the country in which the company operates. It is also common to compare the growth rates and the margins with the same data for other companies in the same industry.

In analyzing the figures, see if the company made acquisitions or divestitures that had some impact on the numbers. This information should be found in the text of the management's discussion in its financial statement and the statement of cash flows in the Investing Activity section.

If the company has made acquisitions or divestitures of assets of a meaningful size, hopefully it will have supplied pro forma information. Pro forma information typically shows what key financial statistics would look like for the company if the transaction had occurred several periods earlier. As an example, if Atlas Corp. bought Neptune Inc. in January of one year the pro forma data might show what the prior year's revenue, EBITDA, and interest expense would have been for Atlas Corp., combined with the revenue and EBITDA of Neptune Inc. and with any additional interest expense related to the financing. Usually pro forma information will be shown in a format that allows year-over-year comparisons to be made as if the acquisition had actually been completed several periods before. These are not projections, but a view of combined past results.

If a company has several business lines, any trend analysis should also try to break out the details of these business lines. This way, it can be seen which ones are causing the greatest changes in the company's overall results. The breakout of business lines typically appears on either the income statement or in management's description of recent results. However, sometimes it appears in the footnotes to the financial statements. Other times, it can only be found in the earnings press release that a company may file. Some companies simply do not break out divisional or business line results.

Additionally, in the notes to the financial statements, the company usually breaks out business done domestically and internationally. This can also help an analyst know if some of the change in results was due to declines or growth in specific business areas or currency changes.

Volatility of Operating Results

When examining the credit quality of a company and comparing it to other debt issuers, the predictability of a company's financial results can be a differentiating factor. When a company has a higher level of predictability (and/or less volatility in its results), it often can give investors greater comfort with owning an investment in that company, and this can cause the debt to trade at lower yields. A common measure of volatility is standard deviation, which is a measure of the average of how much each data point varies from a dataset's average. For example, examine how much volatility various companies have had in their level of EBITDA each year over the last ten years. An average EBITDA of $150 million and a standard deviation of $20 million means that, on average, the annual EBITDA of the company is likely to vary up or down by $20 million from $150 million. Compare this to another company and see which has less volatility. This could imply that the company with the lower volatility has greater predictability and perhaps poses less risk in its level of EBITDA.

There are items to consider when using standard deviation. First, an analyst would want to know if there were any events that might have meaningfully moved EBITDA for one company but not others, such as a significant merger. Second, standard deviation does not distinguish between upside and downside volatility. An investor would not mind volatility if all the big changes to EBITDA were due to exceptional growth rather than wild swings between growth and declines. More advanced analysis might measure upside volatility separately from downside volatility. However, the use of standard deviation is a starting place to compare the stability of a company's operational results.[8]

Industry Specific Operational Metrics

Certain key performance indicators (KPIs) are specific to a sector or an industry. Become familiar with KPIs that are specific to a certain industry to get a sense of relative operational performance between credits in the same business sector. Some examples may include comparing drop and handle per square foot of casino space in the gaming industry, or the cost of acquiring subscribers for a cable television company (cost per gross add [CPGA]), or the net present value of gas and oil reserves for an energy company. Sometimes these industry metrics are focused on change over time. When an industry is in a high growth/low cash flow cycle, the focus may be different than when an industry is more mature and generating more cash. Some industries try to push analysts to certain metrics. When this happens, it is always good to question the reason behind the industry's efforts.

---

8 Standard deviation is usually denoted by the Greek letter σ. To calculate standard deviation for a dataset, you first establish the mean for the dataset. Then for each number in the set, you take the number and subtract the mean. Once each difference is calculated, square each, sum all of these squared differences, and divide by the number of items in the dataset—in other words, take the mean of all these squared differences. Then calculate the square root of that mean.

Margins and Expenses

In our simplified trend analysis exhibit above, there is a line labeled "Margin." This is the EBITDA margin. The EBITDA margin is calculated as EBITDA/revenue, giving a sense of a company's ability to convert revenue to EBITDA. If the company is producing meaningful changes in margins, examine the expense items in greater detail.

One common item for retailers and manufacturers to analyze is the cost of goods sold (COGS). This is usually broken out as a separate item and is labeled the "gross profit margin." The calculation takes revenue less cost of goods, and this totals gross income. Gross profit margin is gross income/revenue. To some extent, this is the value added by the company. In a simplified example, if a can manufacturer buys aluminum as its only material production input, the difference in the company's revenue less the cost of the aluminum should equal the gross profit and is the value added that the company created with that aluminum.

Examining expenses and margins can give a sense of the company's operating leverage, which measures how well its growth in revenue can be translated into cash flow (different from financial leverage or balance sheet leverage).

One aspect of expenses to analyze for a better idea of a company's operating leverage is whether the company has a high portion of its total expenses as fixed expenses, meaning they do not shift when sales go up or down. Expenses that are not fixed are considered variable expenses and tend to move along with the revenue level. Therefore, if there is a high level of fixed expenses, the EBITDA margin can increase significantly as revenues rise. This implies higher operating leverage and margins should go up as revenue rises. Said another way, when there is high operating leverage and revenue is rising, EBITDA should have a higher growth rate than revenue. However, if a company's revenue is declining, fixed costs cannot come down as easily as variable costs, and margins may shrink more rapidly.

Unfortunately, companies typically do not define their fixed and variable costs. Try to estimate these by looking at different time periods and the descriptions of the line items in the expenses (see Exhibit 9.4). Sometimes conversations with management can help, or company presentations can give insights into the level of fixed and variable costs. By looking at many companies in the same industry over periods of time, an analyst can acquire a better sense of operating leverage in an industry.

When comparing margins among different companies in the same business, note whether one has meaningfully better margins than the other, and try to analyze why. The difference in margin may be due to management styles or because one company operates in an area of the country where rents and employment costs are higher or lower. Another common reason is economies of scale. In many industries, a large company has better pricing for its supplies and perhaps has pricing power for the finished goods, as well as being able to leverage fixed costs. Try to analyze what is causing the differences in margins among similar companies.

Exhibit 9.4: Simple Trend Analysis with Costs Annually in $000,000s

	Year 1	Year 2	% Change	Year 3	% Change
Revenue	1,300	1,250	-3.8%	1,325	6.0%
Cost of goods sold	500	489	-2.2%	522	6.7%
Gross profit	800	761	-4.9%	803	5.5%
Gross margin	61.5%	60.9%		60.6%	
Expenses:					
Selling expenses	400	382	-4.5%	397	3.9%
As a % of revenue	30.8%	30.6%		30.0%	
General and administrative expenses	127	126	-0.8%	124	-1.6%
As a % of revenue	9.8%	10.1%		9.4%	
Depreciation and amortization	72	70		68	
Operating income	201	183		214	
EBITDA	273	253	-7.5%	282	11.8%
Margin	21.0%	20.2%		21.3%	

In Exhibit 9.4, the growth rates appear in a separate column to make the data easier to read. Here are a few items to notice:

1. *Gross margin:* This has gone down at least two years in a row, in both a year of revenue growth and a year of decline. This trend is troubling and may begin to be a long-term problem for the business, even though the change is not large.
2. *Selling expenses:* These are variable, but not as variable as revenue. It would appear that selling expenses have a fixed cost component as well as a variable one. This can include sales salaries, fixed costs for a marketing team, and perhaps promotional spending.
3. *General and administrative expenses:* These appear relatively fixed.

Capital Expenditures

The most common way of looking at capital expenditures is as a percentage of total revenue. However, for different industries it may be worth looking at capital expenditures as a percentage of plant, property, and equipment (which is a proxy for business assets), as a percentage of total capital or as a percentage of EBITDA.

Analysis of capital expenditures can be even more valuable if it is possible to break out the difference between maintenance capital spending and the capital spending related to special projects or expansion plans that are more one-time in nature. The maintenance capital spending can be examined as a percentage of revenue to get a sense of the needed rate of reinvestment in the business to maintain the company's operations.

Capital expenditures can also be useful to look at in a time series to see how they have varied versus revenue levels. This can also give an idea of how much is ongoing maintenance capital spending and how much is related to special projects. It is important to remember that when valuing a company, the level of near-term and ongoing capital expenditures can have an impact on the valuation of the company. The fact that different industries have different levels of capital spending can be part of the reason why one industry's average EBITDA valuation multiple is higher or lower than that of another industry.

When comparing different companies in the same industry, it can be informative to examine whether one company has higher growth rates and is investing in capital more than another company does. A company may, for any number of reasons, defer capital expenditures for a period of time. This may make the FCF generation look higher on both an absolute basis and as a percentage of revenue, for a period of time. But the concern when expenditures are deferred is that the firm may have underinvested and may have to play catch-up for a period of time, during which it experiences a spike in capital spending. Another concern when a company is underinvesting in its business is that it could fall behind competitors. It is important to remember that many expenditures can be capitalized. It is not just physical investment. Capitalized expenses could include investments in intellectual property such as media content or software.

It is worth noting that many textbooks and much equity-based research highlight return-on-investment (ROI) analysis or return-on-equity (ROE) analysis. This is done by using a measure of earnings over a denominator, which uses a percentage of invested capital or some valuation of the equity. This type of analysis is certainly helpful in measuring the value of the company's business investment and differences in the management teams or the quality of company assets.

Other Comments on Business Analysis

There are many other layers of business analysis that can be undertaken, including efficiency of sales and manufacturing, and the interaction between capital efficiency and revenue. One of the struggles in undertaking an analysis from outside the business is that many of the more nuanced aspects that are interesting to explore, such as revenue per salesperson, may not be made publicly available. When analyzing a business from the inside, or on a private basis, more of this information may be accessible. Some of the typical ratios that can be used to analyze a business are derived from public information, including the following:

- turnover ratios for assets: net sales (revenue)/average of total assets
- turnover ratio for accounts payable: sales/average accounts payable
- turnover ratio for accounts receivable: sales/average accounts receivable
- turnover ratio for inventory: cost of goods sold/average inventory
- revenue efficiency: sales/average number of employees (or average assets)

Most industries and companies have specific KPIs they will regularly release, either with their financial results or sometimes monthly. Examples of these include the following:

- *Same-store-sales in retailing*: This measures the change in average sales per store for stores that have been open for at least two periods.
- *Book-to-bill ratio*: Common in the semiconducter industry, this measures new orders received, divided by the amount of product delivered. It is used as a measure of new order trends.
- *Average revenue per unit (ARPU)*: This is common in subscriber businesses that measure pricing trends per unit and was common, for a period, in the cable television and mobile phone industries.

The thing to remember about KPIs is that they are usually developed by the companies, which, generally, determine if they want to make them available to investors and analysts. For example, for many years, companies regularly reported same-store-sales and ARPU. Then, many companies stopped providing the data, which was not available elsewhere. Clearly, the data was no longer helping the companies' stories. Question if the KPIs being given are really valuable or a bit of propaganda. Some KPIs have proven quite misleading as a measure of business value. If the vast majority of companies in an industry use a certain KPI, and one company does not, it should definitely be a warning to dig deeper into the company that excludes it and be extra wary of that credit.

You will also want to develop a series of checks for a company's competitive position in a market. This may include comparing its revenue growth rates to those of its peers. If a company reports product volume or customer count comparisons, track these trends versus those of its peers. The data may give insights into whether the company is gaining or losing market share to the competition. Some industries provide good industry data, derived from industry groups, government agencies, or sometimes even third-party private vendors, which can be used to gauge a company's competitive position. Keep in mind that many industry groups are actually lobbyist organizations for the industry, so their information contains natural biases. Industry research by third-party vendors also contains an innate bias: they need to help the industry survive so they can keep selling the information.

Barriers to entry can be a vital competitive advantage. How strong an industry or company's barriers to entry are is not easily defined in a quantitative number, but it is something that has to be considered as a potential strength or weakness when analyzing a business.

In businesses that are in more developmental stages, management will often try to develop an idea of which other industries they may be taking revenue away from, and what their total addressable market (TAM) might be. TAMs can be definitionally dependent, so always be skeptical: examine how well defined these TAMs really are.

It is not enough just to notice a business trend or catch a change in a company's competitive position. Try to understand what is causing these changes and whether they are temporary or permanent. That is where real differences can occur in investment performance.

A Pragmatic Point about Companies Outside the Market

It is easy, when analyzing an industry or a sector, to be very focused on the companies and not beyond that universe. This tendency can lead to weak analysis. Look at closely aligned businesses that could pose a threat or an opportunity. For example, analysts focusing solely on data storage companies may not see software makers and Internet retailers that are moving into the cloud storage market and disrupting the data storage industry.

In most cases, companies in the leveraged debt markets are not the market leaders in their industry. They are often more in the middle of the pack or even at the small end within their markets. Analysts that only examine these companies in leveraged debt markets may miss potential big changes in the industry that could materially impact the companies they are supposed to be monitoring. To avoid this, be sure to pick out some of the industry leaders in any industry that is being examined. They may be public companies with no debt, or investment-grade companies. Look at the trends these companies' operations are going through. Read which strategies they are pursuing or listen to their management teams to glean insights into potential changes in the industry.

Closing Comment

A credit analyst needs to analyze the debt issuer's ability to service the debt, but part of that job is being able to analyze a company's operations. In analyzing the operations of a debt issuer, an analyst wants to get a sense of the consistency and resiliency of the business, as well as the likelihood of future growth or decline in the business. These trends will end up impacting cash flow and debt service. A company that has more volatility in its ability to generate cash flow will worry debt investors more than one that is consistent, so understanding the company's history as well as its outlook is critical to good credit analysis. Understanding business trends and the competitive landscape for a credit can lead to insights about likely event risks as well.

Chapter 10

Financial Issues: Expectations, Modeling, and Scenarios

What's in this chapter:

- guidance and forecast construction
- revenue modeling
- EBITDA and free cash flow modeling
- debt structure
- scenarios
- a pragmatic point on bank maintenance covenants and expectations

H ISTORICAL DATA IS very important to credit analysis, but an analyst has to develop a forward-looking analysis framework as well. This involves utilizing historical data to get an idea of what the company is capable of and which trends are likely to influence future performance. This forms the basis for developing an idea of what the company might look like going forward and whether the company is going to be better or weaker over time. The analyst can build a single model of what the future might look like for the credit, or a series of scenarios. As prediction is hard, scenarios are the better path when time permits.

Guidance and Forecast Construction

Many companies give guidance for a few selected metrics. This is often used as the basis of projections or scenarios. Company guidance is typically given for the next quarter or the next year or both. Companies with public stocks can be very sensitive about making sure they give guidance that they can beat or come very close to. For companies with public stock, there are also areas that provide a composite of sell-side equity analysts' earnings estimates. These are often called consensus estimates and can be viewed as a measure of how investor expectations might be set.

In the bank market, investors who choose to go private on a company can generally get three- to five-year projections from the company, but they are prohibited from sharing that information with others who are not private. They may also be prohibited from trading in the company's public bonds or stock. A company's guidance, or longer-term projections, serves as the basis from which an analyst can judge the company's performance and build a model, or set of scenarios. If guidance is available from a number of companies in the same industry, look to see if there are any meaningful differences in the trends they are outlining.

Most forecasting involves a certain amount of extrapolation from past performance and some insight into whether recent trends are going to be maintained, accelerate, decline, or reverse. Forecasting is often categorized as either bottom up or top down: it can come from the bottom up by building from expectations for each operational division within the company and expanding to look at overall company performance to see how that performance fits with industry expectations and how that industry fits into the outlook for the general economy. Top-down categorization starts with the overall economic picture and works down to specific revenue and expense drivers. In reality, forecasting should involve both macro and micro factors. The macroeconomic outlook will be more important for cyclical businesses and less so for more defensive businesses, but they are all intertwined.

When building a forecast, it is common to start with what drives revenue and then work down through expenses. Ideally, certain KPIs that would drive revenue should be identified. They could be data made available by the company or industry data. As an example, a software company may regularly give updates on how many customers it has subscribed to its service. This could be used to derive a revenue model and build scenarios to see the sensitivity to changes in the customer count and changes in the average revenue per customer. Another example would be a company involved in the automotive space, where available industry and government data on total car sales can be used to build up a revenue model based on estimates of the company's market share.

Revenue Modeling

When building a model, ideally, there are certain items that drive revenue and expenses, such as units sold or contract renewals. Keep in mind that any model should be built so that it can be sustained over time. Choose inputs that can be obtained regularly, because the model should be updated as new data becomes available. For example, if there is a great data point that could be used to drive a model, but it only becomes available once every ten years, and another slightly weaker data point is updated every year, it is better to use the more frequently available one in the model. Rarely is the ideal information needed to build a model available. There will always be levels of uncertainty. Anyone doing credit analysis has to balance thoroughness and precision with timeliness and reality.

A decision has to be made as to how detailed to make the revenue model. For example, should there be a line item for every business division, or will it be enough to model the overall revenue? The level of detail for various line items may vary depending on what the biggest questions or concerns are surrounding the credit. If revenue is volatile and margins are more stable, it may be worth spending more time on the line items that build up revenue forecasts than on expense items.

One typical way to start building any model is from the top down by trying to derive which macro numbers influence revenue. It can start with GDP. However, often, data more specific to an industry can be gleaned. It can vary by industry and company. Often, specific projected data is available from companies, industry groups, or government entities. Do not underestimate the amount of data on government websites that have industry outlooks, and projections from government agencies and other organizations around the globe such as OPEC and the OECD.

After the key macro drivers are chosen, the next step is to figure out how those drivers impact revenue. One methodology would be to back-test relationships and go through results for the last several years to see how well correlated a company's revenue is to these macro factors. For example, historically, has the company's change in revenue moved in unison with changes in GDP or with computer sales?

It is also important to include any plans for expansion or divestiture that the company is undergoing. For example, in looking at a retailer, the model may use a consensus outlook for national consumer spending for the next year as a driver for that retailer's revenue expectations. However, if the retailer plans to build ten new stores a year, this expansion must be incorporated into the model as well. It might make sense to project sales per square foot for the retailer (this refers to square feet of selling space in the stores). As the company expands new stores, simply add more square feet to the model. It might look something like Exhibit 10.1.

Exhibit 10.1: Sample Model Driver

	A	B	C	D	E	F
	Year 1 Actual	Year 2 Actual	Year 3 Actual	Year 4 Projected	Year 5 Projected	Year 6 Projected
1 Consensus retails sales growth				1.00%	3.50%	1.00%
Company Data						
2 Sales/ sq. ft. (in $)	420	418	421	425	440	444
3 Growth rate		-0.5%	0.7%	1.0%	3.5%	1.0%
4 Total retail sq. ft.	200,000	200,000	205,000	215,000	225,000	245,000
5 Total sales (in $)	84,000,000	83,600,000	86,305,000	91,420,150	99,020,779	108,900,852
6 Growth rate		-0.5%	3.2%	5.9%	8.3%	10.0%

In this simple example, columns A, B and C are historical results. The next three columns are projected estimates. This model is driven by sales per square foot, in line 2, and total retail square feet, in line 4. It assumes that the company's sales per square foot, or retail space, grow with the industry consensus and that the company grows its total sales (line 5) above the industry rate by adding square feet of retail space in the projected years. The first thing that someone with a healthy level of cynicism should notice is that the growth rates in the projected years are much higher than in the historical years. The main factors appear to be both higher growth in sales per square foot and more square feet owned by the company. This assumes that new retail space will capture as much revenue per square foot as existing retail space and thus implies that simply by adding square footage, the company can capture market share. This could be true, but it can be viewed as a fairly aggressive optimistic outlook.

There are more detailed aspects that could be added to the modeling. For example, there could be a breakdown of different components of the retail square footage by how much was dedicated to various products, or stores could be analyzed to see if they do better in some regions than in others. However, some of this data might not be available. An analyst could look at the historical data to see if this modeling concept would explain previous actual results.

There are simpler revenue modeling techniques. Rather than try to create a model with data that derives the revenue, such as in Exhibit 10.1, an analyst could take historical data and build projected revenue from the historical data. This could be as a simple as applying an anticipated industry growth rate to the most recent year, or just extrapolating future growth from the most recent period. If revenue has had a highly predictable growth pattern in the past, it might be easy to rationalize; but clearly, a situation could be oversimplified, especially if an industry is going through transition.

When preparing a financial model on a company that is entering a new operational phase, such as opening a new hotel or introducing a new product line, it can become harder to project revenue. Try to study similar projects undertaken by competitors to see how they evolved, how quickly revenue ramped, and where cost overruns occurred. Then, apply judgmental techniques to the size of project that is being undertaken at the company being analyzed.

For some companies, revenue mix can be a very important aspect of cash flow volatility. A company may have some high margin revenue lines and some lower margin revenue lines. Some sales may have a much longer selling cycle, and some much shorter. The business mix is important to consider when modeling both revenue and EBITDA.

Sales models can change, too, and this can impact the revenue. This is true of technology-driven fields such as mobile phone services, enterprise software, and the music industry; in all of these the revenue shifted from a product sales model to a subscriptions model. Changing sales models have to be considered when building out any projections. A shift in how products are sold, priced, or distributed can be very disruptive in the near term and increase the need for short-term cash, even if, in the long term, the plan seems sound.

Thoroughness versus Timeliness

Some analysts are modeling junkies. They build elaborately detailed and interconnected models. There are clearly times when this is necessary. But be careful not to spend too much time on elaborate models when a simpler one can give the same results. An analyst always must balance thoroughness against timeliness. A model should be easily adaptable so it can be used to react quickly to breaking news on a company. If a more elaborate and complex model is appropriate, it is wise to have a much simpler submodel that can be used and updated rapidly. Even the best analysis loses its value if the opportunity has passed and if the rationale and conclusions cannot be communicated coherently.

EBITDA and Free Cash Flow Modeling

The model in Exhibit 10.2 goes from revenue through expenses, EBITDA, free cash flow and then to modeling the important debt metrics and capitalization. This model uses a maker of car tires as an example. Columns B through D represent historical results. Columns E through G represent projections.

Exhibit 10.2: Actual and Projected Model Sample for a Tire Company (in 000,000s Unless Noted)

		A	B	C	D	E	F
		Year 1 Actual	Year 2 Actual	Year 3 Actual	Year 4 Projected	Year 5 Projected	Year 6 Projected
	Drivers						
1	Car sales	19	22	21	20	19	22
2	Inflation	1.00%	2.00%	1.00%	1.50%	1.50%	1.50%
3	Replacement units	15	14	15	15	15	15
4	New car units (mkt. shr. *4)	15	19	18	18	17	19
5	New car market share	20%	22%	22%	22%	22%	22%
6	Price per unit (in $)	30	30.343	30.499	30.75	31	31.25
7	Price growth		1.1%	0.5%	0.8%	0.8%	0.8%
	Income Statement Data						
8	Revenue	906	1,012	1,021	1,002	983	1,074
9	Revenue growth		11.7%	0.9%	-1.8%	-1.9%	9.2%
10	Cost of goods sold	589	668	679	677	669	736
11	Gross profit	317	344	342	325	314	338
12	Gross margin	35%	34%	34%	32%	32%	31%
13	Selling, general, and administrative	181	192	194	195	197	204
14	Depreciation	85	83	82	81	81	80
15	Operating income	51	69	66	49	37	54
16	Total interest expense	28	28	28	27	27	27
17	Cash taxes	9	15	14	8	4	10
18	EBITDA	136	152	148	130	117	134
19	Margin	15%	15%	15%	13%	12%	12%
	Free Cash Flow						
20	EBITDA	136	152	148	130	117	134
21	Capital expenditures	72	71	70	69	69	68
22	Interest expense	28	28	28	27	27	27

		A	B	C	D	E	F
		Year 1 Actual	Year 2 Actual	Year 3 Actual	Year 4 Projected	Year 5 Projected	Year 6 Projected
23	Cash taxes	9	15	14	8	4	10
24	Working capital uses	12	14	14	-5	12	15
25	Free cash flow	15	24	22	31	5	14
	Debt						
26	Bank debt (4%) due year 5*	300	300	290	280	270	270
27	Senior notes (8%) due year 6	200	200	200	200	200	200
28	Total debt	500	500	490	480	470	470
	Other Data						
29	Interest expense	28	28	28	27	27	27
30	Cash	20	44	66	98	103	117
	Credit Metrics						
31	EBITDA/total interest	4.9×	5.4×	5.3×	4.8×	4.3×	5.0×
32	Bank debt/ EBITDA	2.2×	2.0×	2.0×	2.1×	2.3×	2.0×
33	Total debt/EBITDA	3.7×	3.3×	3.3×	3.7×	4.0×	3.5×
34	Net debt/EBITDA	3.5×	3.0×	2.9×	2.9×	3.1×	2.6×
35	FCF/debt	3.00%	4.80%	4.60%	6.50%	1.40%	3.00%

* Amortization begins in year 3. This assumes the debt is refinanced at the end of year 5 at the same rate.

The macro drivers for the model include national car sales in line 1 and inflation in line 2. We assume these come from third-party sources, such as industry association or government historical data and projections. The sales are driven by replacement tires (line 3), which remain relatively constant, new car sales, and an estimate of the company's market share of tire sales for new cars. Revenue is simply driven by unit sales and price (line 3 + line 4 multiplied by line 6). Note that the price per unit, both historically and in the projected numbers, does not keep pace with inflation; the prices actually rise at only about half the rate of inflation.

Cost of goods sold is on line 10 and represents raw material and direct manufacturing costs. Line 13 has other operating expenses. The cost of goods sold should be impacted by the number of sales as well as inflation. This exhibit shows that cost of goods has been rising, and the model projects that it will rise more quickly than revenue, more in line with overall inflation, and this is causing gross profit margins to decline. Selling, General and Administrative (SG&A) expenses move along relatively consistently as a percentage of revenue.

It is usually not worthwhile to try to build a model of expenses with items that cannot be tracked in the future. If a company is not going to make certain detailed data on expenses available, it will likely not make sense to break it out in the model.

Even though companies do not usually break out costs into categories of fixed and variable, it is helpful to try to think of business expenses in this way. It is a good exercise to try to estimate the breakdown of expenses in this way, but it is hard to maintain a model based on this type of breakdown from the public documents typically available to an analyst.

When raw material inputs are part of the expenses, they can sometimes be modeled separately, such as crude oil for a refinery or paper costs for a printing plant. It is helpful to run scenarios with different commodity pricing environments. It is also helpful to factor in wage inflation and pension costs if applicable. Interest expense appears on line 22. It is derived from the debt capitalization. Usually, it is best to build a separate capitalization section of a model, run the interest expense from that section, and link it to the income statement. This model takes the average debt amount outstanding during a given year from lines 26 and 27. It multiplies the average amount outstanding by the respective interest rate for each tranche of debt and adds them together. Models can get more complex, particularly for floating-rate debt, and factor in scenarios with increasing or decreasing interest rates.

Starting on line 20, a section is set up to derive FCF. We start with EBITDA and then begin to subtract other selected cash uses. Capital expenditures are usually the most important item that needs to be included. Company management often gives guidance on these expenses, particularly if large projects are being undertaken.

A typical method of modeling capital expenditures is as a percentage of revenue. However, look at other factors. For example, if a company has been expanding or contracting its businesses, this could cause a shift in capital expenditures. Also, some types of capital expenditure can be lumpy, where very little has to be spent for several years, but then there is a large increase for the replacement of a major item.

Depreciation figures shift due to changes in capital expenditures, but also from adjustments for changes in tax accounting, write-ups, write-downs, or write-offs of asset value. It can be insightful to try to examine, over various periods of time, how well depreciations and capital expenditures are aligned. If they are materially different, try to understand why. It can give insights into the consistency and predictability of a company's capital investment. Mergers and acquisitions are often the cause of a mismatch between depreciation and amortization versus capital expenditures. Tax codes can also cause changes as they sometimes allow for companies to undertake acceleration of depreciation. The footnotes to the financial statements often discuss the useful life of the company's major assets, at least for accounting purposes. If capital expenditures are very low as a percentage of depreciation over time, it may be a sign that these expenditures need to spike suddenly. Similarly, if a major asset is nearing the end of its accounting useful life, explore whether there might be a pickup in capital spending.

When calculating FCF, always check if there is a difference in the interest expense reported on the income statement (total interest expense) and actual cash interest expense paid (cash interest expense). The latter is typically broken out on the statement of cash flows.

Cash taxes can usually be calculated based on a pretax net income figure when modeling FCF. However, many leveraged companies do not have to pay taxes if they do not generate pretax net income or because they have built up excess tax losses (net operating losses) that can be used to defer tax bills. So do not fall into the trap of assuming that a tax line on the income statement is actually a cash item. Always check the statement of cash flows and the footnotes.

Changes in working capital can also impact FCF. This can be hard to model going forward, and it is not something on which management always offers guidance. It is helpful to see how working capital has changed relative to revenue levels in the past and look at historical trends during various cycles.

Do not forget to explore the financial statement footnotes of a company to find details of pension obligations. While details may appear elsewhere in the statements, they are commonly set out in the footnotes. Pension-related expenses sometimes are large for companies with a legacy of a large employment base and may need to be modeled separately from other expenses.

Debt Structure

It is useful to build out a separate debt and liquidity portion of the model. In Exhibit 10.2 there is just a summary section on the debt, starting on line 26. The primary source of liquidity is cash, on line 30. In this model, the tire company generates positive FCF. A decision must be made as to what to do with the cash in the model. In this case, for the first two years of historical results in columns B and C, the company simply adds the FCF to its cash position. In year 3, in column D, bank amortization begins. Some FCF is used to pay down bank debt ($10 million), and then the balance is added to cash. Based on this historical pattern, the model assumes that the company will do the same in the projected years. Depending on what the covenants in the bank debt and bonds allow, the company could also deploy the cash for uses that are not as debt friendly. These uses could include buybacks of stock, dividend payments, minority investments in other companies, or acquisitions.

In the debt sections, break out each piece of the debt structure in as much detail as possible. Read through the footnotes or the separate exhibits that describe the debt instruments and note the maturities of debt and any scheduled principal amortization. It is recommended that a separate section in the model be set up, highlighting the debt amortization (debt paydown). This can be linked to the amount of debt outstanding so that these figures reduce in line with scheduled amortization. Generally, the more links the better, and it means fewer numbers have to change when new information arises, or it is decided to adjust scenarios. It is not uncommon for analysts to color-code entries that need to be regularly updated versus those that are linked and changed automatically.

In the model in Exhibit 10.2, the bank debt matures in year 5. An assumption has to be made about how this debt is paid off when it matures. This model assumes that the bank facility can be refinanced with a new loan at maturity. Debt is commonly not retired at maturity with cash that has been saved up for the repayment. More often, it is refinanced with a new debt instrument or a combination of funding from debt and some other source such as cash on hand or asset sale proceeds. However, do not assume that a refinancing can automatically be accomplished. First, look at the leverage in the model at the time the debt matures. In this model, the debt is maturing in a year when car sales have declined, and margins have dropped for the tire company. This could make it more difficult to refinance. Looking at the bank leverage in Exhibit 10.2 at the time the current bank agreement matures and needs to be refinanced, the ratio is 2.3×; net of cash, it is about 1.4×. Based on those relatively low leverage ratios (the analyst could compare the leverage to other recently completed bank loans), this should give the analyst comfort about the ability to refinance this maturity. The next step will be to develop a view on the cost of refinancing. For example, in this case, given that the bank debt is being refinanced in a relatively weak operational year, would the banks demand a higher interest rate? It is likely that the banks would insist on a higher interest rate than the historical level. Include this in the model for the years after the refinancing, and this higher cost of debt will impact FCF. If the debt of a company is trading at a discount to par, it is a strong signal that when that debt comes due, the company will have to pay a higher interest rate because the market is already showing that to attract buyers of the debt, a higher rate than the stated coupon rate is required. If a debt instrument is very close to maturity and is trading at a discount, it may imply that the market thinks there is a high risk that the company cannot refinance the debt and may face default.

In this simple model, we have footnoted what the debt amortization is and what we assume happens in year 5, when the bank debt matures. Everyone who builds models should become a big fan of footnoting so that anyone looking at the model can determine the major assumptions that are being made. Some people prefer to have a separate section outlining assumptions being made in the model. Whichever method is preferred, any time the model is updated the assumptions and/or notes section needs to be too.

This model shows the cash line as a source of liquidity. In a more complex capitalization, there might be a section on other liquidity sources. Along with cash, there should be a line item for any other borrowings that are available. Most commonly, this is in the form of a bank revolver. However, there are other possible sources of liquidity, such as asset-backed lines and vendor financing. Any borrowings under the available facilities should be linked to the model's debt section, and if these short-term borrowings go up or down, this should impact the interest expenses.

What happens if there is not enough cash or available borrowings to meet a required debt retirement, or perhaps the leverage is too high for a typical refinancing? The modeler would have to make some decisions about what the company could and would do. There are several ways this can be addressed in a model:

- *Funding needs*: The model can have a separate line, labeled either "Deficit" or "Funding Needs," that simply shows what the company needs to raise.
- *New financing*: You can assume that the debt can be refinanced and create a new line labeled "New Financing," making an assumption about whether it is in the bond or bank or even equity market. Then include the new debt and related expenses in the model going forward.
- *Financing options*: You can begin to explore the possibility of asset sales or unconventional financing options.
- *Scenarios*: You can assume that this is a trigger for a default and/or a major asset sale and start to run scenarios for restructuring.

The bottom line is that when there is a shortfall to meet an obligation in a model, the analyst must begin thinking about options for the company and what the possible outcomesmight be for the holder of a bond or bank loan in the company. In these cases, it is vital to start running scenarios and considering decision trees with various probabilities for different outcomes.

You can build models in a multitude of ways. It is important to remember that sometimes models vary depending on what the analysis is trying to solve. For example, suppose the company being analyzed is doing well and the focus is on how quickly it can deleverage and get a rating agency upgrade. In this case, a model could be built to show FCF going to pay down debt as rapidly as possible. In another example, a company may have a number of debt maturities coming up and not have the cash to meet them. The analyst may be more interested in how much cash can be built up and in analyzing which avenues might be available for new financings. This might include looking at the bank covenants and determining if there is room within the bank agreement to raise more borrowing, or which assets outside the lending group might be available to sell or securitize.

Avoid Extrapolation

One of the biggest dangers in building any model is becoming too dependent on extrapolation from historical trends. When building models, don't just automatically assume that the conditions of the recent past will continue. It is rare to see a company that is not facing major changes either due to changes in the macroeconomic environment, a shifting competitive landscape in its industry, or internal operational changes. An analyst wants to learn from the past and look for operational trends, but simple extrapolation from the past will not prove helpful without layering in some careful thought about how a business is likely to change in the future.

Scenarios

With many variables in a model, minor changes in one or two assumptions can alter a company's outlook, especially over a longer time period. Therefore, rather than building a single model and using that as an ideal projection or estimate, it is often preferable to look at a few scenarios to analyze how sensitive a company's credit quality may be to different operational conditions.

You might want to build scenarios to solve to a given event and see if they look realistic. If a bond issuer is a candidate for an upgrade to investment-grade, instead of building one model that estimates cash flow and leverage, the drivers of the model could be reversed. The model could be run to see how much deleveraging would have to occur for an upgrade and if that could be reasonably achieved over a given time period. In a more stressed credit, the model could be designed to see how much of an EBITDA decline has to occur for a company to see its FCF go negative and figure out if that level of decline is realistic. Or the model could simply run financials assuming various business trends to see how the company performs during a recession, during a raw materials price increase, or in a growth scenario. Then two different companies can be compared to see how well they do in each of these scenarios.

Good scenario analysis can apply a probability to each case, and this makes it easy to develop a probability-weighted outcome. In a developing situation, the use of scenarios has an advantage over a single estimate. The use of scenarios, probabilities, and a probability-weighted estimate allows the modeler to make changes to both the scenarios and the probabilities, as new information becomes available. This can be particularly helpful in stressed situations and contentious merger and acquisition transactions.

In the simplest scenario analysis, an analyst could run a base case with a downside and an upside scenario. Exhibit 10.3 takes our tire company model, looks at the projected years, and reduces EBITDA by 10%. In this case, it appears that the FCF and the EBITDA/interest expense ratio are the metrics most sensitive to the decline.

Exhibit 10.3: Scenarios Down 10% (In $000,000s Except for Metrics)

	E	F	G
	Projected Year 4	**Projected Year 5**	**Projected Year 6**
EBITDA	117	106	120
Margin	12%	11%	11%
Free Cash Flow			
EBITDA	117	106	121
Capital expenditures	69	69	68
Interest expense	27	27	27
Cash taxes	8	4	10
Working capital uses	(5)	12	15
Free cash flow	18	(5)	1
Debt			
Bank debt (4%) due year 5*	280	270	270
Senior notes (8%) due year 6	200	200	200
Total debt	480	470	470
Other Data			
Interest expense	27	27	27
Cash	84	79	80
Credit Metrics			
EBITDA/total interest	4.3×	3.9×	4.5×
Bank debt/EBITDA	2.4×	2.5×	2.2×
Total debt/EBITDA	4.1×	4.4×	3.9×
Net debt/EBITDA	3.4×	3.7×	3.2×
FCF/debt	4%	-1%	0%

*Assumes this debt is refinanced at the end of year 5 at a comparable interest rate.

Exhibits 10.4 through 10.6 show a very simple scenario analysis for a company's projected operating income. Exhibit 10.4 shows the most recent historical results for the company, which will be the base for the projections. The revenue drivers in this model are for units sold, multiplied by price per unit. In this simplified example, the expenses are made up of two items: 1) the cost of goods sold (COGS), which is also driven by being multiplied by units sold, and 2) other expenses, which are less variable than COGS. In Exhibit 10.5, the assumptions for each scenario are laid out and should be linked to the model so if changes in assumptions are made, they roll through the scenarios. Exhibit 10.6 shows three years of projections for each scenario. It can be seen that the year 3 operating income varies materially in all three cases.

Exhibit 10.4: Historical Result for Scenario Analysis of Operating Income

Historical

Units sold	500,000
Price per unit	1,000
COGS per unit	350

Income Statement in $000s

Revenue	500,000
COGS	175,000
Gross profit	325,000
Gross margin	65%
Other expenses	200,000
Operating inc.	125,000

Exhibit 10.5: Scenario Assumptions

Change in Units Sold

Scenario 1	3.0%
Scenario 2	-3.0%
Scenario 3	10.0%

Change in Price of Average Units Sold

Scenario 1	3.0%
Scenario 2	-3.0%
Scenario 3	10.0%

Cost of Goods Sold Inflation Rate

Scenario 1	0.8%
Scenario 2	1.5%
Scenario 3	3.0%

Cost of Other Expenses Inflation Rate

Scenario 1	0.6%
Scenario 2	1.0%
Scenario 3	1.2%

Exhibit 10.6: Three Scenarios for Year 3 Operating Income

	Scenario 1			Scenario 2			Scenario 3		
	Year 1	Year 2	Year 3	Year 1	Year 2	Year 3	Year 1	Year 2	Year 3
Units Sold	515,000	530,450	546,364	485,000	470,450	456,337	550,000	605,000	665,500
Price per Unit $s	1,030	1,061	1,093	970	941	913	1,100	1,210	1,331
COGS Per Unit $s	353	355	358	355	361	366	361	371	382

Income Statement Date in $000s

Revenue	530,450	562,807	597,176	470,450	442,693	416,636	605,000	732,050	885,781
COGS	181,795	188,310	195,598	172,175	169,832	167,019	198,550	224,455	254,221
Gross Profit	348,655	374,498	401,578	298,275	272,861	249,616	406,450	507,595	631,560
Gross Margin	66%	67%	67%	63%	62%	60%	67%	69%	71%
Other Expenses	201,200	201,200	201,200	201,200	201,200	201,200	201,200	201,200	201,200
Operating Inc.	147,455	173,298	200,378	97,075	71,661	48,416	205,250	306,395	430,360

Each of these scenarios show very different operating income in year 3. It is also not likely that all of these outcomes have an equal probability of occurring. More likely, scenario 1 is a base case outlook, while scenario 2 is a downside case, and scenario 3 is a more positive case. Therefore, it would appear worthwhile for the analyst to apply a probability to each outcome. In Exhibit 10.7, a probability is assigned to each scenario and multiplied by that scenario's year 3 operating income. When these products are added together, the analyst will have a probability-weighted year 3 operating income to utilize in future analysis. For this to work, the probabilities need to total 100% when added together. The spreadsheet in Exhibit 10.7 totals all the probabilities as a check that the analysis is complete.

Exhibit 10.7: Probability-Weighted Year 3 Operating Income

	A	B	C
	Probability	Year 3 Op. Inc.	A × B
Scenario 1	60%	197,842	118,705
Scenario 2	20%	43,412	8,682
Scenario 3	20%	423,970	84,794
Total	100%		212,182

Scenario Paralysis

While scenarios are exceptionally valuable as an analytical tool, they can also become a time-wasting labyrinth if they are taken too far. An endless number of scenarios can be run on any situation, so the analyst has to be very conscious of building too many scenarios that have only minor changes and do not really help to answer the concerns about the situation. Careful planning should be undertaken before building out scenarios, and the scenarios chosen should show some meaningful differences and have a realistic chance of occurring.

A Pragmatic Point on Bank Maintenance Covenants and Expectations

Bank loans sometimes have maintenance covenants, such as minimum EBITDA/ interest ratios or maximum leverage ratios. These are normally expected to show improvement over time. It is useful when building estimates, or scenarios, to include them in the model's ratio section to see how much headroom, or cushion, is anticipated from the expected results relative to these covenanted maintenance tests in each scenario. A violation or potential violation of these covenants certainly is an event that needs to be noted, as it will generally trigger a negotiation between the company and the bank lenders.

The maintenance tests are usually based on company projections that both the company and the banks are comfortable with. The covenants might typically be designed to give headroom of 25% over these projections, or less in stressed situations. This can sometimes be used as a roadmap for public analysts to ascertain the company's internal projections.

Keep in mind that the measures used in the loan document, such as an EBITDA minimum level, may be a carefully defined term and may differ from how the model may be calculating the data. For example, in the covenant leverage ratio, the definition may allow add-backs of one-time cash charges to EBITDA and allow cash to be counted against total debt. In this case, it is good to have separate lines in the model for covenant EBITDA and covenant debt.

Even when there are no maintenance tests in the debt documents, it can make sense to include a covenant calculation in a model. A common item to monitor is how much room a company might have under its restricted payments covenant limiting its ability to pay dividends. An estimate can be run, in the model, of how much capacity the company has, based on the covenants and the definitions in the loan documents.

Another item to keep in mind is expectations. In stock market commentary, when a company releases earnings, there is often much focus on whether the company met consensus expectations of analysts' estimates. The stock may frequently trade up or down, based on how well the company did versus these expectations. The leveraged finance market typically does not have the same degree of sensitivity, but the movements and reaction in the equity market can be a valuable gauge for sentiment. Therefore, for short-term trading around earnings, a credit analyst should try to have a good understanding of the expectations for quarterly results. If there is a significant reaction upon the release of results, it should be analyzed to determine if it will have a short-term or long-term impact on the debt securities, because sometimes, when there is a surprise result, the markets over-react, initially.

Closing Comment

The development of models showing what the credit quality of a company is likely to be in the future is a very important part of credit analysis. These models are rarely a perfect predictor of the future, but they are a valuable tool and should be revised as new operational trends evolve. They help investors understand which operational changes can trigger the biggest changes to the credit quality of a debt issuer. Scenario analysis is generally more useful than building out just one model, as long as some real thought is put into the analysis and the probabilities. The next level of scenario analysis would apply an expected value to the related debt instruments in each scenario to estimate where the debt instruments might trade in each scenario.

Chapter 11

Structural Issues: Coupons

What's in this chapter:

- loan coupons
- bond coupons
- deferred pay coupons, zeros, and PIKS
- how the coupon is determined
- modeling changes in coupons

L EVERAGED FINANCE DEBT instruments have several types of coupon structures. Most coupons are floating rate or fixed rate, but other structures do occur, especially in private debt markets and when new debt is issued in financial restructurings. The most important structures are the cash-paying fixed and floating-rate coupons, but an understanding of deferred pay structures is important as well. While price movements and the associated widening and tightening of spreads are an important focus of understanding the leveraged finance markets, over longer periods of time, the bulk of the return in leveraged finance is interest income from coupon payments.

Loan Coupons

The interest rate on bank loans is usually a floating rate, not a fixed rate. This means that the interest rate moves at a set spread to some base rate: as the base rate moves, so does the coupon. The base rate is usually a short-term rate that is readily accessible and has a liquid market. Most loan floating-rate structures use a one- or three-month rate and typically the reset of the coupon date matches the duration of the rate, so the coupon does not move every day with the base rate but is reset periodically. If the coupon resets quarterly, the instrument uses a three-month base rate.

The most common base rate used in the leveraged loan market for many years was LIBOR. However, LIBOR is being phased out in many markets, and different countries are promoting various market-based short-term rates. In the USA, it appears that SOFR will be the most common. It is is based on the cost of short-term borrowing, securitized by US Treasury securities. In the United Kingdom, it appears that SONIA will be the replacement; in Europe ESTR; and in Japan TONAR.[9] Which region's base rate gets used is typically determined by the currency that the debt is issued in, not by where the company is based. If a Japan-based company were to issue Euro-denominated floating-rate debt, the base rate would utilize ESTR.

A typical US-dollar-based bank loan might be said to have a rate of LIBOR (or SOFR) plus 625 bps. This means that the rate would be 6.25 percentage points over LIBOR. If the LIBOR rate is 2.5%, the company that borrowed this bank loan would be paying 8.75%. It is common for bank loans, generally, to pay interest based on their base rate; if a loan is using three-month LIBOR, it would pay quarterly.

Some bank agreements include other features that can impact the coupon. For example, some loans may have a LIBOR floor that is triggered if LIBOR goes below a certain rate. If LIBOR drops from 2.5% to 1.5% for a loan without a floor, the terms require the company to pay its lenders 7.75% (the 1.5% LIBOR rate plus 625 bps). However, loans with a floor of 2% use 2.0% as the base rate and pay 8.25% (or 2% floor + 625 bps rate).

---

9 SONIA = sterling overnight index average; ESTR = European short-term rate; TONAR = Tokyo overnight average rate.

Some loans also have what is known as a pricing grid, shown in Exhibit 11.1. This was very common for a period of time but is less common now in syndicated institutional loans. In this structure, the rate the company pays on the loan may move, depending on some financial metric—usually a debt/EBITDA or a senior secured debt/EBITDA (the loan would typically use the secured leverage test because bank debt is usually ranked senior secured). The grid moves the spread if the ratio moves up or down significantly.

Exhibit 11.1: Pricing Grid

If the quarterly senior secured debt/ EBITDA ratio is between		the spread to LIBOR is
<	2.00×	+250
2.01×	4.00×	+350
4.01×	6.01×	+450

Bond Coupons

Leveraged finance bonds have several types of interest structures. By far the most common is a fixed-rate structure. This is where the bond pays a set rate, such as 10% per year. Bonds typically pay interest semi-annually. Buyers who purchased €1 million of a 10% bond would be paid two installments a year of €50,000 each.

Some bonds have a floating-rate structure, as described in the bank agreements. Floating-rate bonds usually have a floor, but this type of bond is atypical.

Some bonds have step coupons. They take two typical forms:

1. *Step coupon occurring upon an event:* It is not uncommon for a weaker investment-grade company to have a provision that if the bond gets downgraded to high yield (assume BB+), then the coupon on the bond increases by +25 bps, which may step up for each downgrade. If the initial coupon on the bond was 3%, upon the downgrade, the bond starts paying 3.25% interest to investors.

2. *Bond coupon increasing on a certain date*: If a bond with a ten-year maturity is issued with a 5% coupon, that coupon may step up to 7% on the fifth anniversary of the date it was issued. This is done because the market would likely require a higher interest rate than 5% to buy the bonds at the time they were issued. However, the company might not be able to service the debt initially, but is expecting to grow its cash flow. So, it will offer investors an increase in the coupon in later years.

Deferred Pay Coupons, Zeros, and PIKs

Periodically, deferred pay bonds are issued. The four common types of deferred pay bonds are zero-coupon, zero-step, pay-in-kind, and toggle bonds.

A deferred pay bond pays no cash interest for all, or part, of the bond's life. So usually, if investors forgo cash interest during the life of the bond, they require a higher yield than they would if it were a regular cash-paying bond. The deferred pay structure also, as a rule, makes the bond more volatile to changes in interest rates than a similar-yielding cash-paying bond would be. Generally, deferred pay structures are issued by companies going through a start-up phase or major transition of some kind, and cannot afford all the interest payments that investors would require to be attracted to buy the debt. For this reason, they tend to be higher risk and also require more yield. Typically, these companies are expected to see meaningful growth rates or deleveraging through asset sales at high multiples.

Zero-Coupon Bonds

A zero-coupon bond is the simplest deferred pay structure and has not been that commonly used in leveraged finance, but it is an important base to start from. With a straight zero coupon for life, the company issues a bond to buyers at a deep discount from par. For example, suppose the company sells a five-year bond at 55.75% of face value. If it were selling a face amount of $100 million in bonds, it would raise $55.75 million from investors. Bondholders would pay $55.75 million. If investors were to own the bond until maturity, they would get $100 million from the company when the bond matures in five years, which would be equal to a 125 return. The bond's value goes up each day (accretion) as it gets closer to maturity. Exhibit 11.2 shows the amount of the bond when it was issued and what the accreted value is on selected dates. If the bond were bought on that date in Exhibit 11.2 at the accreted price, the yield (return to maturity) would be 12%. If the purchaser were to pay more than the accreted value, the yield would be less than 12%. If the purchaser were to pay less than the accreted value, the yield would be more than 12%. This is just like buying a cash-pay bond at a discount to par. The YTM is higher than the coupon. However, the accreted value is the claim value of the bond and changes each day. The return on the investment comes in the form of this principal accretion, as opposed to coming from cash interest payments.

Exhibit 11.2: Annual Accretion on a $100 Million Five-Year Zero-Coupon Note

Date	Accreted Value in $000,000s
At issuance	55.75
End of year 1	62.74
End of year 2	70.50
End of year 3	79.20
End of year 4	88.90
End of year 5	100.00

Deferred Pay Bonds and the Balance Sheet

When working with deferred pay bonds, or any debt that is issued at a discount and accretes to par, it is important to understand the differences between looking at the whole debt issue as it appears on the company financials and looking at an individual bond.

When looking at a financial statement model for a credit or a company's financial statement, the focus is on the whole bond issue. Using the data shown in Exhibit 11.2, the company issued $100 million bonds at 55.75% of face value. On the balance sheet immediately after the bonds were issued, a new debt obligation of $55.75 million would appear. One year from now, that bond would appear on the balance sheet as $62.74 million because it accreted to that amount. The difference would have been recorded on the income statement as an interest expense of $6.99 million ($62.74 million – $55.75 million). The statement of cash flows would show this as a noncash interest payment.

When figuring out how the bond will trade, and when talking to a trader, the analyst must think on a per-bond basis. The typical bond is in $1,000 increments for trading purposes and must be translated into a per-bond basis and quoted on a percentage of face value basis.

Continuing with the example, 100,000 bonds were issued. Because a round number such as $100 million is outstanding, it is not difficult to figure that at the end of year 1, if investors wanted to buy the bond at the accreted value to equal a yield of 12%, they would pay 62.74 per bond.

To change this example, assume that the company issued $200 million in bonds. At the time the bonds were issued, the accreted value was 55.75% of face value. However, on the balance sheet this would not appear as $55.75 million, but as a debt of $111.5 million ($200 million × 0.5575). At the end of year 1, the balance sheet would show a debt of $125.48 million ($200 million × 0.6274). However, if an analyst were informing a portfolio manager of the price of the bond if it were supposed to trade at the accreted value, the analyst would not say, "111.5 at the time of issuance" or "124.88 at the end of one year," but would still quote 55.75 or 62.74, respectively. This is because bond prices are quoted as a percentage of par value.

Exhibit 11.3 shows, as an example, the balance sheet accreted value for the $200 million of bonds and how the bond's trading price (accreted value per bond) would be quoted.

Exhibit 11.3: Annual Accretion on a $200 Million Five-Year Zero-Coupon Note Issued @ 12%

Date	Balance Sheet Accreted Value in $000,000s	Accreted Value Per Bond in Percentage
At issuance	111.50	55.75
End of year 1	125.48	62.74
End of year 2	141.00	70.50
End of year 3	158.40	79.20
End of year 4	177.80	88.90
End of year 5	200.00	100.00

This accreted value is an important concept in bankruptcy because the principal claim that a bond has in bankruptcy is only for the accreted value.

Note that the accreted value changes every business day. We show only the difference annually for illustrative purposes. Most bond-calculating systems show this calculation for any given day. Bond-calculating systems typically give the accreted value on a per-bond basis. The analyst must multiply it against the face amount to calculate the full amount of the debt on the balance sheet. For all these deferred pay structures, keep in mind that the accretion, or growth in the debt, must be modeled onto the debt structure section of any model, and the distinction between cash and noncash interest must be modeled correctly.

Accretion in Cash-Pay Bonds

This concept of accretion also can be a factor in cash-paying debt. Sometimes a loan or a bond with a cash-paying coupon is issued at a slight discount, enhancing the return to investors to entice them to invest (this happens quite often in the leveraged loan market). This discount is referred to as an original issue discount (OID). It is usually not that large, perhaps one to two bond points. However, it appears on the balance sheet and is amortized over the life of the bond, just as would happen with a zero-coupon bond. Similar to what occurs with a zero-coupon bond, if a company goes bankrupt, the claim in bankruptcy of the holder of the bond, or loan, with an OID will not be par but whatever the accreted value is on the day that the bankruptcy was filed.

Zero-Step Coupon Bonds

Another type of deferred pay issue is a zero-fix or zero-step coupon bond. We will use the term *zero-step* because the interest rate, or coupon, steps up. These bonds are issued as a zero coupon and, after a set number of years, begin to pay cash interest.

A typical structure is for the bond to be issued at a discount, accrete for five years to par, and then begin paying cash interest. The bond accretes from its discounted issue price to par (the face amount) during the period in which it is not paying cash interest. When the bond begins to pay cash, it pays on the full face amount. The rate at which the bond accretes during the zero period is usually the same as that of the cash coupon when it starts paying. The bonds are generally callable at a premium on the date that the cash interest begins accruing. Exhibit 11.4 is a schedule of what the accretion and cash interest payments on an eight-year bond might look like.

Exhibit 11.4: $100 Million Zero-Step 12% Eight-Year Bond; Goes Cash Pay at the End of Year 5

Date	Accreted Value in $000,000s	Annual Cash Interest Payments
At issuance	55.75	-
End of year 1	62.74	0
End of year 2	70.50	0
End of year 3	79.20	0
End of year 4	88.90	0
End of year 5	100.00	0
End of year 6	100.00	12.00
End of year 7	100.00	12.00
End of year 8	100.00	12.00

PIK and PIK Toggle Bonds

Another type of deferred pay bond is pay-in-kind (PIK). In this structure the bonds are usually issued at face amount. However, for a period of time, most commonly three or five years, interest is paid not in cash but by issuing additional bonds, thus paying the interest in kind rather than in cash.

You should remember a few things about this type of structure:

- *Increasing payments*: After the new bonds are issued, the next interest payment is made on the new number of bonds outstanding, so each successive next interest payment is actually larger (see Exhibit 11.5). When modeling the bond, the number of bonds increases by the amount of the interest payment (similar to the accretion of a zero coupon).

- *Par value*: If bonds are trading at a significant discount, the coupon payment will initially be valued at less than par. The same could be true if the bonds were trading at a premium. This can impact how the bonds trade. An investor who owns $1 million of an 8% PIK bond on a semiannual coupon payment would receive $40,000 of new bonds. However, if that bond were trading in the market at 105, the market value of the interest payment would be $42,000 ($40,000 × 1.05).
- *No accrued interest*: Although cash-pay bonds are traded with accrued interest, PIK bonds do not trade with accrued interest. Theoretically, during the period between interest payment dates, the price rises for the amount of interest that is accruing. It declines after the interest payment is made by a like amount.

After the bond finishes its PIK period, it begins paying cash interest.

Exhibit 11.5: Interest Payments on a $100 Million 10% PIK Bond in $000,000s

Date	Amount Outstanding	Amount of PIK Payment	New Amount Outstanding
At issuance	100.00	-	-
Issuance + 6 months	100.00	5.00	105.00
Issuance + 12 months	105.00	5.25	110.25
Issuance + 18 months	110.25	5.51	115.76
Issuance + 24 months	115.76	5.79	121.55
Issuance + 30 months	121.55	6.08	127.63
Issuance + 36 months	127.63	6.38	134.01

An innovation to the PIK structure is a PIK toggle note. In this structure, during the period in which the company would typically use the PIK structure, the issuer may choose, at the beginning of any interest period, to pay the coupon with a PIK payment or cash payment, or frequently, a combination of the two. Sometimes this type of note has a different coupon rate if the company chooses PIK versus pay cash (the coupon is usually lower for a cash payment).

Deferred pay bonds are typically used to help preserve cash during a company's developmental or transitional period, when it would probably be difficult to service the full interest payments on the debt if it were all cash pay. Another way this type of problem has been addressed is with overfunding. In this overfunded structure, the bond is issued in an amount more than the company actually needs. The extra money is put in an escrow account to service the interest payments for a period of time, generally two or three years.

How the Coupon Is Determined

The interest rate or coupon is determined when the bond or bank loan is issued. Multiple factors influence the rate. They include the general interest rates currently prevailing in the country where the bonds are being issued and the average rates on high yield bonds and loans in the same industry and with the same rating. If the company has bonds or loans outstanding, the level at which these bonds are trading will be a factor, based on the outstanding yields and spreads when the new debt is issued. The better the issuer is perceived, and the better the structure of the new debt, the lower the coupon. Maturity, seniority, covenants, and other structural issues will be factored in by investors when comparing a new bond or loan to existing investment opportunities in the marketplace. Additionally, market supply and demand at the time of issuance can be a factor in determining the coupon. Frequently, the stated intention of the use of a new debt issue's proceeds is to retire existing debt. This can sometimes increase demand for a new issue, as holders of the debt that is being retired may want to roll into the new issue.

If an issuer has improved considerably over the years after its issuance of the debt, and interest rates have not moved much, the bonds will trade over the issue price and will offer a lower yield. In this case, the company may start thinking about trying to refinance the notes or loans at a lower rate to save money.

Modeling Changes in Coupons

Impending debt maturities can be a significant factor for a company. Depending on how the company is doing and the marketplace, there may be refinancing risk. At the very least, the new financing may change a company's cost of capital and impact its financial liquidity.

Refinancing risk can be hard to estimate over a longer time period or during a phase of exceptionally high interest rate volatility. When modeling scenarios, consider modeling fixed- and floating-rate debt and factor in a sensitivity analysis with increased interest rates.

Interest rate hedges also have to be considered. Companies can purchase a hedge to lock in rates and effectively turn a floating-rate coupon into a fixed rate. This hedge has a cost. It usually has an expiration as well, so a company may be hedged for two or three years and then face floating-rate risk. Always read the footnotes to financial statements with an eye toward seeing if some or all of the debt is hedged to make sure the model is showing the correct interest expense and understand the risks to the cost of capital.

The high yield market can move with interest rates, but historically, it is much less sensitive and less correlated to interest rate movements than many other fixed-income markets. Other large segments of the bond market live and die by minor moves in general interest rates. These include government and/or sovereign bonds and those of related entities, mortgage-backed securities, and high-grade corporates. All these other debt markets tend to have much longer duration than the leveraged debt markets.

This lower correlation with interest rates for high yield debt is due to a number of factors. The first is that credit improvements and declines in high yield companies tend to have much more influence on the yields the bank debt and bonds trade at than relatively small moves in general interest rates. Second, the coupon on these notes tends to be much higher than that on other types of fixed-income securities mentioned here, so a change in interest rates has a smaller impact on these issues. Third, it is rare for leveraged companies to issue bonds with maturities much longer than ten years; longer maturities are fairly common in government and high-grade bonds. Intuitively, the longer the bonds are outstanding, the more sensitive they can be to a minor change in rates. The coupon and the maturity are major influences when calculating the duration of a debt instrument, and duration helps to measure the sensitivity of a debt instrument to changes in interest rates or credit spreads. Below-investment-grade debt tends to have a much lower duration than asset classes such as investment-grade corporate bonds.

Closing Comment

The coupon is the contractual return that an investor gets for loaning the money to a company, and it is a major component in the cost of capital for a corporate issuer of debt. On the surface, the coupon on leveraged finance debt instruments looks like a relatively straightforward part of the structure. There are several nuances and potential variability in the structure of coupons that can make the analysis of coupon structures more complex. When undertaking forward-looking credit analysis, it is important to always consider that the average interest expense that a company has to pay changes over time as new loans and bonds are issued to retire older debt securities. These changes in the cost of servicing debt impact the ability of a company to generate FCF.

Chapter 12

Structural Issues: Maturities and Calls

What's in this chapter:

- maturities
- calls
- a quick review of YTC
- benefits of calls and call options
- clawbacks
- 10% annual call
- cash flow sweeps
- other bank prepayments
- open market repurchases
- a pragmatic point on early debt retirement

DEBT INSTRUMENTS HAVE a finite life: they have a maturity date at which time the borrower has to pay back the money borrowed from the lender. A shorter maturity generally represents less risk than a longer maturity, because the longer a debt stays outstanding, the greater the probability that something will go wrong with the borrower. Where a debt instrument stands in line by maturity and where it stands in line by seniority can make a difference in what yields and spreads the debt will trade at. Many debt instruments have features that give the company an option to buy the debt back before it matures and retire it. An option to buy something is called a call option. These call options are a benefit to the issuer rather than the borrower.

Maturities

For a bond or loan, the maturity is the date on which the company must repay principal to the investors. There is no standard maturity. For below-investment-grade bonds, a ten-year maturity from the time of issuance is quite common, but maturities have ranged from three years to five, seven, and eight years as well. They can also be longer, such as a twelve-year bond. However, longer maturities are not common in the leveraged debt markets, given the uncertainties and changing nature of many leveraged companies. When there are structures of twenty-year maturities or longer in the leveraged debt markets, they are typically bonds that were issued as investment-grade credits but have since been downgraded to the high yield market.

Within a company capital structure, the bonds usually mature at a later date than bank loans. Usually, bonds are not only structurally subordinated to bank loans; they are more junior on a temporal basis as well. In some situations, a bond matures ahead of more senior bank debt. However, bank lenders (and other senior lenders) often require a springing maturity in these cases. This feature typically states that if the more junior bond is not retired at some point prior to maturity, say six months before it actually matures, the maturity of the bank loan springs forward and becomes due immediately. This feature helps the more senior security in a distressed company to have more control over forcing a company into bankruptcy or other actions related to the payment of debt.

Leveraged finance bonds usually do not require any payments of principal on the notes before maturity. Some bonds, in the past, had what was known as a sinking fund, which required the company to retire a small portion of the bonds in selected years ahead of maturity. This feature is rarely seen anymore.

Bank loans tend to have shorter maturities than bonds. It is not atypical for a loan to have a maturity of five years or less. While many institutionally placed leveraged loans do not have any required debt amortization payments during the life of the loan, it is more common to see an amortizing bank loan in leveraged finance than to see a bond with a sinking fund. In many cases when an institutional tranche of debt does require some principal amortization of the debt, retirements are very modest. An amortization schedule retiring one percentage point per year of the face amount of the loan would not be uncommon.

Calls

The most common way, other than a maturity, for a company to retire a bond or loan is through a call. A call gives the company the right to buy back the notes or loan (or call them) beginning on a specific date at a specific price. In a typical high yield bond that has a ten-year maturity, the bond may be noncallable for five years. Then, after the fifth anniversary of the bonds' issuance, the company starts to have a call option. Investors will say the bond is callable. In this situation, it is typical for the bond's first call price to be equal to par plus half the coupon. After that, the call price would reduce each year so that it is callable at par one year before it matures. Exhibit 12.1 shows common language for a call schedule for a 12% bond; in year 5, the bond is callable at par plus half the coupon, or 106. The debt-issuing company could call the whole bond outstanding or just call half of the issue. The company usually has to announce the call price thirty days before it can retire the bonds. This type of call data is typical of what is often seen in the market, but there are all sorts of variations.

Prior to December 30 year 6, these bonds were not callable. After this date, they were callable at the prices shown as a percentage of face amount, as laid out in Exhibit 12.1.

Exhibit 12.1: Call Schedule

From December 31, year 6 until December 30, year 6	106
From December 31, year 7 to December 30, year 7	104
From December 31, year 8 to December 30, year 8	102
From December 31, year 9 and thereafter	100

Bank loans usually do not have the same level of call protection as bonds do. Traditionally, bank loans could be called at any time at par, but over the years, some call protection has become more common. Loans frequently offer some premium for six months or a year. So, while they are still callable, the buyers get a slight premium, such as 101% of face amount. This can make it less attractive for the issuer to repurchase the debt. Depending on market conditions, a new loan might be issued with an original issue discount, which effectively makes any call premium a bit higher. When a debt security is callable immediately, but with a premium, it is sometimes called soft call protection.

A Quick Review of YTC

When calculating the yield on a bond, investors typically want to use the most conservative yield calculation. When a bond is callable and is trading at a premium, the most conservative yield calculation is probably not YTM.

When a bond is trading at a discount to its face value, the yield calculation that is most conservative will be the YTM, as shown in Exhibit 12.2. If it rises in price, the most conservative yield (or lowest yield) might be a yield calculated to one of the call dates and call prices. For example, if a bond is trading at 112, as shown in Exhibit 12.3, it may not actually be trading on a YTM; it may be trading on a yield to its worst call. In this case, the bond is trading to its call date in year 3, because if the bond is called in that year, it will result in the lowest yield. Exhibit 12.2 shows that if the same bond is trading at 101, the lowest yield is to the call date in year 5. Bond investors are always looking at the possible downside, so they tend to look at the most conservative yield and use the YTW measure unless otherwise specified.

The call schedule has an impact on the yield calculation when the bond is trading at a premium. For example, if the bonds are trading at a very high premium and investors buy the bond based on YTW, but the bonds are not called on that date and remain outstanding longer, they get a higher return than the YTW. Understanding that a company may leave a bond out past a call date can be an important part of the analysis as a bond starts to trade on a YTC basis. Call prices also adjust the duration of a bond. When a bond starts to trade to a call date, the duration calculation will assume that the bond is more likely to come out on that date, so as callable bonds trade at higher prices, the duration can move more with fairly small price changes. Duration measures the price sensitivity of the bonds to changes in interest rates or spreads. It is an important measure to watch because if a callable bond trading at a premium starts to see the bond price decline, its price can become increasingly sensitive to rate and spread movements and the duration will become longer.

Exhibit 12.2: Call Schedule for a 10% Bond Callable in Three Years Trading at a Price of 101

Call Date	Call Price	Yield	Spread
First call year 3	105.00	11.05	1,097
Call year 4	102.50	10.21	979
Call year 5	100.00	9.74	916
Maturity	100.00	9.78	897

Exhibit 12.3: Call Schedule for a 10% Bond Callable in Three Years Trading at a Price of 112

Call Date	Call Price	Yield	Spread
First call year 3	105.00	7.02	694
Call year 4	102.50	7.06	664
Call year 5	100.00	7.10	652
Maturity	100.00	7.48	668

Benefits of Call Options and Call Protection

Having an option is usually advantageous. The right to call the bonds or the bank debt is usually an advantage for the issuer (the company) as opposed to the buyer (investor) of the bond or loan. For example, if a company issues a 12% seven-year note, and the company dramatically improves as a credit over the next three years, that bond should trade up and may deserve to be trading at a yield of 7%. This would equate to a price of 117.2 if the bond could not be called before maturity. It also implies that the company could issue new debt at close to 7%. If there were no call protection, the company could retire these bonds at 100 and issue new debt at 7% and investors' bonds would never have had a chance to trade the bond at a price as high as 117.2. No one would buy the bond at 117.2 knowing the company could force people to sell back the bond at 100 at any time. Even if the bond were callable at a normal call schedule, it might be callable at 106 at the end of year 3, and it would trade higher than if it were callable at 100 at any time. However, the price level would still be below where the investor could sell the bond if it were noncall for life. The call is really a benefit and an option for the issuer of the bond, not the buyer. The stronger the call protection is, the more attractive it is for the debt holders.

Investment-grade bonds generally see fewer extreme changes in credit quality than those rated below investment grade. Investment-grade bonds often are noncall for life. Another term for these bonds that are noncallable is bullet bonds. This structure is attractive to the buyer. Most leveraged companies hope to see meaningful improvements in their operations and therefore want opportunities to lower their cost of borrowing in the future. Issuers that want to refinance a bullet bond prior to maturity will probably have to pay a significant premium to get bondholders to sell back the bonds to the company.

Clawbacks

There are other types of call option that appear in some debt instruments. *Clawback* is a fancy word for a call option. Typical language for a clawback is as follows:

> Prior to the call schedule, the Company may at its option on any one or more occasions redeem the Notes in an aggregate principal amount not to exceed 35% of the aggregate principal amount of the Notes originally issued at a redemption price of 110% of the principal amount thereof, plus accrued and unpaid interest thereon, if any, to the redemption date, with the net cash proceeds of one or more Equity Offerings; provided that: at least 65% of such aggregate principal amount of the originally issued remains outstanding immediately after the occurrence.

What this means is if new money is raised in a stock offering, the company can retire some of the bonds earlier than otherwise allowed. Using this type of call usually requires a fairly high call price; the standard is par plus the full coupon. This option usually is available only for the first three years after issuance, or at least before the standard call structure is in effect.

Investors do not want their bond issue to be so small that it may not trade regularly. Therefore, this clause often has a restriction that after the clawback, a certain percentage of the original bonds still must be outstanding. The concept behind the clawback is that raising equity money for the company is usually a credit improvement and something that bondholders would like the company to do. Therefore, if the company does this relatively soon after issuing the bonds, the bondholders are willing to give the company a call option as an incentive to retire debt early.

There are a few other points to note about this clawback option. Typically, a company's bank agreement requires the proceeds, or at least part of the proceeds, from an equity offering to be used to reduce bank borrowing. But companies can frequently get a waiver from the banks. Read the terms of the clawback and the defined terms carefully. The chapter titled "Structural Issues: Covenants" discusses defined terms in more detail. Usually, whenever a term is capitalized in a loan agreement, bond prospectus, or indenture, it is being used in a form that is defined specifically in the document. For example, in the clawback language shown at the beginning of this section, *equity offerings* appears to be a specifically defined term. When going to the definition section in the bond prospectus, read the definition of *equity offerings*. It may be defined as a new public share offering, or it may include private share offerings as well. In case this does not sound like enough fun, there is frequently a defined term within the definition of another defined term. So read these terms carefully and have something nearby to take notes on. Just because a bond has an equity clawback, do not assume it is standard. The defined terms can be critical to how the bondholders are treated.

Ten-Percent Annual Call

Another type of call feature is the right to call a certain percentage of the issue each year. This usually occurs when a bond is being issued on a senior secured basis in place of bank loans. The normal structure is that, at the company's option, it can use cash to call up to 10% of the original amount of bonds outstanding annually at a price of 103. The rationale for this feature is that bank debt usually is callable immediately, and the company can deleverage by retiring bank debt. Companies that issue bonds with these structures typically have bonds outstanding and no bank debt. The company wants to be able to deleverage in the early years when the bonds are outstanding, and this feature allows it to make the bond more like a bank loan substitute from the issuer's perspective.

Cash Flow Sweeps

Cash flow sweeps are most common in bank loans for leveraged companies, though they occasionally appear in bonds. The excess cash flow sweep takes several forms but utilizes a predetermined portion of a calculated net FCF number to retire, or make an offer to retire, existing debt at a preset price. This type of call is usually an annual option. This is done in part because cash flow calculations can utilize fully audited numbers. It sometimes is structured as a call, where the company has an option to call the loans or bonds, but it sometimes is a requirement for the company to offer the payment and it is the debt holders' option to accept this offer or not. This clause usually does not utilize the entire portion of the calculated excess FCF. Normally, it would not use more than 50%, or less, of the calculated excess FCF. When it is the company's option or a required excess FCF sweep, the debt retirement works like a partial call.

When the company is required to offer a FCF sweep, the company has an obligation to make a mandatory offer to purchase using a certain percentage amount of the defined excess FCF. The holder can either sell the bonds into the offer or not. If more debt is put back to the company than the size of the offer, the debt usually is accepted on a pro rata basis. Suppose the defined excess FCF is $90 million and the sweep requires 50% of it to be used to make an offer to retire a bond at par. The company makes an offer to all holders of its bonds to buy up to $45 million of its loans at 100. If less than $45 million is put to the company, all the bonds put are retired. For example, if $120 million is put back to the company, each holder would have only 37.5% of its loans retired ($45 million/$120 million = 37.5%).

This is another place where careful reading of the terms and defined terms can be very important. For example, within the definition of FCF, EBITDA may be defined. In the terms of one bond, the EBITDA definition might include one-time charges, but in another bond from the same issuer it might not.

Other Bank Prepayments

Bank agreements typically require mandatory prepayments upon the occurrence of a number of events. These often include all or a portion of the proceeds from asset sales. There is usually also some limitation on how much of the proceeds of an asset sale has to be in cash. In addition, usually, a minimal threshold must be met to trigger this feature, such as an asset sale of over $10 million.

Generally, there are also mandatory prepayments for all or a portion of the proceeds from the issuance of equity, and sometimes for the proceeds from the issuance of more junior debt securities as well. In practice, if one of these events occurs, the company can often negotiate a compromise with the banks for a partial paydown with the proceeds because this is often a credit-improving transaction.

Open Market Repurchases

Although they are not actually calls or puts, open market repurchases of debt by companies are important for analysts to understand, as are the differences in how this can be done with bank loans and with bonds.

Open market repurchases typically occur when a company utilizes cash on hand, or sometimes bank borrowings, to buy back bonds in the open market. Repurchasing bonds in the open market usually has to be allowed by the covenants in the bank loans and any more senior notes. Generally, a test such as a leverage test and a restricted payment covenant must be met. Also, in most cases, a basket of a certain amount of excess cash flow must be met before a company's bank loans, or more senior debt, allows these purchases to be pursued.

However, if the company is permitted to pursue open market purchases, it can buy bonds at any price. If the company's bonds are trading at a discount, it can buy them at that price. Another way of looking at it is that the company can buy them for less money than it would be required to pay at maturity, thus reducing its debt by more than the cash it is using. When doing such a trade and capturing the discount in the bonds, the company effectively uses $1 of cash to retire more than $1 of debt. Therefore, the company actually books a gain on its income statement (noncash) and reduces the amount of debt on its balance sheet. A company can also make a specific offer to purchase bonds in the market, through what is called a tender offer. A tender offer may also ask bondholders choosing to sell into a tender to vote to change the covenants or some other feature of the bonds.

Normally, the company cannot do discount buybacks in the bank debt. Generally, the company is restricted from buying back bank debt at a discount, even if it is trading at a discount in the secondary market. Bank agreements usually require any paydown of bank debt to be paid pro rata to all holders of the bank loans, so companies are not likely to benefit from open market repurchases of bank debt. But there have been cases where waivers have been given.

If a company's debt is trading at a meaningful discount, and the company has enough cash on hand to retire debt, it is often most attractive for the company to look to retire its bonds rather than bank debt; the bonds usually have higher coupons and therefore are more expensive for the company.

Holding Bonds Rather Than Retiring

When buybacks happen, the bonds are not always retired. For various structural reasons, companies sometimes hold onto the repurchased bonds rather than retire them. Additionally, when a company is owned by a PE firm, the PE firm may buy back the company's bonds. Remember not to confuse the sponsor buying the bonds with the company buying back the bonds. The sponsor is a separate legal entity, and if it owns the notes (or the bank debt), they remain outstanding. The sponsor can also buy loans without the various par and pro rata restrictions that might apply to the company if it were purchasing them.

A Pragmatic Point on Early Debt Retirement

When a bond is trading at a yield much lower than its coupon, analysts often try to analyze whether the company will look to refinance the debt. Typically, this is done by running a net present value of leaving the bonds outstanding versus a net present value of issuing the new debt and retiring the old debt. This must include any premium payments necessary to call the old bonds and fees associated with issuing the new bonds and an assumption on the interest rate of the new financing.

A quick way to get a glimpse of whether it makes sense to do this is to take the existing bonds' call price; this gives a proxy for how much funding is needed to retire the existing bonds. Then multiply this amount by the likely new-issue coupon. (The YTW on the existing bonds is a good proxy.) Finally, see if this new figure, which is a proxy for new financing costs, is meaningfully less than the bonds' existing coupon. If it is, then it is usually worth exploring refinancing possibilities in more detail. Exhibit 12.4 shows an example.

Exhibit 12.4: Quick Check on Refinancing

Existing Bonds	Coupon	Call Price	Recent YTW
Senior notes	10%	104.00	7%
Cost to retire bonds	104.00		
Assumed new coupon	7%		
Annual interest cost on new notes (104 × .07)	7.28		
Annual interest cost on old notes	10.00		

Also, if a bond is not callable, or is not callable yet, the company can tender for the bonds. This offer to repurchase bonds is made to all holders. Typically, the company prices this offer so that the yield on the bonds would equate to a yield that is at a spread of only 50 to 100 bps wide of the equivalent maturity Treasury or other government bond. Most bonds, even noncall bonds, have a make-whole provision that lets them call bonds at an equivalent Treasury note plus a 50 bps spread (typically referred to as $T + 50$) at any time.

Closing Comment

Call structures have a significant impact on the yield and duration of debt instruments and the return profile of these investments. Understanding how call prices impact the potential return profile of different debt instruments can be a major part of relative value analysis. Call structures also influence what corporate finance actions a company might look to pursue. While there are some standard aspects in call structures, each document can vary. Diligence is needed when analyzing the terms and definitions in the loan documents.

Chapter 13

Structural Issues: Ranking of Debt

What's in this chapter:

- ranking
- structural subordination
- subsidiary guarantees

D EBT SECURITIES HAVE different priority rankings within the capital structure of a company. During a bankruptcy, the debt with the most seniority in ranking has the first claim on the assets and the value of the company. Assuming there is enough value for the senior-most debt, the second-most-senior piece of debt would have the first claim on the remaining value, and so on, until any residual value would be available for the equity owners. This is sometimes called a waterfall. The priority ranking impacts how bonds and loans trade even if the risk of bankruptcy is remote because things can always go wrong. Even if a company appears far from being worried about a bankruptcy, the ranking and structure of loans and notes will impact how they trade relative to each other and to other investments. In general, the less risky a company appears, the less difference in yield the market will demand for differences in seniority. Ranking is critical when investors are looking to protect their downside. Many nuances in the legal language describing seniority and security can make what looks like a simple waterfall priority ranking vary greatly from its initial appearance.

Ranking

The ranking of securities affects the coupon that is decided at the time a bond or loan is issued and will affect how the bonds and loans trade throughout their life. When a company is strong and doing well, the difference in yield between more senior bonds and more junior bonds may be small. The riskier a credit is, the more of a spread between more-junior and more-senior securities is likely to be seen.

In some structures, there are many layers of debt; and in others it is quite simple, with maybe only one level of debt. Sometimes the corporate structure is quite simple, and all the debt resides at the same entity. In other cases, debt sits in different parts of the company: some debt has priority claims at one entity and other debt may have priority claims at another.

Bank loans usually are the most senior, but sometimes bonds or other securities have equal claims or even, occasionally, more senior claims. In legal parlance, having an equal claim on the same asset is often referred to as being pari passu (on equal footing). This phrase is used frequently in debt markets to indicate that two debt instruments rank equally.

A typical bank loan has a senior ranking and also security. The security is a priority claim on specific assets that lenders can, theoretically, take possession of if the contractual payments owed to them are not made. This is similar to a mortgage on a house: if the payments are not made, the mortgage holder has a first claim on the house. The key is how the security is defined. The agreements can be specific.

As an example, we'll look at a hypothetical company called Cedar Corp. As shown in Exhibit 13.1, it has three factories and also owns 50% of the stock of another company called ACBar Co. Cedar has a secured bank loan and senior-unsecured bonds outstanding. The security agreement (which is part of the loan document) may list all three factories as assets that are secured (as indicated by the shaded boxes in the figure). Other ways to describe this type of secured claim for the loan are that 1) it has liens on these assets, or 2) it is collateralized by these assets. In this case, the 50% stake in ACBar Co. is not part of the collateral. What does this mean for the loan holders? If the company were to go bankrupt, the loan would have first claim on all the factories' value. If the value of the factories were not enough to pay off all the loan, it would look toward the company's other assets—namely, the ACBar Co. stock. Because the stock is not part of the security agreement, the loan only has a senior-unsecured claim on these assets. It must share any value from this stock equally with other senior claims, such as the senior-unsecured notes. In theory the three factories are worth $400 million, and the stock is worth $100 million. In a bankruptcy, the $500 million bank loan would get back $400 million of value from the shares with the notes on a pro rata basis. If the notes were senior subordinated notes instead of senior, their claim on the stock would rank behind the claim of the loans.

Exhibit 13.1: Cedar Corp. Debt Structure
(Shaded Areas Represent Secured Assets)

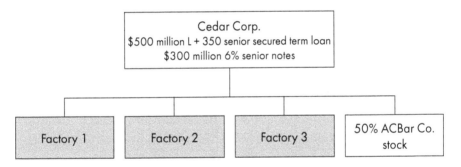

Even if the security agreement says something such as "substantially all the assets of the company," it's important to read the definitions and the actual collateral agreement. Foreign subsidiaries are often not included in the security packages as they are often more difficult to securitize. Here is a simple ranking of priorities:

1. senior secured debt
2. senior-unsecured debt
3. senior subordinated debt
4. subordinated debt
5. preferred stock
6. common stock

Senior secured debt is the most common bank debt. Senior secured debt and senior (but unsecured) notes rank as a senior class of debt. Secured debt simply has the secured priority claim on selected assets that are in the security agreement. Bank loans sometimes are senior unsecured, but more often, senior-unsecured debt is in the form of bonds. There can also be several rankings of secured debt. For example, there can be a first priority secured issue, usually called a first lien and second lien.

Ranking below senior debt is subordinated debt. There can be senior subordinated debt and subordinated debt, which would rank lower. Senior subordinated has historically been the most common type of high yield bond issued. Bank debt is almost never subordinated. It is important to recognize that subordinated bonds have an actual subordination agreement. These become important documents in a bankruptcy. Be sure to read the subordination agreements, which can include an important intercreditor agreement. Sometimes they have unusual features or exceptions as to when these notes actually are subordinate to other debt.

Sometimes preferred stock is involved. This is an equity claim in the capital structure but comes ahead of common shares, and some structures have more debt-like features—for example, a preference date on which the shares are to be repaid, and a set dividend rate resembling debt more than equity. Typically, if the company does not meet the maturity or misses several dividends, there is no meaningful recourse relative to the survivability of the company. In other words, the preferred cannot, on their own, trigger an event of default. Perpetual preferred shares do not have a set debt to be repaid but typically have a set dividend rate and look more like straight equity. Preferred shares usually have a set face amount and a dividend. Sometimes the dividends are PIK. If the preferred is not paid, the dividends usually accrue, meaning the preferred holders' claim doesn't go away; it just builds. Sometimes the terms of the preferred share agreement offer other recourses for the company if dividends or repayment dates are missed. A typical recourse is that the preferred shareholders get to vote for a certain number of board seats. If a remedy is not spelled out in the preferred stock document, which is not the norm, the shareholders could, theoretically, sue in court for lack of payment, which could eventually lead to a default. The preferred shares do have preference over the common equity, and if the payments are not honored in the preferred agreement it is difficult for the common equity to monetize its value or receive any distributions.

The common equity/stockholders come last in the priority ranking.

Now that the priority ranking has been explained, it is important to understand there are some common ways in which bonds, and sometimes loans, are structured that can circumvent these traditional rankings. There are structural ways to make debt rank more junior or more senior regardless of its priority ranking. The two most common ways are through corporate structures and subsidiary guarantees.

Structural Subordination

Corporate structures usually do not consist of just one legal entity; normally, there is a parent company and several subsidiaries operating underneath the corporate umbrella. In most of these cases, the structure is such that the parent company owns the stock of each subsidiary. Debt can be issued at any number of these entities, meaning the parent holding company or any of the subsidiaries.

When some debt is issued at an entity closer to the operating assets while other debt is issued at an entity that is further away, such as a holding company, the debt at the holding company is often referred to as being structurally subordinated. In a simple structure, if there were debt at the holding company and debt at subsidiary A, then the debt at the holding company would be structurally subordinated in its claims on the assets of subsidiary A to the debt at that subsidiary, regardless of the rankings of the two pieces of debt.

A common type of structure is shown in Exhibit 13.2, in which a holding company does not have any assets itself except for owning the stock of the subsidiary. This entity is called Tapas Inc. HoldCo (Tapas HoldCo) in our example. Its only asset is 100% of the stock (or a 100% ownership stake) in its main operating entity, Tapas Co. OpCo (Tapas OpCo), which performs its operations through four subsidiaries. These subsidiaries are where all the cash flow is produced and where the value of the company is generated.

Exhibit 13.2: Structural Subordination

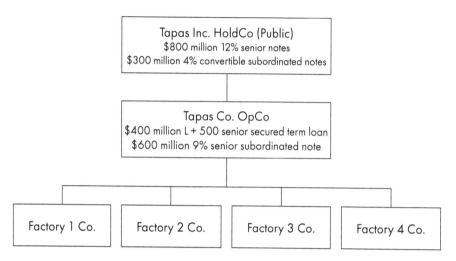

Tapas HoldCo is where the company's public stock is issued. Shareholders who buy stock in the company own a stake in this entity. Exhibit 13.2 shows that two bonds are issued at this level. One is a 12% senior note, and the other is a 4% subordinated convertible note. Tapas HoldCo's only asset is its 100% ownership of Tapas OpCo. At Tapas OpCo, there is an L + 350 (LIBOR + 350 bps) senior secured bank term loan, secured by the stock of the factory subsidiaries. There is also a 9% senior subordinated note. Unless otherwise designated, a debt instrument only has a claim on the assets of the entity that issued the debt. Tapas OpCo's assets are the stock of the three companies that own the factories. In this case, there is no debt at those factory operating subsidiaries.

If this entire entity were to become bankrupt, the senior secured bank loan would have first priority on the cash-flow-producing assets. The Tapas OpCo senior subordinated notes would have the next priority claim on the factory asset value, even though these notes are subordinated and the HoldCo notes are senior. The Tapas OpCo notes were issued by the company that owns the assets. Anything that is left over after paying off the debts at Tapas OpCo would go to the equity shareholders of Tapas OpCo. This is the value available to repay the debt holders of Tapas HoldCo, including the 12% senior notes.

Said another way, Tapas HoldCo's only asset is the stock of Tapas OpCo. Although the 12% senior note is a senior note because of the corporate structure and whichever entity issued the note, it is structurally subordinated to the claims of all the debt at Tapas OpCo. It is critical to be sure of which issuers are the actual entity with the debt obligation and where assets are held.

A logical question is why a company would want to form a more complex structure. It would seem easier to issue junior debt at the OpCo. Corporate structures can be driven by many factors, including managing corporate liabilities to cost-of-capital considerations and operating in multiple jurisdictions.

One possibility is that the more complex structure of this company could be driven by the bank structure. Banks are often focused on how much debt is actually at their issuing entity because of their senior ranking and security and will allow more debt to be issued that is junior to the loan and at another entity. Theoretically, if the company defaults on the holding company debt, those debt holders may get control of Tapas OpCo's stock, but they cannot necessarily force Tapas OpCo into a bankruptcy. (It is not uncommon for a holding company to default and subsidiaries to not default, but there are also many cases where bank loans and bonds also often have cross-default provisions.) The lenders at Tapas OpCo are also likely to be in a stronger position in bankruptcy defending their position against a holding company claim rather than a junior claim at the same corporate entity. Another factor could be funding costs. When issuing the various debt instruments, a company will try to decide which structure will result in the lowest interest expense, or cost of capital. Is it cheaper on a blended basis to get a higher rate on the bank debt and issue all the debt at the operating company? Or is it better to get a lower rate on the bank debt and the senior subordinated notes and pay a somewhat higher rate on the most junior piece of debt issued at a holding company?

A holding company and operating company structure may be in place because not all the debt was issued at the same time. If the Tapas OpCo debt was issued first, the company, several years later, may have wanted to pursue an expansion or an acquisition. The covenants in the existing bonds may not have permitted more debt to be issued at Tapas OpCo. Therefore, the company pursued new financing at the holding company level.

Exhibit 13.2 shows that Tapas HoldCo also has issued convertible debt. Convertible notes are typically held by more equity and equity-like investors than fixed-income investors. They are definitely debt and need to be included in any analysis and also should be considered as an investment option. Commonly, they are ranked on a junior basis and issued at the holding company level because they will be at the same level at which the actual public shares are issued.

It is important to understand the notes' convertibility. These bonds have an option to be exchanged for company stock. This is an option of the debt holder. Therefore, the debt may not require cash for the company to extinguish them. Investors usually see a convertible bond as a hybrid in which part of the value is in the bond component of the structure and part is for the option to convert to stock. For these reasons, the coupon on convertible bonds is usually lower than comparable nonconvertible bonds.

As an example, if an investor had a $1,000 face amount bond of Tapas HoldCo convertible bond, and it was convertible into 100 shares, the investor could convert that bond and create shares at $10 per share ($1000/100 shares = $10 share price). If the stock were trading at $9, that would not create value. But if the stock were at $12 per share, it would be worth converting; the debt would be retired by issuing more shares. In this case, where the stock is trading over the conversion price, the convertible bond is said to be in the money. An investor who bought the bond at $900 would effectively be creating the conversion feature at $9 ($900/100 shares = $9). If the stock trades at a price at which the bond is in the money, analysts must decide how aggressively they want to treat this in their analysis. Can they be aggressive and assume that the bond gets converted and treat it as equity?

Additionally, converts sometimes have a feature whereby if the stock is trading at a big enough premium over the price at which the bond can be converted into equity, the company can force the bondholder to convert. Do not ignore convertible notes in structural analysis. It is important to recognise that they often have their own unique features that need to be understood to fully appreciate how they interact with the rest of the capital structure or may influence management actions. For example, some convertible bonds have puts allowing them to be sold back to the company; some may have mandatory conversions. Management is typically most focused on taking care of the equity holders, and this may prioritize how they handle convertible bonds in the capital structure.

Covenants, Structure and Servicing HoldCo Debt

When there is a holding company and an operating company structure, the covenants on the bonds and the loans at the operating company do not typically dictate what the holding company can do. However, the operating company covenants usually do control how cash or assets could move up to the holding company to service that debt. It is important to understand and analyze how the cash can get from the operating entities through an intermediate-level operating company and up to service the holding company obligations.

Subsidiary Guarantees

Subsidiary guarantees can also bypass typical seniority language. A guarantee from entity 1 on the debt issued by entity 2 effectively makes the debt of entity 2 an obligation of both entities. It gives the debt a claim and a priority ranking at entity 1 even if it did not issue the debt. It is common for bank debt issued at a holding company to be guaranteed by all of a company's principal subsidiaries.

In the earlier example in Exhibit 13.2, if Tapas OpCo guaranteed the 12% notes of Tapas HoldCo on a senior basis, these bonds would have a priority claim on all the assets of OpCo ahead of the senior subordinated notes of Tapas OpCo. If notes of equal rank are issued at the same entity and one bond has a guarantee from an operating subsidiary, this gives it a structurally senior claim on the assets of that subsidiary versus all other notes issued alongside it.

Exhibit 13.3 is a chart for AndBar Inc., which has three operating subsidiaries. The company has an L + 350 bank loan. The loan is secured by the stock of the operating subsidiaries that AndBar Inc. owns and also has senior guarantees from each subsidiary. It also has an old 10% senior note that allows for only $20 million more in secured debt unless these 10% notes are given equal security. This feature in a debt structure is called a negative pledge. The company wants to issue more debt to pay for expansion. It wants this debt to be lower cost and rank ahead of the 10% senior notes. However, the banks do not want all the new debt *and* the existing 10% notes to be secured. Management gets the banks to agree to a new senior-unsecured bond. To give it priority over the

10% senior notes and get a lower coupon, the company gives the guarantees from the operating subsidiaries, which allows it a structural claim ahead of the 10% senior notes on those assets. To make the banks happy, this subsidiary guarantee does not have a senior ranking as the banks do. The guarantee is a subordinated guarantee from the operating subsidiaries. This new 8% senior note effectively has become structurally senior to the old existing 10% senior notes, because the old notes do not have any subsidiary guarantees. But the new senior note is still junior to the banks because the guarantee does not rank as highly as the bank debt's guarantee. It also does not trigger the negative pledge. When this transaction is announced, it will probably cause the old 10% notes to trade down in price because, first, the banks, and now, the new notes have priority claims on the subsidiaries in which all the asset value lies.

Exhibit 13.3: New Issue with a Subsidiary Guarantee

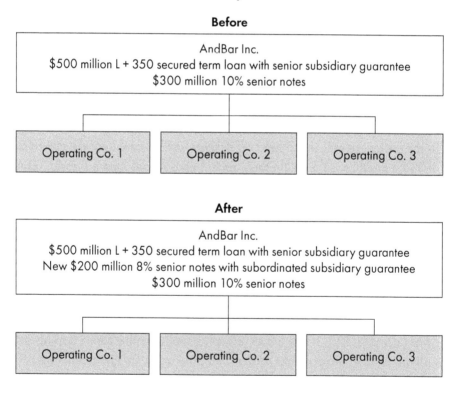

When existing debt has debt issued senior to it, investors often say that the old existing bonds have been primed. Structural subordination and guarantees can prime existing debt and also sometimes get around existing debt covenants, accomplishing the same thing. If existing holders are unaware of the loopholes or features in the bonds they own, and they see the bonds trade down substantially because of getting primed, they often use a more colorful phrase for what has happened to them.

Guarantee Rankings

Subsidiary guarantees have rankings too. For example, a subsidiary could guarantee holding company debt on a senior secured basis or perhaps on a subordinated basis. This is not uncommon where a subsidiary may offer a bank loan a senior secured guarantee and a bond a senior subordinated guarantee, mirroring the structure at the issuing entities.

Closing Comment

Read all the language relating to rankings. For example, suppose a company has a revolver and a senior secured bond. The document may actually state plainly that both are equal (pari passu). However, deep in the document there could be a clause that expressly gives priority to the revolver in the case of a bankruptcy. This effectively gives the revolver what is called a first out. It is not only a factor in bankruptcies. The detailed specific language can also address how the two tranches are treated when proceeds are raised from an asset sale, equity offering, or other event. There may be language that even though they rank equal, the first $25 million of any asset sale proceeds is used to repay the revolver before the equally ranked senior secured notes share in the proceeds. Ranking of securities is one of the differentiating factors when analyzing relative value and it is vital to get the ranking correct.

Chapter 14

Structural Issues: Covenants

What's in this chapter:

- methods to approach covenant analysis
- debt incurrence
- defined terms and carve-outs
- restricted payments
- change of control
- asset sales
- reporting requirements
- other covenants
- affirmative (maintenance) covenants
- restricted and unrestricted subsidiaries

EACH BOND INDENTURE or loan agreement has covenants. These are, effectively, rules that the company has to follow as long as these debt instruments are outstanding. The covenants in leveraged finance tend to be much more complex than investment-grade debt. Debt holders want more control over what a company can do because of the greater perceived risks in lending money to more leveraged companies. Covenant analysis is a vital part of credit analysis.

Methods to Approach Covenant Analysis

There are covenants that are common to most leveraged finance debt, but never assume that a covenant for one issue or one issuer is the same as another. Read them all the way through. Trends in covenant structure change over time. During some periods they shift toward favoring the issuer, and in other periods the buyer of the notes.

Analyzing covenants can be a complex task that has often been compared to peeling off layers of an onion, slowly uncovering each level of the covenant to see how it works; and each time one layer is peeled off, there is another one to peel. Just as peeling an onion causes tears, a few tears are likely to be shed during the process of analyzing covenants. Covenants are best read when in a cynical mood, with an eye toward how the company can harm the loan or bondholder. The covenants are the rules that help protect the loan and bondholders.

Covenants can sometimes show what a company wants to do in the future. For example, if certain types of transactions are specifically permitted under the covenants, such as a type of acquisition or distribution, it could be a sign that management hopes to shuffle its assets around.

Sometimes it is helpful to lay out the covenants in a flow chart or diagram to understand how they work. It is helpful to have a relatively consistent way to chart or diagram covenants when comparing the differences in debt instruments within the same company.

Usually, the most important covenants are negative covenants, which prevent a company from doing something such as issuing more debt or selling an asset. Affirmative covenants in bond agreements are usually less important. Affirmative covenants require a company to do something such as file financial statements or maintain a certain level of cash on the balance sheet. Affirmative covenants are much more common in bank agreements and are more commonly called maintenance covenants. They may require a company to maintain a certain amount of cash on the balance sheet or a minimum EBITDA. The trend in the institutional loan market has been to remove maintenance covenants, or significantly minimize them. Loans with little or no maintenance tests have begun to be called covi-lite loans.

The most important covenants found in bond indentures and bank agreements tend to deal with debt incurrence limits, restricted payments, restrictions on asset sales, and change of control. They are designed to protect the lenders and prevent the company from materially changing the credit quality of the company in a negative way compared to what the credit looked like when the money was originally loaned.

This chapter does not cover every type of covenant. Once ways to examine the details of these key covenants are understood, the thought process involved in analyzing these covenants can be applied to others.

Debt Incurrence

Debt incurrence covenants state under what terms a company is allowed to add to its debt. The basic test is often based on a leverage ratio or a fixed-charge coverage test. If the test cannot be met on a pro forma basis for the proposed new debt, the company cannot issue the debt.[10]

When a leverage ratio is used, the test sometimes uses a total debt/EBITDA ratio and states that, pro forma for the issuance of the new debt, this ratio has to be met. If it is assumed that the covenant uses a 5× leverage test, the basics of the test would work as follows: If the company were leveraged 4× and had $500 million of EBITDA outstanding, this covenant would allow it to issue approximately $500 million more in debt, which would bring the company pro forma ratio to 5× leverage. This addresses total leverage but does not directly address the ability to service the debt. If the new debt is particularly high cost (a high coupon), it could put a disproportionate strain on net FCF.

The other common test used for debt incurrence is the fixed-charge coverage ratio. This ratio is usually an adaptation of the EBITDA/interest expense ratio. In the case of a fixed-charge ratio test, the denominator (fixed charges) is defined. The ratio usually starts with interest expense and then may include items such as noncash interest, debt maturities due in one year, and capital expenditures.

---

10 *Pro forma* is a term for presenting information on a hypothetical basis, adjusted for an event. In this case, it applies to what the ratios would look like after issuing the new debt.

For a simple example, assume that a company has a fixed-charge ratio test in which the denominator is based only on total interest expense and the numerator uses EBITDA. If we were to employ the example from the prior paragraph, it would work as follows: If the debt incurrence test were a 2.0× fixed-charge coverage test (as defined above), prior to the transaction, the ratio would be 2.5×. If the new debt were issued at an interest rate of 10% (see Exhibit 14.1), the company could issue $500 million more debt and pro forma for the new debt would still meet the test of 2.0×. If the rate on the new debt were only 7%, the company could issue $800 million in debt (this would be more debt than the 5× leverage ratio test would allow). If the rate were higher (e.g., 13%), the company would be permitted to issue only $400 million of new debt.

The fixed-charge test ratio is much more sensitive to the overall interest rate environment and the company's borrowing costs than a leverage test would be. Therefore, an improving credit that uses a fixed-charge coverage test under its debt incurrence test should see the combination of its increasing EBITDA and its decreasing borrowing costs combine to give it more capacity to increase the leverage on the company if it chose to do so.

Exhibit 14.1: New Issuance under Incurrence Tests in $000,000s (Except for Ratios)

EBITDA	500

Debt (@ 10% coupon)	2,000
Interest expense	200

EBITDA/interest expense	2.5×
Debt/EBITDA	4.0×

With New Debt at 10% Coupon

EBITDA	500

Debt (@ 10% coupon)	2,000
New debt (@10% coupon)	500
Total debt	2,500
Interest expense	250

EBITDA/interest expense	2.0×
Debt/EBITDA	5.0×

With New Debt at 13% Coupon

EBITDA	500

Debt (@ 10% coupon)	2,000
New debt (@ 13% coupon)	400
Total debt	2,400
Interest expense	252

EBITDA/interest expense	2.0×
Debt/EBITDA	4.8×

With New Debt at 7% Coupon

EBITDA	500

Debt (@ 10% coupon)	2,000
New debt (@ 7% coupon)	800
Total debt	2,800
Interest expense	256

EBITDA/interest expense	2.0×
Debt/EBITDA	5.6×

Defined Terms and Carve-Outs

There are many words and phrases within a covenant that are known as defined terms. When a word is a defined term, its meaning in plain language does not matter in the legal reading of the document. What matters is how that term is defined in the bond or loan document. Defined terms usually are capitalized in the description of the notes or loans and have a specific definition for the purposes of the document. The terms are usually defined elsewhere in the document, often in a section dedicated to definitions. This is where bookmarks and highlighting come in handy. It is common to switch back and forth between the pages with the covenant language and the pages with the definitions. After the covenant ratio is calculated, there is still work to be done. Often the covenant will also include a whole section on exceptions to the covenant, often referred to as carve-outs. As an example, in a leverage test, certain types of debt may specifically be excluded from the debt incurrence restrictions. These carve-outs might include loans to employees or debt related to a specific project.

These concepts of defined terms and carve-outs apply throughout the analysis of covenants and structures in bond and loan agreements. The following sections describe some of the items that are typically defined, starting with the debt incurrence test.

Defined Term Examples

A total debt/EBITDA ratio in a covenant can be made significantly more complex than it seems when the two terms in this ratio are defined in the document.

1. *Total debt*: This may seem a straightforward term, but do not assume so. It may, or may not, include debt at a parent company, or it could exclude analysis of debt junior to the instrument, or it could exclude non-cash-paying debt. It also may be defined if it includes short-term debt or borrowing-based facilities such as accounts receivable facilities. All these exceptions and more have been seen in various debt documents as the loan agreement redefines a simple definition of total debt.

2. *EBITDA*: These definitions can be even more complex and may or may not apply to noncash charges, fees paid to owners, and other items. More interestingly, they can apply to pro forma add-backs, including EBITDA, from a company being acquired and may also include cost savings that the company has budgeted from the acquisition or simply cost savings from its own plans that have not been achieved yet. Furthermore, they may add back the actual cash costs that are related to these cost savings (because there are usually cash costs related to achieving cost savings).

Making all these adjustments for total debt and EBITDA can end up creating a very different set of metrics than what might be produced if simple definitions of the terms were used. Often on a summary spreadsheet, analysts choose to show both debt and EBITDA, as they would typically be calculated for financial purposes and also for comparisons with other companies. An analysis can then also have lines showing covenant defined debt and EBTIDA and the related covenant ratios. Some companies will report covenant EBITDA or covenant ratios. Other companies will not report those figures and may not even report all of the data needed to calculate the covenant data. In these latter cases, an analyst has to estimate these figures. The absence of this type of information made available by the company should be a warning of how the company approaches transparency for investors.

Carve-Outs

Within a high yield bond prospectus or a loan document, the debt incurrence covenant is usually only a small part of the covenant. The bulk of the rest of the covenant typically describes exceptions to the ratio test. These exceptions outline other ways in which debt can be issued even if the debt test ratio is not met and are often called carve-outs. Some carve-outs are fairly straightforward and standard in bond and loan agreements—these might include a lien that is already in place on an acquired property, or a court imposed tax lien.

A typical carve-out may include the existing bank line. The key is how this carve-out is written. Sometimes it allows borrowing on the bank line above and beyond the ratio test. Sometimes the carve-out for the bank line is reduced by permanent repayments of the bank borrowing. This means that prepayments of the bank debt will permanently reduce a company's borrowing capacity, and the company may look to avoid making these prepayments. If the covenant does not reduce the bank borrowings by prepayments, the company could deleverage and then releverage, even if it did not meet the leverage ratio test. The prepayments of a revolver are not normally permanent, and the company may look to repay a revolver ahead of term loans for this reason. How the agreement defines bank borrowing can be a factor too. If it is defined as senior secured debt, the facility could be funded with a bond financing if it is senior secured. If a bank or credit agreement is specified, any financing using this carve-out would need to be in the form of an actual bank loan.

You must read all the other carve-outs because there may be specific carve-outs for acquisitions or refinancing. An investor usually does not mind a refinancing of junior existing debt as long as the new financing is longer-dated and no more senior than the existing financing that is in place.

Another type of carve-out involves early-development-stage companies that might need multiple rounds of funding from various sources and is based on equity value, frequently perceived or real asset value. This carve-out would allow additional debt financing based on new equity funding raised. As an example, for every $1 of new equity raised, the carve-out would allow the company to add $0.50 of new debt regardless of other debt tests.

In this section, we discussed carve-outs using the debt incurrence test as an example. Carve-outs commonly appear in all major covenants throughout the debt documents.

Restricted Payments

Restricted payments covenants try to restrict what the company can do with its cash flow and other assets. The concept behind the covenant is that holders of a bond or loan would want the company to meet certain goals before it can use money to either pay dividends on the equity, do stock buybacks, or be able to retire securities that are more junior to the loan that they hold.

Within the document, what constitutes a restricted payment is defined. As a rule, this definition is not short and includes many carve-outs. From a debt holder's perspective, the definition of restricted payments should specify that money or other assets going to the equity holders through dividends or stock repurchases and early retirement of more junior debt are all included as restricted payments.

There has been some controversy over private-equity-owned firms using carve-outs in this test to transfer assets from a company to the equity holders (entities controlled by the PE firm). There can be debate over how the asset is valued in the transaction and if the transfer is being done under the restricted payments test or through other covenants such as permitted investments.

The core of a restricted payments covenant normally has two parts. The first is a test that has to be met to be able to make such a payment. The second is a basket that limits how big a payment can be made.

Typically, the test that would have to be met feeds off the debt test. It is common to have language in the restricted payments test stating that, pro forma for a restricted payment, the company would have to meet the ratio portion of its debt test and be able to issue at least $1 of debt under that test. When analyzing this covenant, an analyst will have to circle back to the debt incurrence test and apply either the leverage ratio or a fixed charge test that is used in that covenant to meet the restricted payment test.

The basket measures how much is available for a restricted payment, and it can build up over time. It starts from a specific date and builds by cumulatively adding 50% of net income from that start date to the time of the payment. Whatever that accumulates to is what the company can use for restricted payments, and any restricted payment made gets deducted from that basket. However, if the test mentioned in the preceding paragraph is not being met, the basket cannot be used via typical traditional language. More aggressive covenants include a starter basket as well, which may state that in addition to the basket, the company has a certain dollar amount available to pay out through a restricted payment test.

Instead of the 50% of net income test, another common test for a basket builder is any EBITDA over 1.4× interest coverage, or some other ratio.

Here are some items to examine in the definitions and terms of restricted payment basket language:

- How are periods of negative net income counted? Are they deducted from the basket or just excluded?
- How are net income and interest coverage defined?

- What other items can be added to the basket, such as proceeds from equity offerings?

Some higher-quality issuers use restricted payments tests that are much simpler; they have a debt test that must be met. As long as pro forma for any transaction the company undertakes stays within that test (perhaps a 4× leverage ratio), the company has no limits on its ability to make restricted payments.

Restricted payments descriptions tend to have many more carve-outs than debt incurrence tests. In the normal course of running a company, some selected stock buybacks or other payments may have to be made. These are typically allowed to a limited amount. There might be a carve-out for the repurchase of stock from a departing employee up to a total of $10 million in any one year and a total of $100 million over the life of the debt. (These sizes will vary depending on the company's size.) There are often general carve-outs for one-time payments and some carve-outs for refinancing as well. There are also carve-outs that allow proceeds from equity financing to be used to make restricted payments. These carve-outs can be very aggressive, particularly in transactions by PE firms.

PE firms use the leveraged debt markets to help finance companies they purchase. Their primary goal is to get the best returns for their investors, and the more quickly they can get payments back on their equity investment, the better the net present value of their returns can be. Therefore, they look to have very loose restricted payments tests or many carve-outs so they can rapidly begin distributing money to the equity and boost their returns.

Permitted Investment Covenants

If time permits, you should try to look at the permitted investment covenant. Some structures have multiple subsidiaries, and permitted investments can sometimes include moving money or another asset into a legal structure within the corporate organization but out of the lender group. So, effectively, that money used under the permitted investment clause no longer directly supports the loan or bond, which can give a debt investor an unpleasant surprise. Permitted investments can often be in completely unrelated entities too.

Change of Control

Change-of-control covenants generally relate to a takeover of the company or a change in the control of the board. Typically, if a change of control, as defined in the document, takes place, the company that issued the debt must make an offer to repurchase the bonds at 101 of the face amount, usually within ninety days of the event's closing (not the announcement date). There is usually a clause that allows an acquiring company to make the offer as well. Bank covenants for change of control are fairly similar, although often the offer to purchase is at par.

The definition of *change of control* is important and varies significantly from document to document. A common example would be when anyone obtains 35% or 50% of the voting control of the equity or control of the board of directors. Numerous variations exist.

Usually the description of change of control carves out *permitted holders*. This is a defined term that must be examined. Sometimes it applies to the family of the controlling shareholder; sometimes it applies to another company that already has a significant stake in the issuer; or it can be defined in any number of other ways.

Other features sometimes appear in the change-of-control section. Exceptions might prevent the change-of-control offer from going into effect. The covenant may specify that as long as the leverage ratio pro forma for a change of control is no higher than it was prior to the event, the change of control is not triggered. Another common exception might specify that as long as the ratings agencies do not lower the ratings due to the change of control, the covenant is not triggered. They could include a specific ratio target that must be met, or perhaps require a ratings upgrade or an investment-grade rating.

Change-of-control covenants often come into effect in event analysis. This is especially true when two companies are merged. The structure of the transaction and the language of the change of control can be key to whether this put option for debt holders comes into play.

Asset Sale

Asset sale covenants typically define the form that major asset sales can take and how the proceeds from an asset sale can be utilized.

This type of covenant usually first prescribes the size of an asset sale covered by the covenant. It may have a dollar amount, such as any asset sale valued at over $50 million. It may define a percentage of assets, such as any asset sale that would be valued at more than 15% of net tangible assets. Or it may be prescribed in some other manner.

The next section of the covenant may dictate how the asset sale can take place. For example, it may dictate that 85% of the proceeds must be in cash. Or it may allow that a swap for similar assets may be undertaken.

Finally, there is usually a description of what can be done with the proceeds from such an asset sale. Typically, an offer has to be made to repurchase bank debt and any more senior debt. If proceeds remain after this offer, the usual language of a senior subordinated note gives the company 180 days in which to either reinvest the money into permitted assets or make an offer to repurchase the bonds at par. Permitted assets would be a defined term in the document. If no bondholders choose to sell bonds into this offer, the company is typically free to do as it wishes with the balance of the proceeds, within the boundaries of the other covenants.

This type of covenant tends to not have that many carve-outs but does have many defined terms. A common carve-out includes specific types of asset that may be excluded from this definition. If the company owns a large piece of real estate or a nonstrategic subsidiary, this may be excluded from the asset sale restrictions.

Reporting Requirements

Another very important covenant for companies that do not have public stock outstanding is the affirmative covenant to make financial statements available. If a company has public stock outstanding, most countries and exchanges require financial statements to be regularly and widely available, either quarterly or semi-annually. It is not always the same with debt securities.

Leveraged finance debt is usually not listed on exchanges. Some formats of the notes are considered private placements. This maintenance covenant is important to debt holders if the company is private, and even if it is public, in case the company goes private at some point. Additionally, the public financials filed to fulfill the requirements for a company's stock will usually be the holding company financials. Often, the bonds or loans are issued at a subsidiary. In some cases the subsidiary that is issuing the debt may have very different financials from those of the parent or holding company. Debt holders will want to see the financials for the actual credit they are lending to, not necessarily the parent company, so that they can analyze the credit risk at the correct entity. From the issuer's perspective, having to file separate subsidiary financials carries an extra cost and may also make more information available than the issuer cares to have in the public domain. But that should be factored into the management's decision to issue debt at a subsidiary.

How the financials are made available can be important. Some companies may prefer not to have their financials publicly available, for competitive reasons. However, the more inaccessible these financials are, the less liquid the trading in the related debt issues will be. From a debt holder's perspective, if the expectation is that there will be any trading in the debt, it is important that the company make financial results available. The most open forum for financial statements is filing them with a regulatory body such as the US Securities and Exchange Commission (SEC) or making them available on the company's website. A more restrictive practice might be to have them made available to existing debt holders. The company may legally limit these holders from forwarding the financials to others. There are also closed sites that require company approval to obtain the financials and limit their distribution. From a trading and information-flow perspective, this covenant can be important. Some bonds and loans may covenant in a requirement to hold quarterly or semiannual investor conference calls, effectively requiring the management to make themselves available to investors.

Other Covenants

Other covenants may include the following:

- *Business lines*: A covenant might restrict a company's lines of business. For example, an oil and gas exploration company may be limited by this type of covenant to staying in the energy business.
- *Related parties transactions*: Restrictions are often placed on transactions with related parties and include a description of how they need to be handled. For example, if the chairman of the company also owns a consulting business that the issuer of the bonds wants to hire, this may have to be approved by all outside board members. Or the covenant might limit the fees that can be paid.
- *Drop away*: This covenant appears in some bonds and typically states that if one, or a combination, of the major ratings agencies upgrade the bonds to investment grade, a number of the covenants may no longer become operative. These drop-away covenants are carefully defined and usually include the most restrictive ones. One item to look for when reading this type of covenant concerns the reinstatement of covenants if the company is later downgraded.

Typically, bank agreements have negative covenants that are slightly tighter than those found in bonds.

Words to Watch For

There are a few words to always be careful of when reading covenants:

- *And/or:* When a covenant lists criteria that have to be met, it can be very important if the word *and* or the word *or* appears between the last two items on the list. In a change-of-control covenant, it can make a big difference if the change-of-control offer to repurchase does not go into effect because 1) there is a ratings upgrade ___, 2) the leverage ratio is no higher than pro forma for the event. The meaning is quite different depending on whether *and* or *or* is inserted in the blank.
- *Notwithstanding:* For example, after its fourth or fifth paragraph, a covenant might state: "Notwithstanding the prior paragraphs in this section ..." This means that readers should ignore everything they just read when they go on to the next section of the document.

Affirmative (Maintenance) Covenants

Most of the covenants described so far are known as negative covenants. The reporting requirement described earlier is an affirmative covenant because it requires the company to do something. Typically, bonds do not have many affirmative, or maintenance, covenants. Leveraged bank agreements sometimes have a lengthy section of affirmative covenants. Failing to meet these covenants is a covenant default, sometimes called a technical default as opposed to a financial default. Not all loan agreements have maintenance covenants, but they are more common in loans than bonds.

Some common maintenance covenants can include a required minimum amount of cash or liquidity, maintenance of annual appraisals on the security underlying the loans, or other annual information.

The maintenance covenants that analysts most closely monitor tend to be financial maintenance tests. These can include revenue levels, EBITDA levels, and/or some combination of ratio tests. Defined leverage tests are common, such as debt to EBITDA, or interest coverage tests. As with the other covenants, the terms must be read carefully, because definitions can make a major difference. The definitions of these maintenance tests in the bank agreements have an even greater tendency than the bond definitions to include add-backs for cost savings or temporary losses from a single subsidiary.

Financial tests are often not static; they are sometimes constructed to get tougher over time, as lenders want to see credit improvement. When the bank agreement is publicly available, the grids that indicate changes to maintenance covenants can show an analyst what the company's own internal model may look like. Traditionally, bankers who build these covenants work with the company's model to create a grid that makes sense. The covenants usually build in some cushion over the company's projections. It is not atypical to assume that there is about a 20% to 25% cushion versus the company's actual internal models.

Another feature that is commonly found in bank covenants is a springing maturity. If a tranche of bonds or any more junior debt is outstanding and matures on a date ahead of the bank debt, a springing maturity often exists. In this case, the clause typically states that if the more junior debt is not refinanced or retired, say, six months prior to its actual maturity, it will trigger a default in the bank debt.

Modeling Maintenance Covenants

When building a model, if the bank agreement has maintenance covenants, an analyst will often want to show how much headroom there is between a bank agreement's maintenance covenant and the actual figure generated by the company's operating results. The analyst has to be sure to define the actual ratio in the same way it is defined in the covenants, even if it seems to be an illogical way to calculate the data.

Restricted and Unrestricted Subsidiaries

Bank agreements and bond indentures employ the concept of restricted and unrestricted subsidiaries. Restricted subsidiaries are entities that are party to the bond or loan agreements. They must abide by all the covenants and must support the payment of these debt instruments. Unrestricted subsidiaries do not have any obligation to support the bond or loan or follow its restrictions. So effectively, from the debt holder's perspective, management can do what it wants with these unrestricted assets.

For example, assume that a company owns five casinos: Two in Atlantic City, two in Las Vegas, and a new early-stage riverboat casino in Indiana. The four established casinos in Atlantic City and Las Vegas are the restricted subsidiaries, and the property in Indiana is unrestricted. The EBITDA from the restricted subsidiaries must meet any required ratios in the covenants. Any EBITDA gains or losses at the new Indiana casino do not affect these ratios. Additionally, the company could add debt, or sell the unrestricted Indiana assets, and not have to worry about whether this is allowed under any of the covenants in the restricted group debt agreements.

In this example, the casino company will likely report consolidated results for all five properties. When a bond or loan agreement includes the concept of restricted and unrestricted subsidiaries, the company often is required to separately report the results for the restricted group, even if it is public and reported results include all the consolidated operations. If the company is private, the reporting requirements typically require only the results of the restricted group, not the unrestricted subsidiaries, to be reported. Investments or transactions with the unrestricted subsidiaries usually should have to meet the requirements under the restricted payments basket and the restricted investment basket because this effectively results in money leaving the group that is supporting the debt.

When debt agreements contain the concept of restricted and unrestricted subsidiaries, there are also definitions of how a subsidiary's classification can change from a restricted subsidiary to an unrestricted one. Typically, the restrictions are pretty loose, but this type of transaction would not be allowed if it would violate the various restricted payment and debt tests. It is recommended that when these structures are present, the permitted investment covenant is carefully analyzed.

Not all companies and their debt instruments are structured with restricted and unrestricted groups. However, when they are, this is an important concept to understand. In some cases, the restricted group that supports the bonds will own the equity of the unrestricted group so that it may, theoretically, reap some asset value benefits from the entity.

Closing Comment

Understanding covenants can be time-consuming. It can also be frustrating because, in some cases, even after much time is invested in analyzing the covenants, there may not be a clear answer, due to ambiguity in the language. Increasingly, battles over what is actually allowed or not allowed within the covenants end up in courtrooms. The quote that always comes to mind when analyzing covenants is part of Sir Winston Churchill's description of Soviet foreign policy: A covenant is "a puzzle, inside a riddle, wrapped in an enigma."

Chapter 15

Structural Issues: Amendments, Waivers, and Consents

What's in this chapter:

- the process of amending terms
- tenders and exchanges
- distressed exchange offers
- some examples

WHEN A COMPANY wants to change the terms of its debt, it can refinance the existing debt with new debt that has the terms it wants, or it can try to get an agreement to change the terms of the existing debt. Trying to do a refinancing requires a new round of legal, accounting, and financing fees and exposes the company to market risk on interest rates when setting the new coupon for the new financing. The second method is to approach the debt holders and negotiate an amendment or a waiver to the terms that the company needs to change. This usually involves paying the debt holders a fee or giving them an improvement in the terms of their debt. There is a difference between an amendment and a waiver. An amendment is a permanent change to the terms of a debt agreement. A waiver is a one-time or event-specific change to the covenants.

The Process of Amending Terms

Within the terms of the debt securities are details of how changes to the covenants, or other terms, can be made. Generally, the changes require a simple majority of the loan or note holders to approve them based on holdings. (This means that if it is a $1 billion bond, holders of $500.1 million of the bonds would need to approve a change.) Sometimes terms require a supermajority, such as 67%. There are other situations where the terms specify that certain changes require one percentage, and changing another term would require a different amount. It is important to note that what are commonly called money terms require a 100% affirmative vote for any adjustments considered negative for the debt holders (e.g., increasing a coupon is allowed; decreasing the coupon is not). It is difficult to get a 100% vote on anything. Money terms are usually the principal amount due, the interest rate, and the maturity, including principal amortization requirements.

Because bank agreements tend to have more covenants, bank loans more commonly see requests for amendments and waivers than bondholders. This is especially true of affirmative covenants because companies get hit with some disruptions to their plans, and growth trajectories can change. It is generally considered easier to get amendments and waivers done in the bank market. In the loan market, the agent bank keeps track of all holders of the loans. Given that bank lenders usually enjoy the most senior position in the debt structure, they also tend to be more flexible on changing terms in exchange for fees. The concept of lender liability in the bank market comes into play in the context of adjustments on affirmative covenants. Bank lenders have an obligation to not act in a manner that is detrimental to the company they have lent money to.

The agent bank is equivalent to a lead underwriter on a bond but continues to have obligations after the placement is completed. Generally, it maintains communications with all the holders. Because of the nature of how the debt trades (every trade usually has to be approved by the agent bank), the agent bank usually knows who all the holders of the debt are. The agent bank is also often a holder of the debt and is usually the logical entity for the company to use as a lead negotiator on any changes to the debt terms the company wants to make.

The types of holders of bank debt can matter in the process of getting amendments and waivers completed. For example, if the majority of the holders tend to be traditional commercial banks, it is generally believed that they are more focused on the relationship with the company and are more willing to reach reasonable agreements quickly. When aggressive, stressed, or distressed investors tend to hold much of the bank debt, they have a reputation for being more concerned about near-term returns. Other investors, such as structured CLO types and other institutional holders of bank debt such as mutual funds, view this process in many different ways.

Tenders and Exchanges

Other options are available if covenants or structural changes are needed and the bonds are not callable. These commonly involve the use of tenders and exchanges, which are used for permanent changes to the covenants, not for waivers.

A tender is a company's offer to purchase securities. For example, if a company wanted to change a covenant, it could make an offer to buy at least 51% of a bond issue outstanding at 110. Part of this price would include a consent fee for agreeing, almost simultaneously, to the waiver or amendment, and then the bond would be sold back to the company at that price. These transactions are actually a two-step process even though they happen simultaneously, involving a tender to purchase the debt, and a consent. This requires the company to have either existing liquidity or new financing in place. The price for the tender can be expensive for the company, too.

When doing a tender, the company must have cash or raise financing to pay for it. The company's financial team and advisors must weigh the expense of the new debt versus how high a consent fee might need to be to get the transaction done. The bonds' callability, or how close they are to maturity, also becomes a factor in the ability to do this. In bank debt, because of the callability and the requirement to make all prepayments pro rata, tender and consent transactions are not as common.

Another alternative to a straight consent, waiver, or tender is an exchange offer. Debt holders receive an offer to exchange into a new note with the changes in the covenants that the company needs. As opposed to a tender, an exchange allows the company to avoid having to raise new financing or use cash. And unlike a tender, the bondholders are not offered cash, but a new security.

The exchange offer typically offers some incentive to the holders to exchange rather than not exchange (or hold out). Exchanges and tender offers can be coercive by potentially leaving any holdouts with a much weaker position in the credit if they don't tender or exchange. If the company gets the requisite amount to undertake the exchange or tender, all the protection of the old covenants from the notes that do not exchange is sometimes stripped away. In an exchange offer, the new exchange could also be senior to the old notes, thus priming the old notes. The new notes could also have a bigger coupon or a shorter maturity. Or they could even exchange into more debt. Perhaps the holder exchanges $1 worth of old bonds and gets back $1.05 of new ones. These exchanges usually have a minimum acceptance rate. Keep in mind that 100% acceptance is unlikely. Therefore, both the old outstanding issue and the new issue will probably be smaller and may have less trading liquidity.

One type of amendment common in the loan market is an amend and extend. This is actually a new issue that looks a bit like an exchange offer that is negotiated with the banks. In a simple form, the company negotiates with the banks to agree to keep in place the basic terms of the bank agreement and perhaps make a few changes to the covenants; this is the amend part. Then the company also gets holders to extend the maturity and issues a new loan with these terms, using the proceeds to retire the old loans. But even if the company gets 90% of the bank debt to agree to this, it cannot force the other 10% to accept the extended maturity date. This type of transaction effectively works as an exchange does. There are often two tranches of the loan after the amend and extend transaction; or if the new loan is in demand, the company might be able to raise enough to retire any outstanding old loans.

Distressed Exchange Offers

Exchange offers are also quite common in distressed situations. They are usually attempts to improve a troubled or stressed situation. Often, they are structured in hopes of avoiding a bankruptcy and are often structured to be coercive to debt holders. If the debt of a stressed company starts to trade at a significant discount, it may increasingly tempt a company to make a distressed exchange offer to capture some of this discount.

In a distressed exchange offer, the debt holders agree to an exchange that negatively impacts some of the critical money terms but does give them some other advantage in the new security. As an example, debt holders may own $10,000,000 of distressed 6% subordinated bond that matures in two years and is trading at 60. They may accept an exchange offer for 70% of the face amount of their bonds in a new bond that has an 8.625% coupon, is senior secured, and has a five-year maturity. The bondholders have sacrificed a considerable amount of principal but improved their ranking in the capital structure and maintained about the same level of annual interest income. The company has reduced its overall debt and moved out a maturity. Debt holders that didn't exchange have been primed and are now junior in priority, but their full principal matures earlier than the new debt if the company does not default. Some studies and ratings agencies will consider the bonds that were exchanged as having defaulted because they permanently impaired critical money terms of the debt.

Some Examples

The need to change affirmative covenants can be driven by a poor economy or a change in competition. The need to change negative covenants, such as the ability to issue more debt or waive a change of control, is usually driven by an unforeseen event, such as a merger or acquisition or a shift in expansion plans. It is not uncommon to see a company undergoing a transaction to pursue a waiver for the change-of-control covenant. This example focuses on a waiver for the bonds, but it could just as easily apply to loans as well.

Sometimes it appears obvious that a change-of-control put would not be exercised by any holders, but it can still matter. Assume that a company has a 10% senior note outstanding and that the company's bond has a change-of-control put covenant that requires the company to make an offer to purchase the bonds at 101% of face value. Then assume that this company is being bought by a much stronger credit, maybe even an investment-grade company that has bonds that trade at 5%. This implies that those 10% bonds will be trading significantly over 101 when the acquisition closes. Even though a 101 offer to purchase may be made, it is unlikely that any bondholders would sell the bonds, because they would be trading at a higher price than the change-of-control put of 101. However, acquisitions can take a long time from the time they are announced until they actually close, and market conditions can change rapidly. The board of directors of the selling company will want to protect shareholders and will likely require the acquiring company to arrange some kind of financing that can be utilized, if needed, to pay for the change of control in case market conditions vary greatly by the time the transaction closing finally occurs. Then the company management must decide which is more cost-effective: 1) arranging some type of draw-down option for financing the change-of-control put (in case the change-of-control offer gets hit), or 2) trying to get a waiver from bondholders on the change-of-control covenant.

The acquiring company must weigh what it will cost to secure this financing commitment—usually some form of bridge loan fees to a bank or other institutional lenders—versus what it is willing to pay the bondholders to agree to waive this right to put. The bondholders have to weigh how much they can get the company to pay them versus the company walking away from the waiver negotiation and using other financing. In that case, the bondholders would get nothing and would give up a chance to get paid an extra fee in what already appears to be a good transaction for them. The bondholders also have to weigh their assessment of the current fee being offered to them versus the chance that the bonds might trade below the 101 put they could have been offered at the time the transaction closes. With all of these considerations at play, the company will likely make an offer to the bondholders to waive the change-of-control put for this merger, and negotiations will begin. Bondholders will want to make sure that the language of the waiver is very specific and is only a waiver for this transaction and not a permanent amendment to the agreement.

Sometimes a company foresees that it will violate one of the financial maintenance covenants. Because bank holders can be private as opposed to public, the company can start discussing its issue with the agent bank, and hopefully, some of the largest holders, before a violation occurs. The company may be seeking an amendment to the test, or perhaps just a one-time waiver. The company will typically have to pay a fee for the debt holders' consent. The size of the fee will likely depend on the reasons for the request, the company's performance, and to some extent, the makeup of the holders of the bank debt. The fee may not always be an immediate cash outlay; it could be a temporary or permanent adjustment to the coupon payments on the debt. Typically, if a company violates one of these terms, the bank agreement gives it thirty days (or some other set amount of time) to fix the problem before officially causing a default. This is called a grace period. The same is true for a missed coupon payment. Temporary waivers can be passed while negotiations are ongoing for a more permanent amendment or a longer-lasting waiver. Theoretically, these technical defaults could cause a bankruptcy, but it is hard to think of a case where such a technical default has been the sole cause of the bankruptcy.

Another way to cure a technical default is through an equity cure. A covenant may allow a company's owner to cure a financial technical default simply by putting more equity capital into the company. For example, suppose a company is in violation of a debt/EBITDA test, and a reduction in the debt of $50 million would keep the company out of the violation. The company's owner would be allowed to invest another $50 million into the company's equity to cure this default.

Bank covenants often require paydowns of all or a large portion of the proceeds from actions such as asset sales and equity offerings. In the case of asset sales, the company may actually require the bank lender's approval. In reality, the company often negotiates with the banks on what it can do with the proceeds before agreeing to the transaction. It is easier for the company when bank lenders are private because these negotiations may be done well before any transaction is finalized or announced publicly. The bank lenders will often agree to some form of partial payment and then give the company more leeway in what to do with the balance of the proceeds.

Closing Comment

Consents, tenders, and exchanges often come into play because an event occurs or appears likely to occur. The event is often a merger or acquisition, but it could also be the risk of an impending maintenance covenant violation or a default. Similar to covenant analysis, examining these types of transaction involves careful reading of the terms, as there is no standard format. It also involves the use of scenario analysis. When the economy is going through a period of stress or a specific industry is struggling, stressed exchange offers become increasingly common.

Chapter 16

Other Credit Factors: Ownership and Management

What's in this chapter:

- ownership considerations
- management considerations

AN ANALYST SHOULD always understand a company's ownership structure and develop a sense of management's goals as well as their past record in achieving their goals. Ownership and management's first obligation is typically to the shareholders. Sometimes what is good for shareholders may not be good for debt holders, and vice versa. While having a fiduciary priority to the shareholders' interest, a management team has to focus on being fair to a multitude of constituents for the longer-term good of the company and its shareholders. These constituents include employees, customers, and debt holders. Therefore, how the company ownership and management have treated debt holders in the past can impact how the debt securities are valued in the market.

Ownership Considerations

Understanding the ownership of a company can give an analyst insight into potential future actions. If the company is public, it can make a difference if there is one dominant shareholder, or if an activist investor takes a stake and advocates for certain changes. It can also be good to understand how much of the company management and employees own. If senior management have a large stake in the company, they have a vested interest in the company performing well, but if performance falters, it may be difficult to change leadership. When a company is private, the motivations of the owners might be different if it is owned by a financial firm, such as a PE firm, or if the ownership is a family trust.

When a company is publicly owned and has no controlling shareholders, it can be a takeover target. If a stock is materially underperforming its peers, management may be under pressure to do something more radical or depart from current strategy. This may be true even if the company is sound from the debt holders' point of view.

In the USA, for companies with public stock, an annual proxy statement must be filed. It shows the major shareholders and management's compensation and stockholdings, as well as the names of the directors and their holdings and affiliations. The compensation section can be particularly interesting because it may outline options and bonuses for the management team if certain goals are met. This helps to understand management's incentives and the targets they are striving for. Large shareholders can influence how a company operates, and if there are large outside shareholders, these documents are where some of the information can be found. It can be especially valuable to note if their ownership stake is new or has recently been increased. The footnotes in these documents can be very valuable because sometimes ownership stakes are held in trusts or other entities and the footnotes may explain the joint ownership of some of these entities.

The most common private ownership structure in the leveraged debt market is ownership of a company by a PE firm. PE firms usually have a series of investment funds from which they use capital to buy companies. Investors in these funds have a time frame in which they want to see a meaningful rate of return. For these reasons, when a PE firm owns a company, the PE firm typically has in mind a time frame and strategy for how it will get a return on its investment—this may be a shorter time frame than the strategic plan of a publicly held company. Therefore, ownership by a PE firm almost ensures that a transaction of some kind is in the plans in the near future. PE firms vary greatly in their investment focus, their style, and what expertise and value-added features they bring to the company's management. Keeping a separate list of PE firm styles and history can be helpful.

While it is not the norm, there are times when controlling stakes in public companies are held in different classes of common stock, where one class has supervoting power. Therefore, a relatively small ownership stake in these shares may have much more control over the board of directors and the overall vote in key shareholder matters. Often the non-super-voting stake is publicly traded, whereas the supervoting shares may not be publicly traded. The economic benefits to the two classes are usually equal. If the company is sold, each share of voting and super-voting shares would be paid the same value.

Management Considerations

Analysis of management has a much higher level of subjectivity than the analysis of financial statements. A view has to be developed of whether to believe the management team can do their jobs and if they are setting achievable or unrealistic goals. An analyst hopes to have access to both managers and owners through conference calls and meetings. The goal is to try to gain insight into what is going on with the business's operations, and what the key drivers of the business are, and to understand goals and strategies as a well as the metrics management looks at to measure success.

Where possible, look at what management has done in the past, either with the current company or with other companies. Examining management and ownership's history with other companies can sometimes help with analyzing a company's strategy.

Sometimes management has a history from which can be gleaned various aspects of how a company might be managed, including growing revenue, cost cutting, and asset acquiring or selling. This background information can impact how the debt securities trade and can help guide the types of scenarios to model. It is helpful to have a standard list of items to address with every management team, and a subset for specific industries.

An outline of a management checklist could resemble the following:

1. Operational History
   a. Has the company met its guidance?
   b. How have margins compared to the industry?
   c. How do revenue and EBITDA trends compare to the industry?
   d. Is there the ability to grow the company?
   e. What are the operational KPIs that management uses?

2. Strategic Approach
   a. Does management have a reasonable strategy for positioning the company?
   b. How do they expect to compete?
   c. How are they managing technological change?
   d. How have they dealt with any crisis in the past?
   e. What are the financial KPIs?
   f. What is their approach to the balance sheet and long-term financial goals (target leverage)?

3. Governance
   a. What are the structures of management and the board?
   b. What are the management and employee ownership stakes?
   c. Are there potential conflicts?
   d. What is the history of employee relationships?
   e. What is the history of legal and compliance?

One of the advantages of looking at multiple companies in the same industry is that it is easier to see if there are outliers among management teams in terms of operational results, expectations, or strategies. Outliers are not necessarily bad, but they should be examined carefully. For example, a manufacturer of auto parts announces that through cost cutting, it will get EBITDA margins up to 15% from 9%, without hurting its revenue. The company would seem to be well on its way to improving the credit. Look at five or six comparable companies, and if none of them have EBITDA margins better than 12%, it is reasonable to be skeptical of the announcement the company just made.

Management incentives are important to understand. Investors tend to favor situations where management has a meaningful stake in the firm. In the case of a PE firm, investors will often examine how much of their initial investment the PE investors have recouped to try to understand their likelihood of pursuing equity sales or dividends and their level of interest in how the company is performing.

The composition of the board of directors is important to look at. Investors want to see some outside independent directors who are not aligned with management or ownership. The idea is that outside independent directors help balance those who may be closer to the company. The independent directors also should represent minority shareholders' views equally with the larger shareholders and management. A more diverse board can be very beneficial to bringing outside views and checks and balances to a company. The board has certain legal responsibilities, including analyzing risks, and should be a good governor of any extreme plans proposed by management. Significant changes to a board of directors should be analyzed as to what the differences are in the interests and background of those who left the board and those who joined.

Closing Comment

Management, ownership, and board composition are a vital part of credit analysis. Understanding how management acts can be an important guide when prioritizing scenario analysis and event analysis. Often views and insights about a management team can be garnered from other operators in the industry, though it is important to understand their motivations for sharing their views. More candid views often come in person-to-person conversations as opposed to electronic forms of communication. If an analyst wants to be ahead of the market and prepared to react quickly, it is critical to develop a thoughtful view of management styles, likely motivations, and the strategies of management teams.

Chapter 17

Other Credit Factors: Environmental, Social and Governance Factors (ESG),Socially Responsible Investing (SRI), and Impact Investing

What's in this chapter:

- Environmental, Social and Governance (ESG)
- Socially Responsible Investing (SRI)
- impact investing and green bonds
- engagements
- a few pragmatic points on ESG and SRI

ESG, SRI, AND impact investing are often grouped together in discussions, but while they are inter-related, they are also very different. The definitions for all of these fields are evolving and can be subjective, but they do overlap in many ways. Many of these investment factors have been an important aspect of credit analysis for a very long time and have impacted investment results. However, attempts to codify the characteristics have escalated in recent years. The issues in ESG and SRI are vital considerations when making investments, as they can create both large risks and opportunities. These issues are part of the core of credit analysis.

ESG

ESG factors should be integrated into all aspects of making investment decisions. From the most basic pragmatic stance, considering these factors is part of risk mitigation in the investment process. If a company has bad practices in managing or addressing ESG, it increases risks to the financial viability of the credit and can also be an important differentiator in making relative value decisions between a group of credits.

To research ESG factors, an analyst often has to review the company's financial documents as well as other resources. The financial documents will usually have a section focused on risks, which may cover some of these areas, and there may be information in the footnotes to the financial statements. These areas may contain any specific risks on ESG, but often will only include major issues and tend to focus on areas where there have been legal or regulatory actions taken against the company. This will typically be couched in legal commentary and give very limited information on the situations but can be a good starting point for more research. Typically, companies do not draw attention to these sections and try to limit what they include.

For every company, do news searches and enter search keywords such as "lawsuits," "labor relations," or "environment." A good source to search can be the databases of government agencies, and activist and lobbyist groups. There are also for-profit third-party resources that supply research on ESG and SRI issues. Most of these organizations will have some biases in their data and reporting, and this is important to be aware of. All of these resources can and should be used for SRI research as well.

In the environmental arena, there are some industries that have higher risks than others. Companies in industries such as natural resources or manufacturing require an analyst to inquire about environmental processes, controls change, or improvements they are undertaking as well as any regulatory or legal challenges or investigations. However, environmental issues can be a factor in all businesses. As an example, there have been controversies over packaging and single-use products in the retail and food industries that have impacted operating costs. Every business interacts with the environment. Some have products and production that have more obvious impacts; others pose more passive risks for the environment. Some companies may face risk of its business being hurt by environmental issues out of its control (e.g., wildfires or rising sea levels). Poor management of environmental issues can increase the risks of an investment in any credit.

Some environmental risks are easier to measure. For example, reporting on carbon footprints and sustainability is increasing. Some companies release reports on their carbon footprint, but they are usually larger companies that can afford to have the staff prepare and monitor this kind of reporting, and therefore are usually not in the leveraged finance markets. Because of the availability of quantitative data on environmental issues, this ESG risk can receive more focus in ESG and SRI analysis than other issues, but they are all of great importance when doing analysis.

Social issues can be as significant a risk to a corporation's well-being as any other ESG factor. They can build up surreptitiously and result in a sudden flare-up of risk. This could come in the form of poor employee management that results in a strike or lawsuit. Social issues can cover a broad swath of topics, from a product that unintentionally offends a large part of the public, including customers and investors, to poor hiring and recruitment practices. Social issues involve interaction with stakeholders in the business, which can include employees, customers, suppliers, investors, and members of the community in which the business operates. This can also involve employee and product diversity issues (which can easily fall into the governance category as well). Sometimes it is hard to blame a company for social issues such as a long-time product or brand suddenly being viewed as offensive as social norms change, or a senior employee acting inappropriately. It is important to monitor how management handles these events and also to ascertain that there is not a culture at the firm that has created the problem. It is important to find out if a company has established controls, policies, and monitoring within its organization to address these types of issue. Investigating and analyzing social risks in a credit should involve searches of databases to look for problematic employee relations or customer lawsuits and complaints. The websites of governmental agencies can be a valuable source for data as well. Be sure to check websites of both local and national entities such as labor, environmental, and health agencies.

Governance is an area that is more natural for debt investors to gravitate toward, as debt holders are commonly involved in negotiating covenants and monitoring how a company treats debt and equity holders. Governance can cover how the company manages relationships with investors in both the debt and the equity, and how aggressively it might try to circumvent covenants or not. However, governance concerns go well beyond these capital market issues that naturally attract investors. They can also involve how well a company manages existing and potential conflicts of interest, board diversity, executive pay, uses of FCF—broadly, how the company is managed.

All of these factors need to be examined and considered when making an investment. Regardless of anyone's personal view on these topics, a company that mishandles any of these areas could face major consequences. This could come in the form of lawsuits, legal action from governments, a backlash and loss of customers, and/or more limited access to funding.

Companies can have a mixed scorecard in ESG. A company may have an exceptionally environmentally friendly business but terrible governance. There are also risks from ESG that have to be considered that could pose a risk to companies even if they manage their own business very well. Climate change could endanger a business in an area where wildfires become more prevalent or rising water levels could endanger a plant near certain bodies of water. These same types of risk could disrupt supply chains for a company. Tracking and discussing ESG factors are necessary risk mitigation tools, and a company that is exceptional in these areas may see benefits in attracting new customers, cheaper capital, or significant government support.

One of the best tools to analyze ESG risks at a firm is a conversation with management. If the management takes these types of risk seriously, it is a good sign. However, it is important to probe how well they have established the organizational structure within the firm to manage these types of risk.

SRI

Socially responsible investing has a high level of subjectivity. Two people might care passionately about investing with a socially responsible set of rules, but may, quite reasonably, want to focus on different SRI characteristics in their investing. One person may be more concerned about nuclear risks and want to avoid investing in companies associated with atomic energy and atomic weapons; another may feel that a bigger threat to society is the health of individuals and want to avoid investing in companies involved in alcohol and tobacco.

SRI usually involves negative screening, which means making decisions to ban certain types of investment. Decisions about SRI investing rules are usually made at the allocator level, but some funds may have their own rules about exclusions to attract like-minded investors. SRI exclusions will vary greatly and can be driven by the type of investor. As an example, a religious organization may have certain negative screens it wishes to introduce into its investment portfolios because of its religious beliefs (e.g., no investments associated with gambling or adult entertainment), and a health insurance company may have SRI bans on very different categories (e.g., no investing in alcohol or tobacco).

There is not one set of rules within SRI, and it is important that the personal biases of analysts and investment teams do not tilt analysis in this arena. It is important for analysts to get a sense of how widely certain negative screens are being instituted in the market and how they might impact a company's, and an industry's, capital costs and ability to refinance debt.

Analysts are often asked to determine if a company should fall into a negative screen category. This is usually done by analyzing revenue sources, but the more precise the guidelines are for negative screens, the easier the job is to do. However, the lack of corporate disclosure on some topics can make such screening very difficult.

Theoretically, SRI could have positive screens too. This could involve investing only in companies that do not produce carbon emissions beyond a certain threshold, or in specific social trends. More often, this type of investing is categorized as impact investing.

Impact Investing and Green Bonds

Impact investing is a definitionally dependent area, with many investors taking different approaches to the field. Generally, it involves making investments to specifically promote and encourage a type of activity by corporations or nongovernment organizations related to environmental or social issues. This can come in the form of equity or debt, including venture-capital-like investments. As examples, impact investing can fund a start-up clean renewable energy company or offer funding to help an existing company change how it addresses environmental issues, such as refurbishing a factory to switch from using coal-fueled power to renewable power sources.

Impact investing is intended to generate some type of change that the investors view as positive, whether it is increasing corporate diversity, addressing environmental issues, or improving education. Ideally, impact investing should intentionally produce measurable results in achieving whatever goals are being aimed for and also produce good investment returns.

Some believe that impact investing has to be done through equity investments giving a group control over a company or at least enabling it to bring pressure on the company, through shareholder votes, to change certain behavior. One could argue that, unless the equity affords a controlling ownership position, impact investing through debt could be more effective than equity. The contractual nature of debt could allow for covenants that require the company to achieve certain KPIs. The failure to achieve them could trigger events such as coupon increases or additional security. Impact investing is often done through private investments, such as debt private placements, but can be done in the public markets as well. Some investors consider investing in green bonds as a form of public impact investing.

Green bonds began to appear around 2007. Initially, green bonds were focused on funding specific projects in the public or private sector to improve the environment. The market has since expanded to include projects viewed as likely to improve social conditions as well. These have often been issued by nongovernmental organizations such as the International Monetary Fund (IMF), and also by private companies.

There are agencies that have various ratings or certifications for green bonds. However, these entities may have different agendas and prioritization from each other and from investors. One area of green bond issuance that can be controversial involves providing funding to a company generally viewed as negatively impacting the economy (e.g., a coal fuel utility) to reduce this credit's negative impact. For example, a company in a business that produces a large carbon footprint—perhaps an energy production company—might issue bonds that get a green certification for a project that can reduce its footprint, even if the company overall still has a huge carbon output.

Regulators continue to generate more standards in determining what allows a bond to be counted as green or what investments can be labeled as ESG. They do so to make sure that investment management companies are not greenwashing (appearing to be more robustly addressing ESG issues than they actually are to attract assets).

Engagement

Engagement is an important part of ESG, SRI, and impact investing. If the goal is to improve behavior by corporations, just penalizing a company through negative screens does not necessarily affect how that company acts. It is more powerful to communicate to the company the issues that are impacting the investment thesis and what can be done to address them.

Engagement is also vital to understand how a company approaches certain issues and can give an analyst a better sense of whether the company is in a position to effectively address ESG issues, or whether management is ignoring these risks. Engaging with management can be very helpful in clarifying ESG analysis, as public disclosure on these topics may be of limited value. This can be especially useful in understanding a management team's approach to ESG issues.

Typically, engagement with management on these issues is associated with equity ownership. Equity owners generally have the right to vote on many issues impacting the company, including who gets to serve on the board of directors. Equity holders can use this power as a source of engagement with management to push agendas. Debt holders should not shy away from engaging with management just because their relationship is more contractual. Many issuers, especially PE firms, are regular issuers of debt in the institutional market. It can be pointed out to them that their reputation on ESG issues in the debt markets can impact their funding costs and possibly even their ability to issue debt in these markets. Governance issues are an obvious focus for debt holders, and negotiations on covenants, as well as tender and exchange offers, can speak to how a company's management and ownership view their obligation to debt holders and how they address governance issues with other stakeholders.

A Few Pragmatic Points on ESG and SRI

There are numerous companies that attempt to score and rate ESG issues. This can imply a false level of precision in analyzing ESG risks and benefits, especially numerical rankings. Purely objective rankings can be difficult in ESG versus financial data. Financial data can more easily be categorized—for example, when one company's leverage ratio is lower than another's, this is an objective fact. When entities are trying to apply a scoring and rating system that can be sold to others, there may be too much of an effort to derive a quantitative answer. This may cause the few areas of ESG that are objectively measured (e.g., carbon footprints) to be significantly overweighted to the detriment of other factors when deriving a rating or score.

It is difficult in any rating or scoring system to quantify some of the conflicts on ESG issues that invariably exist, often within the same company. As an example, a company focused on sustainable energy development has very poor employee diversity and a history of employee conflicts. So, it would be hard to determine what kind of score it would get. More importantly, one investor may want to more heavily weight the environmental factors while another may be more focused on the social issues. With these inherent difficulties, any single rating agency is likely to differ greatly from other rating agencies and certainly will not align with every single investor's ESG interests.

Even if some of these ratings and categories are misleading or wrong, they will likely evolve anyway and should be monitored. If the market participants increasingly use these services, they cannot be ignored in any analysis.

Closing Comment

ESG and SRI factors are very meaningful risks that companies face. An analyst has to consider these factors in their analysis and weigh them in a consistent and structured approach. It is best to develop a checklist or grid to review all of these topics on companies so there is consistency to the approach. It is vital to understand how management approaches these issues as well. While management cannot control all factors and events, an understanding of a corporation's structure of controls and its approach to ESG factors gives important insight into the level of risk a company might face. Good ESG practices can also enhance an issuer's credit quality and be a positive as well.

Chapter 18

Other Credit Factors: Fallen Angels

What's in this chapter:

- crossover credits: fallen angels and rising stars
- special considerations when analyzing fallen angels
- fallen angels' impact on the market

THE MAJOR RATING agencies rank bonds using letter grades going from AAA down to D (for defaulted) or a similar pattern. One of the biggest delineations in credit markets is between debt rated investment grade and debt rated below investment grade (sometimes referred to as speculative). Corporate debt issuance rated below investment grade makes up the leveraged debt market. Most entities that invest in the debt markets are bound by rules covering what they are allowed to invest in. A common restriction involves the range of debt that an investment vehicle can own defined by its credit rating. Many investors are not allowed to hold debt rated below investment grade, or their portfolio in debt with speculative ratings is restricted to a certain percentage. In some cases, they may be allowed to own below-investment-grade debt, but they get a capital charge against these holdings (i.e., they need to hold some excess capital against this debt, which lowers their return). Many managers of leveraged debt are restricted from owning too much investment-grade debt as well. When a bond is downgraded from investment grade, it is often referred to as a fallen angel. When a below-investment-grade credit is upgraded to investment grade, it is often called a rising star. These transitional credits represent both risk and opportunity. There are also nuances in fallen angel structures that can cause these credits to differ from debt that was originally issued in the below-investment-grade market.

Crossover Credits: Fallen Angels and Rising Stars

Some of the biggest price movements in debt instruments can occur when a bond becomes either a fallen angel or a risen star. These large price movements occur as changes take place in the universe of those who can hold the debt transitions and the peer group for relative value analysis. Large price movements can also occur if an investment-grade credit looks as if it is going to become a fallen angel but then avoids the downgrade and rebounds.

Analysts and portfolio managers often try to identify potential fallen angels and rising stars early. There are certain characteristics in the ratings data that can identify likely falling angels and rising stars, including looking to see if debt is rated just on the cusp of remaining investment grade. For the largest rating agencies, potential fallen angels would be Baa3 or BBB- (any rating below these levels would no longer be investment grade). For potential rising star ratings, Ba1 or BB+ would be the highest before becoming investment grade. Usually rating changes move by one notch (e.g. Ba2 to Ba1). There have been cases when the agencies have moved a company multiple notches (e.g., Ba2 to BBB-), though often this involves a major event.

Rating agencies also have various watch lists and outlook ratings, such as a "negative" credit outlook or a credit watch positive. This can imply a greater or lesser probability of an upgrade or downgrade. Sometimes when a major event is announced by a company, a rating agency may put out a press release announcing that it is putting the credit under review. This may occur if a merger gets announced. The agencies typically prepare credit write-ups for their subscribers as well, and within these documents they will often outline the target credit metrics the company would have to achieve to get an upgrade or a downgrade.

It is not uncommon for one of the credit agencies to do an entire industry review, at which time a slew of debt in one industry could see major rating changes. Even if an entire industry is not being reviewed all at once, it is not uncommon for an industry rating downgrade or upgrade to be followed by more credit rating changes in the same industry. In an era of rapid technologically driven industry disruption, these industry-wide rating changes may become more frequent.

Indexes Often Define the Markets

There are different definitions of what qualifies a credit as falling below investment grade. This is often driven by how various market indexes define the cut-off. Sometimes, below-investment-grade debt will be defined by its lowest rating among the agencies; other times, it will be based on the average rating of two or three agencies; or it might be based on whether two out of three agencies rate a credit below investment grade. It is important to realize that indexes can change their inclusion rules, so the definition can change. These indexes are followed closely by many investors, who often use them as performance benchmarks.

Special Considerations When Analyzing Fallen Angel Credits

Fallen angel bonds were initially issued as investment-grade bonds. There are certain structures that are more common in investment-grade bonds than in below-investment-grade bonds that analysts should be aware of.

Investment-grade credits are more often structured as bullet bonds, meaning they do not have call features in them. Investment-grade issued bonds often have longer maturities than high yield issued bonds. While leveraged debt bond maturities are not usually much longer than ten years, it is not uncommon for investment-grade bonds to be issued to mature in twenty to thirty years or even longer. These features tend to cause fallen angel bonds to have much longer duration than debt that has originally been issued in the high yield bond market. This means that fallen angels will tend to have more price sensitivity to movements in spreads and yields than high yield issued bonds.

Bonds issued in the high yield market will usually have a cadre of covenants. In different periods of issuance, these covenants may be stronger or weaker, but they usually still include a number of restrictions on the issuer of the debt.

It is not uncommon for fallen angel bonds to have little or no meaningful covenants. One covenant common for investment-grade bonds is a change-of-control covenant. Some investment-grade bonds include a feature in which the coupon increases if the bonds are downgraded below investment-grade rating levels. Sometimes these coupon enhancements are structured so that the coupon increases for each notch the bond is downgraded, meaning if a bond went from Baa3 to Ba1, the coupon would move up once (e.g., +0.25%); and if it were downgraded a year later to Ba2, the coupon would increase again.

The differences in the typical structures between bonds of investment-grade credits and those of below-investment-grade credits are important to consider when analyzing potential rising stars and looking at total return scenarios. A rising star bond that has a noncall bullet structure may be more attractive to investment-grade buyers, and it will then trade better when upgraded than will a callable bond issued by the same company. This is because it may fit better into high-grade portfolios that are familiar with that structure and can be more easily used to match with liabilities. Additionally, the price of the noncallable bond is not constrained by the call feature. When a callable bond is upgraded to investment grade, it will increase the probability that the company will call the bond, as it can refinance the debt at lower rates and with fewer or no covenants.

There are specific analytical factors to consider when analyzing fallen angel credits. When a company gets downgraded and is no longer investment grade, the liquidity sources may change. Revolving credit lines, asset-backed facilities, and perhaps commercial paper or trade credit may become unavailable or require a reset of terms when a company is no longer investment grade. The information about these agreements is usually in a credit's financial statement's discussion of liquidity and footnotes about corporate debt. The full documentation may be in attachments to the financial statements.

An analyst will want to get a sense of whether the finance team at the company understands they will have to operate in a different set of capital markets and liquidity sources may change. When talking to management, an analyst will try to get a sense of whether getting upgraded and reinstated to investment grade is important to them and whether they have a realistic plan to achieve it. This can also be significant when analyzing potential rising stars. In some industries, the cost of capital can be more of a competitive edge than in others.

It is not uncommon for fallen angel/investment-grade credits to be larger in size and market share than those in the leveraged debt markets. Sometimes they have greater business diversification than leveraged finance credits. However, since the fallen angel credit has recently been downgraded by the agencies, the credit often is going through some negative event, or it may be undertaking a transaction that is meaningfully leveraging or facing negative business trends. Analysts will want to make sure that if they are considering recommending the purchase of a fallen angel, it does not become a falling knife.

Fallen Angels' Market Impact

Usually, periods in which there are a significant number of fallen angels occur when either the broad economy or a specific industry is going through turmoil. A large number of fallen angels results in new credits entering and increasing the size of the leveraged debt markets. This can disrupt the supply-and-demand balance in the leveraged debt markets. It can also impact pricing in the market, as the downgraded debt affects relative value within the market. It is also important to consider that this new supply usually occurs when the broad market, or a specific industry, is undergoing some stress.

A large addition of fallen angels to the market can initially hurt pricing levels but can also create some great opportunities. This is especially true if analysis shows that the disruption is likely to be temporary, or that the credit rating agencies may have over-reacted. Rising stars tend to happen more selectively, but industry trends and acquisition activity can lead to an increase in upgrades and to an improved supply-demand balance in the market.

Whether an analysis on a specific issuer agrees or disagrees with the credit agencies, following credit rating movements can sometimes be helpful in looking at broad market trends. It can also be helpful to watch the ratio of rising stars to fallen angels over time, to get a sense of whether the business environment is improving or declining, and to look at the broader market upgrades to downgrades ratios to get a sense of corporate trends.

Closing Comment

Fallen angel credits should be analyzed in the same way as any other credit, but there are some nuances in their bond structure, capitalizations, and business organizations that differ from the typical leveraged finance credits. An analyst has to be aware of these differences. Having an understanding of how and why rating agencies may create fallen angels or rising stars can help an investment team find opportunities to invest in credits that are going through these transitions. Investors have to be aware how trends in these rating changes can cause technical supply-and-demand pressures on the markets.

Chapter 19

Other Credit Factors: Distressed Credits, Bankruptcy, and Distressed Exchanges

What's in this chapter:

- distressed credits
- default and bankruptcy
- classes of claims
- subordination
- claims arising from bankruptcy and debtor-in-possession loans (DIPs)
- valuing the company
- sale or restructuring
- restructuring without bankruptcy
- a few pragmatic points on bankruptcy reorganizations and net present value (NPV)

COMPANIES SOMETIMES GET into financial trouble, and this can lead to default. This is more common for below-investment-grade companies than for investment-grade companies. The risk of default is part of the reason why yields are higher on leveraged debt instruments. Many studies show that over the long term, across a diverse portfolio, investors are more than compensated for the risk of default by investing in the leveraged finance market. While good analytical work is often designed to avoid investing in a default, mistakes happen. It is important to understand how defaults happen and how debt instruments are treated in bankruptcies. This can impact how debt trades on a relative value basis, even in situations that are not likely to lead to default. There is a large portion of capital that is structured to specifically invest in distressed debt situations and bankruptcies.

Distressed Credits

There are numerous reasons why a company might become distressed, but generally, they fall into two broad categories. One is that the company has had operational declines that resulted in a drop in financial results, especially impacting cash flow. The second reason is that too much debt was put on the company in anticipation of growth or high-multiple asset sales that did not materialize.

Financial results can decline for numerous reasons, including:

- A dramatic shift in costs and expenses, such as a spike in energy prices.
- Changes in the competitive landscape, such as price cutting by a stronger competitor, new product development, or product obsolescence.
- Secular changes in an industry, such as the switch from analog to digital.
- Changes in government policies, such as health-care payment changes forced by the government.
- Weak management and poor strategic choices.

In situations where a company has done well financially but not well enough to deleverage and refinance its debt, it is often said to be a good company with a bad balance sheet. Sometimes these companies were overleveraged when the debt financing was originally put in place and valuations were too robust. Sometimes growth was anticipated, and expansion was funded with debt. Perhaps deferred pay coupon structures were put in place, and debt grew, but cash flow did not.

When a company is distressed, potential sources of liquidity and new cash flows become the more pressing aspects of credit analysis. Even relatively small events that impact cash flows need to be analyzed as these might cause the company to run out of money, such as the actual dates of interest and principal payments.[11]

---

11 On income statements, the interest payments are averaged straight-line over the year. But in reality, bond interest payments typically are made in a lumpy fashion, semi-annually. Bank interest payments are usually monthly.

Seasonal working capital needs can also cause strains. It is good to create a chart of potential dates when the company might fail to fulfil a financial obligation. It might look something like Exhibit 19.1. In this exhibit, the available liquidity does not go down by the exact amount of the cash payment due, because it is assumed that the company is generating some positive net FCF, about $2 million per month. In many cases, if the company realizes it will not be able to complete a financial obligation, it may look to file bankruptcy before that date to try to have better control of the case. In other circumstances, the company may go into a grace period or seek to negotiate a forbearance agreement if it believes it is close to rectifying the default.

Exhibit 19.1: Sample of a Chart of Potential-Failure-to-Pay Dates for a Distressed Credit

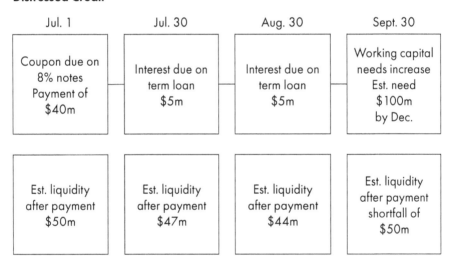

Looking at cash needs is part of the equation, but scenarios need to be analyzed as to what other sources of liquidity might be available:

- Are asset sales available, such as sale leasebacks of real estate?
- Frequently, covenants allow certain assets to be securitized, such as receivables or inventories. Is this a possibility?
- Can availability be drawn under a revolver? If covenants have not been violated, the revolver should be available.

- Although it's usually difficult to do when liquidity is an issue, consider whether an outside investor could be attracted to fund the company with new debt or equity. This might include the sale of the company.

After analyzing the potential payment violation dates and running scenarios of other potential funding sources, be sure to have a sense of when the credit may hit the wall. Keep in mind that the company management will also understand the liquidity risks and usually will not wait until the last minute to start a restructuring process.

Default and Bankruptcy

Bankruptcies are almost always driven by money issues rather than technical issues. Money issues are missed payments that are due. Technical issues include items such as violation of an affirmative covenant. There are times when legal obligations, such as a lost lawsuit, cannot be met, and that is what drives the default as well.

In most cases, the default occurs when a company cannot, or will not, make an interest or principal payment that is due on its debt obligations. The company usually has a thirty-day grace period in which to cure the default on an interest payment. After that time, the parties that have not been paid can begin forcing the company to file bankruptcy. There are often cross-default arrangements among the debt, in which if the company defaults on one debt instrument, it triggers a default in others.

Bankruptcy law varies from country to country. In some countries, a company that enters bankruptcy effectively gets liquidated, and proceeds are used to pay down debt obligations in strict order of priority. The USA and many other countries employ the concept of restructuring and reorganization. There are two varieties of business bankruptcies under the US Bankruptcy Code:[12] a Chapter 7 liquidation and a Chapter 11 reorganization. In a Chapter 7 liquidation, the debtor generally ceases business operations, and a trustee is appointed to administer the assets of the estate, liquidate those assets, and distribute the proceeds to creditors. In a Chapter 11 reorganization, the business debtor, referred to as a debtor-in-possession (DIP), generally continues to

---

12 The Bankruptcy Code is set forth in Title 11 of the United States Code, 11 U.S.C. §§ 101–1532.

operate as a going concern and ultimately seeks to reorganize its business and financial affairs through a confirmed Chapter 11 plan. In a Chapter 11 restructuring, the judge has great power in directing how this reorganization will take place. Generally, the judge tries to avoid liquidating the company because, ultimately, the bankruptcy court must confirm any proposed Chapter 11 plan of reorganization or a sale of the debtor's assets. In some countries, a third-party receiver or administrator is appointed to monitor the company during the process, and there is an extended period to see if creditors can be repaid. This chapter focuses on US bankruptcy laws.

After it is determined that a credit will probably need to restructure, analyze the recovery potential for each tranche of the capitalization.

Realize that even if the company can avoid a bankruptcy and undertake a restructuring with the debt holders outside of the court system, the potential recoveries under bankruptcy form the basis of how the parties would negotiate such a transaction.

When a company files for bankruptcy, the debt obligations are considered claims, which are ranked by seniority and priority. The basic idea is that any value created from a restructuring is first used to repay the highest-ranking claims. If those claims are satisfied, the residual value can then be applied to the next most senior level of claims. This is often referred to as a waterfall. Claims from vendors, tax authorities, courts, and pensions also get ranked, as do the fees and costs related to the restructuring (which typically get administrative priority). Below is a simple ranking of claims:

1. senior secured claims
2. junior secured claims
3. unsecured administrative priority claims
4. general unsecured claims
5. equity interests

A debt obligation's claim typically includes the principal amount owed and any accrued but unpaid interest, up to the date of the bankruptcy filing.

For most claims, interest does not get paid or accrue during the bankruptcy process. Postpetition interest means getting paid, or accruing, interest payments during the bankruptcy. This typically occurs only in respect of secured claims, either as part of an adequate protection arrangement and/or where the case of the secured creditor is oversecured. If, for example, the value of the assets that secure the debt is large enough to cover the value of the principal of the debt obligations and the interest expense, and assuming there is enough liquidity, the judge may require that the interest payments on the secured debt continue to be paid, or accrue, throughout the bankruptcy. The judge focuses on the value of the collateral that secures those debt obligations, not the company's overall value. Before postpetition interest is granted, various parties—such as the company, secured debt holders, and subordinated debt holders—will likely get into a debate and make their cases to the court for and against granting postpetition interest.

Accreted value is an important concept in bankruptcy as it affects the size of the claim of a bond or loan. The claim size is based on accreted value, not the face value of debt. This can be significant if some of the debt was issued with deferred pay structures. The claim that zero coupon bonds, or those with an original issue discount, have in a bankruptcy is only the accreted value up to the date the bankruptcy is filed. Take, for example, a $100 million face amount of bonds originally issued at 61% of face value. On the day the issuer filed bankruptcy, the accreted value of the bonds would be 83.3% of the face value, or $83.3 million. That would be the bondholders' claim in bankruptcy. If these bonds were zero fixed, with a five-year zero period, and the bankruptcy took place after these bonds had fully accreted to face value in year five, the claim would be the full face amount, or 100%—in this case, a claim of $100 million, plus any unpaid interest.

As another example, assume a $500 million ten-year bond was issued with an 11% coupon, but it was issued with a discount of three points at 97 to yield 12%. That three-point discount will accrete in value over the life of the bond, and the claim of bondholders in a bankruptcy will, again, be only what the accreted value is, not the full $500 million. This discount is generally called an original issue discount (OID). The chapter on coupons has more details on accretion.

Classes of Claims

Claims in bankruptcy are divided into classes based on priority. Each claim within a class of security should be treated equally. For example, these classes may be divided into secured, senior unsecured, subordinated, and equity. The division of claims into classes can become complex.

One of the important concepts is that when a class is considered impaired, it gets to vote on any proposed Chapter 11 plan. If the court rules that a class is getting all that it is legally entitled to on its claims, it is considered unimpaired and does not vote on the plan, because it is deemed that this class will approve the plan. If a class is getting nothing, it is deemed to have rejected the plan, and it does not get to vote either. If a class is receiving some compensation but not 100% of its claim, it is impaired. It must approve the bankruptcy with both two-thirds of the class's dollar amount of claims and 50% of debt holders. In negotiations, if an investor controls 33.4% of the amount outstanding of debt in an impaired class, typically, it can block the class from approving the plan. This position size is usually called a blocking position. If an impaired class cannot get the requisite votes for a plan, it is within the court's power to force the plan to be accepted, or to cram down the impaired class. Bankruptcy courts generally do not like to force through plans on impaired classes. For this reason, very small classes that may have no true value on a strict priority basis are sometimes given a token stake in a reorganization.

The class of claims can matter. Assume there are two tranches of secured debt—in this case, a first and second lien. Generally, a second lien can be structured in two ways: It can be party to the security agreement of the first lien, or it can have its own security agreement. If it is part of the same agreement and a bankruptcy filing occurs, the holders of first and second liens are typically made part of the same class of claims. This causes a few things to happen. One is that the second liens may not have as much say in the restructuring, because their class will likely be dominated by holders of the first lien. A second consequence is that the collateral would need enough value to cover both issues (i.e., first and second liens) for the judge to consider postpetition payments. If the second-lien debt has a separate security agreement, holders would be in their own class. The first liens would only need enough value in the collateral to cover their loan to receive postpetition interest. Intercreditor agreements that outline the priorities and waterfalls between different pieces of debt can be a factor in how the debt instruments get treated.

A considerable amount of time in bankruptcy cases is often taken up by arguments over various claims ranking. Disagreements and maneuverings over ranking and classes may not just involve debt claims, but also claims from the trade, leases, and pensions, among others.

Subordination

Another area for debt holders to focus on when examining priority of claims is the idea of subordination. Usually, if not otherwise stated, debt is assumed to be senior. A common type of issuance in the leveraged debt bond market is a senior subordinated note. What makes this note subordinated is part of the indenture called the subordination agreement.

This subordination clause may state that "the notes are subordinated in right of payment to Senior debt." As covered in the chapter on covenants, because "Senior" is capitalized in this covenant document, it is a defined term and may be tightly or loosely defined. If no further clarification is given and the language simply refers to senior debt, it is loosely defined, and many claimants may argue that the bonds should be subordinated. In another case, assume the definition of *senior debt* in an indenture is "the existing bank loans at the time of this indenture and the 8% Senior Notes." This could be interpreted to mean that the subordination agreement is recognizing that the subordinated note is only subordinating its claim to these two items, and therefore any other senior claims should rank equally with these notes. This could include other senior debt that was issued after this indenture was written.

Exhibit 19.2 shows a simple capital structure laid out with only three claims and how each might be treated in a bankruptcy. It is assumed that the equity will get zero, so it is not included in the exhibit. The valuation of the assets of the demolition services company BlowUp Co. is $250 million, and this will be distributed among the claims. It is also assumed that the subordination clause in the subordinated notes only expressly subordinates the notes to the senior bonds.

The pro rata share for all the claims is established. Then some of the enterprise's value is taken from the subordinated notes to make the senior notes whole—in this case, $37.5 million. The other claims are not party to the subordination agreement, and their recovery remains unchanged.

The recovery is shown in the dollar amount and on a percentage basis. The dollar amount is the amount that would be modeled with regard to the balance sheet. The percentage amount equates to the value per bond a holder would receive. It equates to the price at which a trader would quote the bonds or loan, a percentage of the claim value.[13]

Exhibit 19.2: Simple Subordination Example for BlowUp Co. in $000,00s

		Pro Rata Recovery in $	Pro Rata Recovery in % of Claim	Adjusted for Subordination	
				Recovery in $	Recovery in % of Claim
Enterprise value	250.0				
Claims:					
Senior notes	100.0	62.5	62.5%	100.0	100.0%
Other senior debt	50.0	31.3	62.5%	31.3	62.5%
Sr. sub. notes	250.0	156.3	62.5%	118.8	47.5%
Total	400.0	250.0		250.0	

Claims Arising from Bankruptcy and DIPs

Claims can arise during the bankruptcy process and the process can be very expensive. Claims related to the bankruptcy process (e.g., administrative expense claims) typically have a higher payment priority than pre-petition, general, unsecured claims. Analysts must factor these administrative priority claims into their liquidation or recovery analyses. Included among the administrative expense claims are the fees and expenses of estate professionals, such as the debtor's lawyers, accountants, and financial advisors. In some cases, additional debt needs to be issued to help the company remain a going concern. This super priority debt is called a debtor-in-possession loan (DIP), which in some bankruptcies has been huge and in others very marginal. An analyst will try to estimate how much of a DIP might be required. To estimate the size of the

---

13 If the subordinated notes' face amount and accreted value are the same, this would equal the price per bond. If the accreted value on the senior subordinated notes were less than 100% of face value, the price would be adjusted as such if the accreted value were 90% of par: (accreted value 90) × (recovery value 47.5%) = value per par (or face amount) 42.75%.

DIP, examine operational cash burn, working capital needs, and the estimated length of the bankruptcy. In most instances, a DIP or consensual cash collateral arrangement will be accompanied by a rolling thirteen-week cash flow budget, which provides a roadmap for the debtor's financing needs on an interim basis in the course of the bankruptcy case. The bankruptcy court must approve the terms of the DIP or any cash collateral arrangement. Counterbalancing the cost of the reorganization and any DIP may be the company's ability to build up cash during the restructuring process when it is likely to not be paying interest.

DIP financing can be an attractive investment for certain investors. It is given the highest priority and is often priced with an attractive coupon. It is also usually refinanced upon the company exiting bankruptcy or very soon afterward, so it is a very short-dated investment. In many situations, the holders of the senior-most debt tranche in the capital structure—usually the senior secured first-lien holders—offer to fund the DIP and will crowd out others from participating. This is done with the hope that the DIP will be attractively priced and retired soon after the completion of the restructuring. This can help increase their overall return on the bankrupt investment. The additional debt can also impact the recovery value for the more subordinated tranches of debt and effectively change the profile of the return for holders of the same class of debt (i.e., senior secured first-lien holders) who do not, or cannot, participate in the DIP funding.

Valuing the Company

Establishing enterprise value is very important in bankruptcy analysis. Even if the company has an offer from an entity to buy the company in bankruptcy, the various creditors, including the equity, will want to compare the price of the bid for the company to what they believe the company could be worth on a restructured basis.

Deciding on a company's value involves a high level of subjectivity and assumption. However, several valuation methodologies are widely used. One methodology uses valuations based on a cash flow multiple for a number of publicly traded comparable companies, and the average is applied to the bankrupt company's estimated cash flow. An analysis may also be run using a sample of acquisitions of comparable assets if the sample set is large enough. A third common type of analysis is to run a longer-term model of the company and calculate a discounted cash flow analysis. Once various asset valuations are prepared, usually by advisory firms representing each class of claims, various parties involved in the bankruptcy are likely to debate the valuations for some time in front of the court.

These valuation methodologies capture only the value of cash-flow-producing assets. Other assets that are not producing cash flow need to be considered as well. There are some obvious assets to look for, including cash on the balance sheet and separable assets that are not producing cash. In the latter category, suppose the bankrupt entity is a lodging company with several hotels that are losing money, but another manager might find value in owning these assets, even though they currently produce negative cash flow. Digging deeper, there may be undeveloped real estate or real estate on which a sale leaseback could be done. These non-cash-flow-producing assets could also be intellectual property, from software code to trademarks, that are not currently being used or are in development. There may also be minority stakes in other companies that could be sold.

Another factor to consider in the company's valuation is how well the assets are being run. If all, or some, of the assets are operating at margins that are below industry averages, analysts might want to factor this into the valuation analysis. For example, suppose a manufacturing company is making its products at a 12% margin, and all its peers are operating at an 18% margin. A buyer hopeful of achieving 18% margins would probably pay a higher multiple than the industry average, because the buyer's projected adjusted EBITDA is higher than the historical average.

Sale or Restructuring

In some cases when a company enters bankruptcy, there may be interest in buying the company. An analysis has to be undertaken to estimate what the new reorganized enterprise could be worth, after all restructuring costs, in order to compare it to any bids that are being made to buy the company. An analyst cannot just assume a company can get sold. There has to be a buyer. If it is assumed that the company will be sold, part of the analysis should include a list of potential buyers. The more potential buyers with a realistic interest in the company, the more likely it is that the company could actually be sold at an attractive price.

The US Bankruptcy Code provides mechanisms for asset sales either under a Chapter 11 plan or outside a Chapter 11 plan pursuant to Bankruptcy Code § 363.[14] There are several benefits to utilizing the bankruptcy process to conduct an asset sale, such as 1) the ability to bind non-consenting creditors, lessors and other contractual counterparties; 2) the ability to transfer title to the assets to the purchaser free and clear of liens and claims; and 3) the oversight of the bankruptcy court, which substantially reduces the risk of a subsequent challenge to the sale.[15]

Most bankruptcy sales are conducted through a public auction process, which helps ensure that creditors and other stakeholders obtain the highest and best value for the debtor's assets. The auction procedures often include at least one bid for the company (a stalking horse bid), which ensures at least a minimal sale price for the assets, subject to higher and better bids at the auction. Sometimes this comes from a group of creditors. In most instances, secured creditors are entitled to participate in the auction and credit-bid the amount of their secured debt as part of the purchase price consideration.

More frequently in a bankruptcy, the company in bankruptcy is not sold, but reorganized. In the reorganization, the existing claims are given new securities in the reorganized company. The potential outcomes of this type of reorganization are endless. They usually evolve through various rounds of negotiation, sometimes while the arguments over valuation and priority of claims are ongoing. Bankruptcy investors and lawyers can be very creative, and different trends can be in vogue during various bankruptcy cycles.

As an example, assume a company was originally leveraged at 7× adjusted EBITDA, but over time, adjusted EBITDA declined, and now the company is in bankruptcy with a total debt of $1.170 billion, which equates to 9.0× adjusted EBITDA. After all types of experts have submitted their reports, and arguments have been made, the courts determine that a valuation should be no more than 5× adjusted EBITDA, or $650 million. After much wrangling between the claimants, the court determines that no more than 3× leverage

---

14 See 11 U.S.C. §§ 1123(b)(4) (stating that a plan may "provide for the sale of all or substantially all of the property of the estate, and the distribution of the proceeds of such sale among holders of claims or interests") and 363(b) (stating that the debtor, "after notice and a hearing, may use, sell, or lease, other than in the ordinary course of business, property of the estate.")

15 See, generally, 11 U.S.C. §§ 363(f) and (m).

should be on the company. This leverage may be determined by taking into consideration that it can pay a reasonable interest rate on its debt and meet its capital expenditures and still generate FCF while leaving, say, a 15% cushion for operational declines. Exhibit 19.3 is the capital structure of this company before the restructuring, including the DIP financing.

Exhibit 19.3: Capital Structure during Restructuring in $000,000s

DIP loan	40
Pre-petition claims:	
Senior secured bank debt	350
Senior subordinated debt	500
Subordinated debt	320
Total debt	1,210

In this hypothetical case, upon exiting bankruptcy, the company gets a new secured bank line for $40 million to pay off the DIP financing. The bank debt gets a new senior bond in the same amount outstanding as its claim. Together, this new debt totals $390 million to equal 3× EBITDA, which would cover the full claim value of the DIP and the secured debt. The bank creditors who are now the holders of the new senior bond will want to make sure that the new debt instrument they are receiving will be structured to trade at least at par so that the market value of its new security equals its prior claim. This may entail a high coupon or significant covenants. The more junior securities in the debt structure will receive equity. They realize that the higher the coupon and the more restrictive the new senior note will be, the more downward pressure it could put on the value of the stock it will receive. These more junior classes will argue in the courts for lower coupons and more lenient covenants versus what the former bank debt holders want.

Under this scenario, the company is worth $650 million, and $390 million of that value has been allocated to the debt for the DIP and the bank claims. The remaining $260 million would go to the senior subordinated debt. However, its claim was $500 million, so this class and the subordinated debt would be considered impaired classes. The most senior class of debt that is impaired and not paid in full is sometimes called the fulcrum security. This impaired class needs to vote on approving the plan and also frequently controls the equity, postbankruptcy.

Theoretically, no value should be allocated to classes more junior than the senior subordinated debt. In reality, some token value is often given to expedite the process. In this case, 3% of the equity value is given to the subordinated debt, and warrants that had a strike price equal to a valuation of 7× current EBITDA were given to the equity. The allocations and recoveries are outlined in Exhibit 19.4. Except for the DIP facility, the securities are getting their value not in cash, but in a package of securities. The true value of the consideration they are getting will depend on how these securities issued during the reorganization will trade in the market post bankruptcy.

Exhibit 19.4: Capital Structure and Recoveries (in $000,000s unless Noted)

	Claim	Received in Bankruptcy	Valuation	% Recovery
DIP loan	40	Cash	40	100.0%
Pre-petition claims:				
Senior bank debt	350	New senior debt	350	100.0%
Senior subordinated debt	500	97% of equity*	252	50.4%
Subordinated debt	320	3% of equity*	8	2.4%
Total debt	1,210		650	

* Based on equity value of $260 million

The equity ownership of a company typically changes during a bankruptcy. Some class of debt holders often ends up controlling the equity. This can make for strange combinations of equity holders controlling the company. Major shareholders may have varied views on what they want to do with the equity and may have varied time horizons for their investments. Often post reorg equities are not that liquid so the positions may not be easily exited. Some investment structures that are designed to invest in debt may not be allowed to own equity or have a limit on how much equity they can own, and this can be problematic.

Non-US Jurisdictions

Bankruptcy laws vary by country. Where the company issuing the bonds is domiciled will often dictate which bankruptcy laws will be involved. This location may be different from where the company is operating. A company may form a separate subsidiary to issue the debt. Luxembourg is a popular country for bond-issuing entities. There have also been cases of shifting venues as creditors and the company may vie for different jurisdictions to oversee the bankruptcy. Some codes favor liquidations; some use the concept of restructuring under what is known as controlled management, using the courts and commissioners. With many legal structures leaning more toward liquidations, frequently corporations and creditors spend an extensive amount of time trying to negotiate an out-of-court restructuring plan in European cases; and in some countries, there are structures to protect the company while it tries to address these issues. These nuances in bankruptcy codes appear to be part of the reason for companies and bondholders in Europe to be more reluctant to pursue bankruptcies as a strategic alternative for a struggling credit.

Restructuring without Bankruptcy

A company typically exhausts many other avenues to finance or fix its liquidity situation before filing for bankruptcy. These alternatives often include looking to undertake asset sales, bring in new investors, and negotiate with existing lenders to try to arrange some type of debt exchange out of bankruptcy.

One of the many reasons companies want to avoid bankruptcy are the costs associated with the process. These include not just the legal and transactional costs, but also less direct costs to the business that can hurt the company's long-term value. They could include the loss of customers and the ability of customers and/or suppliers to potentially break contracts. There can also be ramifications for the company's ability to win new business, especially if it's dealing with government entities. These factors need to be added to any analysis of a stressed company.

There is also the concern that as soon as the legal filings have begun, the management and equity owners tend to lose control of the process, and sometimes lose their jobs and their equity stakes. For these reasons, management, equity holders, and many debt holders usually prefer to avoid bankruptcy.

Frequently, management and the debt and equity owners try to work out a reorganization that may look like a bankruptcy, but in reality is an out-of-court restructuring in the form of an exchange offer. This can help preserve more equity for the owners. The more senior creditors tend to get a package of securities relatively comparable to what they might get in a bankruptcy, but without the time, risks, and impact associated with a bankruptcy. There are endless possibilities for how these exchanges could take place. However, it is not always easy to get the various parties to agree to terms without going through the courts. Holdouts can be an issue for completing these out-of-court restructurings. This occurs when a small group of holders of a security choose to not go ahead with an exchange. In many cases, by holding out, they can improve their position and get a better return on their holdings, which is also referred to as a free-rider problem. If holdouts become too large, they tend to jeopardize the entire exchange.

One method to avoid the holdout problem and a long bankruptcy process is to prepare a prepackaged bankruptcy. In this case, the company reaches a prenegotiated agreement with two-thirds of each class of creditors to go ahead with the proposed plan. It then files the bankruptcy plan. By doing this through a bankruptcy process, with the majority votes already in place, the courts can force holdouts to go along with the plan. This process also looks to be in and out of the courts in approximately ninety days. This time frame is accelerated for a typical bankruptcy. Such a filing may have challenges, but the courts are usually anxious to move the process along.

Another method to avoid the complexity and difficulty of addressing the entire capital structure is to simply try to address the most urgent issues in the capital structure. This can be done through exchange offers, which can be structured to be coercive to holders who do not, initially, want to go along. Assume a company has a debt maturity in eighteen months that is in the form of a $200 million 4% subordinated bond. If the company covenants allow for the issuance of senior secured second-lien debt, the company could offer the subordinated bondholders $150 million of a 7% second-lien bond with a six-year maturity. If the company chooses, it could structure the exchange with a consent that could strip all the covenants from the old 4% bond. This addresses a large portion of the near-term maturity issue. But if the company still faces a default and enters reorganization, the 4% bondholders who do not accept the exchange are materially disadvantaged in the bankruptcy—a risk that could coerce them to accept the exchange offer.

A Few Pragmatic Points on Bankruptcy Reorganizations and NPV

The examples in this chapter involve simple structures. Companies that have more complex structures can take a very long time to wind through the legal system. This can occur when multiple entities have issued debt within the corporation; when there are various cross-guarantees between subsidiaries; and when significant transfers have occurred between restricted and unrestricted groups. Additionally, if a company has a large number of foreign subsidiaries, foreign laws can add to the complexity of a restructuring.

It is also important to note that bankruptcy courts are rather unique in the legal system. Bankruptcy judges have considerable power and sway over the outcome in these cases. The bankruptcy judge has been referred to as the most powerful person in the room.

When looking at recovery values, one has to consider the securities that are being received in the restructuring. Frequently, postbankruptcy securities are fairly illiquid, especially equities. Because of the negotiated nature of the bankruptcy process, some of the more unusual features seen in a debt instrument often appear in the structure of a new bond or loan issued out of a restructuring. This can add to the illiquidity of the consideration that bondholders and loan holders receive.

The amount of time that a reorganization can take has to be considered when trying to reach an investment conclusion about a stressed credit. As an example, for the company described in Exhibits 19.3 and 19.4, if an investment team's analysis reaches the same conclusion as shown in the exhibits, the senior subordinated notes are worth a price of 50, postreorganization. Bankruptcy can take a very long time. If a decision is being made at the beginning of the bankruptcy process whether to invest in these notes or not, a view has to be established as to how long the process will take and then what the present value is for that recovery, especially as no interest income will be getting paid on the investment. If the expectation is for a two-year bankruptcy and the return that is being sought is a 20% internal rate of return, the day the company files bankruptcy, an investor should be willing to pay 34.7% of face value for a bond, using the net present value[16] (NPV) formula as follows: $(50/(1.2)^2)$. The more complex the structure is, the longer the bankruptcy can take, which may increase the risk for the recovery, so a higher rate of return might be sought as well.

Closing Comment

Many investors look to avoid stressed credits and restructurings; others look to specifically invest in these situations. Whether or not an investor expects to be involved in reorganizations, understanding how securities get treated in a bankruptcy is key to having a clearer understanding of the relative value of debt that has different rankings, such as what the yield spread should be between a senior secured debt instrument and a senior subordinated instrument.

---

16 The desired internal rate of return is used as the discount rate in the NPV analysis. The internal rate of return that is chosen should factor in the potential return on other investments as well as the level of risk of achieving that return.

Chapter 20

Market Information: Why Does Equity Matter?

What's in this chapter:

- valuation based on equity markets
- monitoring equities

EQUITY MARKETS CANNOT be ignored when analyzing leveraged finance credits. This is true whether or not the company has public stock. The equity markets are an easily accessible and fluid signal of what corporate valuations are for public companies and for valuation trends generally. Equity markets are significantly more liquid than leveraged finance investments so that when events break on a company or an industry, the price reactions in the markets can often show a quick response if the news is viewed as positive or negative. Stock market moves are not perfect. Prices of stocks can move rapidly, and sometimes the moves have nothing to do with an individual company but are a response to macroeconomic or technical events. A credit analyst has to be careful not to become overly dependent on an equity market valuation for a company or over-react to short-term price movements. Equity market valuations can fluctuate wildly, and any analysis using public equity market valuation should not be anchored on a point-in-time valuation. It is better to look at averages over time, as well as peaks and troughs. An equity price that has more volatility cannot be trusted as much as one with less. The stock prices of the companies that are being followed in the credit markets and their peers have to be monitored for any sudden or unusual activity as well as for long-term trends. The equity market is not always right, but it should not be ignored and can be a powerful early warning system to changes in a credit or investor sentiment.

Valuation Based on Equity Markets

Equity market valuations can be used to arrive at an estimated asset value for a company. To undertake the analysis, comparable companies need to be carefully chosen. A classic way of biasing results in any analysis is through the sample group that is chosen for comparative purposes, so careful thought should be involved in choosing the constituents for a peer group. It is unlikely that the perfect public comparable will be found, so differences in business lines, ownership, size, growth, and operating margins have to be considered. Stock valuations can also differ depending on whether a company is paying dividends or not, or whether a company is undertaking significant stock repurchases or not.

A key task is to make sure that the most up-to-date stock information for the company is being used. This can include making sure the right number of shares is being used in the analysis. This may seem simple, but various items such as multiple stock classes, options, and convertible securities can complicate the issue. Analysts must be consistent in how they choose to count in-the-money[17] options or converts and be sure to count preferred shares if any are outstanding.

One of the decisions that has to be made when looking at the equities is which valuation metric to use. Leveraged finance analysis usually assumes that the equity is being valued on a multiple of adjusted EBITDA. This may not always be the best metric to use. Sometimes stocks are valued using FCF, net earnings, or even revenue, for higher-growth, low-cash-flow companies. Even nonfinancial metrics have been cited as a valuation metric, such as a value per subscriber for an early-stage mobile phone company or proven reserves for an oil and gas company. If the equity market is believed to be using a metric other than an EBITDA multiple, forcing an analysis of equity-market EBITDA

---

17 This means a stock option or convert that has the right to convert to common stock on a per-share price that is below the stock's current trading price. If the conversion price were above the current stock price, it would be referred to as out of the money.

multiples may prove to be a misleading metric. Equity markets do seem to shift key valuation metrics depending on the life cycle of the business and the industry. This is prevalent in newer and rapidly developing industries. The example in Exhibit 20.1 employs the widely used metric, which in leveraged finance is total enterprise value (TEV) to adjusted EBITDA.

This example is based on a hypothetical provider of broadband service and analyzes what multiple of EBITDA the company is trading at and where some of its peers are valued. Note that the cash is subtracted from the valuation. This is done to get a sense of the value of the business, not the excess cash on the balance sheet, and makes comparisons cleaner. When developing a total value for the company, the cash could be added back, as could other non-cash-flow-producing assets.

Exhibit 20.1: Sample Enterprise Valuation (in $000,000s Unless Noted)

		My Broadband Company	Their Broadband Company	Another Broadband Company
1	Total number of shares	110	50	90
2	Recent share price (in $)	$35.00	$10.00	$12.00
3	Public market equity value (line 1 × line 2)	3,850	500	1,080
4	Total debt	2,000	1,500	2,300
5	Cash on hand	100	100	200
6	Total enterprise value (line 3 + line 4 − line 5)	5,750	1,900	3,180
7	Adjusted EBITDA	800	300	500
8	TEV/adjusted EBITDA (line 6/line 7)	7.2×	6.3×	6.4×
9	Net debt/adjusted EBITDA (line 4-5/line 7)	2.4×	4.7×	4.2×
10	TEV cushion (line 8/line 9)	303%	136%	151%

When there are variations in valuations, the analysis should try to discern what other factors might be the cause this variance. The following is a list of some examples of items that could cause a differentiation in valuation multiples:

- If a significant number of shares are not outstanding or free to trade, it can be said that there is not enough float.[18] If a stock does not have enough float, it may limit larger investors from looking to own shares in the company and may cause it to trade at a lower valuation.
- One company might be a more likely takeover target than the others because of ownership or other items. This may cause it to trade at a higher enterprise valuation.
- One company could be a significantly better operator or face more competition.
- A company could be paying dividends on its stock or doing stock buybacks. Both of these actions can help the valuation but are not necessarily good for the debt.
- The equity market does not ignore leverage. It often looks at leverage as a risk and may put a discount on the more leveraged companies in an industry sector. In Exhibit 20.1 the equity valuation is higher for the least leveraged of the comparable companies (i.e., My Broadband Company).

The easiest thing for an analyst to do is to compare this valuation to the debt leverage and see what kind of public enterprise valuation cushion there is for the debt. This cushion is shown on line 10 in Exhibit 20.1.

It is interesting to compare these average valuation metrics across industries. Too often, investors apply the same range of reasonable leverage to all industries. For example, an analyst may look at My Broadband Company and also at a chemical manufacturer (That Chemical Company) and see that both have 2.4× leverage. If the bonds of That Chemical Company were trading at a higher yield, the conclusion might seem to be that the chemical company bonds represent better value. However, after doing equity market valuation analysis, it is clear that broadband service company equities trade at over 6× EBITDA and chemical companies at about 4× EBITDA. Because broadband companies tend to trade at higher multiples, My Broadband Company actually has much better enterprise value protection even though the two companies have the same leverage. These differences should also lead to different yields and spreads in the valuation of these companies' debt instruments.

---

18 The float is generally the number of shares that actually trade. For example, if a company has fifty million shares outstanding, and the chairman owns fifteen million of them, the float would generally be considered to be thirty-five million.

The principal goal of the leverage ratio is to get a sense of how well protected the debt is relative to asset value. Different industries and different types of asset have different valuation ranges, for a multitude of reasons. The major point is that leverage ratios cannot be assessed in a vacuum; they have to be compared to the cost of funding and asset valuations.

A healthy stock multiple can often help give a company more financing options. Consider this when doing scenario analysis for a company. Stock can be used in lieu of cash to make acquisitions and can have certain tax advantages in mergers and acquisitions. Additionally, a healthy stock valuation may lead a company to issue stock and utilize proceeds to deleverage.

The stock price at which a company is valued is not the be-all and end-all of valuations. The stock market does not price everything to perfection; there will always be disputes over a company's value. If stocks were consistently valued perfectly, there would be much less trading volume and much lower price volatility in the equity markets. Sometimes the market is wrong and misvalues a company or industry. The public stock price is typically based on a few shares of stock trading in a company and does not give someone control over that company. Usually, someone pays a control premium to actually control a company. The stock market also does not often factor in synergies and cost savings that a strategic buyer could achieve. This is why, when doing asset value to debt analysis, a database on the valuation of mergers and acquisitions in various industries and a record of what multiples of EBITDA (or other metrics) are being paid in those transactions can be very valuable. All it takes is one person with lots of money who really wants to own a company to change that company's valuation and make the prior stock multiples look wrong.

Databases of Equity Valuations

Some databases can spit out equity multiples. However, they tend to use cookie-cutter rules and not make the typical adjustments an analyst may want to make to EBITDA or OIBDA. Additionally, these databases do not always adjust for share count accurately when factors such as convertible securities and options are significant and close to being in the money. If they are third-party systems, be sure to understand how they are defining their terms and gathering the data.

Monitoring Equities

Whatever market monitoring systems are available to analysts, it is strongly recommended that the stocks of all the companies they are responsible for should be followed. It is best to keep the peers grouped on the computer screen. Stocks tend to be more liquid than bonds, and stocks typically trade on listed markets where prices are updated rapidly. Monitoring these stocks for unusual changes in trading patterns in prices or volumes can sometimes be an early alert to news.

Analysts should also follow the stocks of leaders in an industry, whether they have leveraged debt outstanding or not. Although they are usually investment-grade companies and much larger than the leveraged companies, analysts want to know what trends the industry leaders are facing and try to understand how that will impact the credits they cover.

Monitoring stocks can be especially helpful during earnings season. If certain peers report early, an analyst can often develop a sense of how the industry may have performed for the reporting period and how the equity markets are reacting to these types of result.

It can also be helpful to monitor the volume of trading in a sector or an individual company's stock. Unusual spikes in volume can indicate that stories are beginning to circulate about a company or industry, or that some investors are either buying or selling large meaningful positions. There can of course be many false signals from stock price movements.

Closing Comment

Following equity market movements can be a valuable tool to understand valuation trends in different companies and industries. It can also be valuable to get a sense of how investors are reacting to news events about an industry or a company. It is important to not become too dependent on using equity valuation to make credit decisions. It is also important to not be too dependent on the most recent stock price. Rather than using just one spot in time, it might be useful to use the average stock price over a period of time. When using an average, an analyst may choose to use an exponentially weighted moving-average price to give more weight to recent prices. The value of public equity valuations can be fleeting and should not be the linchpin in coming to a conclusion about a credit.

Chapter 21

Market Information: Reacting to News Events

What's in this chapter:

- scenario: issuer makes an acquisition
- scenario: issuer gets bought
- scenario: issuer announces an IPO
- scenario: issuer is facing a maturity
- a pragmatic point on the blended price to retire debt

WHILE THE LEVERAGED finance market is not as reactive to news events as the equity market, it does tend to be more responsive than most other fixed-income markets. These below-investment-grade companies also tend to have more transformational events than companies in the investment-grade market. Unfortunately, no set of rules governs how a company's debt securities will react in response to a certain type of news event. Often, the entire market may view an announced event as positive, but investors may have significantly different views on how much the news should impact security prices. There are times when news is positive for both the equity and debt of a company; but there are times when a headline is positive for a company's equity but negative for its debt, and vice versa.

Most credit events come with a fair amount of uncertainty. When there is an acquisition announcement, an initial public stock offering, or a new debt financing, the transactions do not close immediately when they are announced, and there is market risk of these transactions never closing. In some cases, all of the terms of the transaction are not announced, so the impact on the prices of debt instruments cannot be fully analyzed. This should cause the bonds and loans to trade at some discount (or premium) to the true pro forma value of the investment. This risk discount, or premium, can rise or fall prior to a closing as the probability of closure changes. This chapter reviews some common scenarios and some of the thought process that should go into analyzing these events.

Scenario: The Issuer Makes an Acquisition

In the first scenario, the restaurant chain Fast Food Co (FFC) announces a plan to buy a smaller competitor, Good Food Co (GFC). The following are some key facts about the acquisition. Sometimes not all of these items are included in the announcement.

Fast Food Co (FFC) Facts

- revenue: $1,500 million; EBITDA: $300 million
- debt: senior secured, bank debt, term loan $800 million L + 350, due in five years
- bonds: $400 million, 8% senior subordinated notes, due in seven years
- leverage: bank debt/EBITDA 2.7×; total debt/EBITDA 4.0×
- cash on hand: $100 million; net leverage: 3.7×
- preannouncement trading levels: bank debt at par, bonds at 8.5% YTW

Good Food Co (GFC) Facts

- revenue $500 million; EBITDA: $80 million
- debt: revolver $50 million; term loan: $50 million

Deal Facts

- FFC is paying $480 million, including assumption of GFC's debt, $380 million for the equity and $100 million of debt (often the revolver would not be counted if it were seasonal). The acquisition is being made in cash (as opposed to doing all or some of it with a stock swap).

- The acquisition price is 6.0× EBITDA multiple.
- FFC expects $60 million of cost savings in the first twelve months.
- Both boards have approved the transaction. Board members represent more than 50% of the voting rights of the stock of both companies.
- Quick pro forma analysis assuming 100% debt financing to pay for the equity:
  - pro forma debt of $1,680 million
  - pro forma EBITDA of $380 million
  - pro forma EBITDA with cost savings $440 million
  - leverage: pro forma debt/EBITDA 4.4×
  - with cost savings 3.8×

These are some of the analytical observations that will arise once this transaction is announced:

- If FFC uses debt to finance the entire transaction, the leverage will initially go up. But if and when cost savings are achieved, the pro forma leverage will actually be relatively unchanged, and the company will be bigger. The analyst must decide how much credit, on day one, should be given for the planned cost savings. A cynical analyst never gives the company 100% credit.
- The analyst should ask whether the cost savings look reasonable. In this case, it can be seen that GFC's operating margins are meaningfully lower than those of FFC, and there is a difference in scale, so it can be assumed that FFC should be able to get some meaningful operational gains.[19]
- There appears to be a low level of deal risk because a majority of shareholders and the boards have both approved the transaction. The major risk would likely be from a regulatory basis.

Here is a partial list of unknowns:

- Will GFC be assumed by the main operating entity of FFC where the FFC debt is currently outstanding, or will it be kept as a separate wholly owned subsidiary, and the GFC debt will be at that entity, having less impact on the FFC debt issues? If GFC will be a subsidiary, where will the new financing debt be issued?

---

19 Also note that if the cost savings are applied to the combined company, the margins are not out of line with FFC's historical margins, so this would appear reasonable.

- How is the transaction being paid for? To be conservative, it was assumed that the company was using all debt to fund the purchase. However, FFC could plan to sell some stock. Another factor is that FFC could plan to use some of its cash on hand. However, given its cash position and that it appears to have no revolver, it likely uses the cash for working capital.
- The analyst needs to look at the debt incurrence covenants and see if they would allow the transaction to be funded with all debt under the debt incurrence test. It would also be worth investigating the covenants' definitions of EBITDA to see if pro forma cost savings could be included in the calculation.
- What cash costs are expected to achieve the cost savings? Savings rarely happen for free. Are there system integration costs, severance payments, or costs related to breaking leases?

Other questions could include the expected timing of the closing; potential breakup fees if the transaction doesn't close; whether GFC management has noncompete clauses; whether GFC's capital spending needs are greater than, equal to, or less than those of FFC; and what GFC's operating trends have been.

There are also a few tangible items to consider about the transaction as well:

- Is making an acquisition such as this a departure from FFC's strategy? (If so, this increases risk to the credit.)
- Is this a good fit for FFC? For example, is there much geographic overlap? Do these two companies operate similar/complementary types of property?
- How did FFC management communicate the acquisition? Did they put out a short, tersely worded press release and nothing else? Or did they offer a more detailed press release with the rationale for the acquisition and other details? Did they hold a conference call to make themselves available to investors? If so, were they responsive or nonresponsive to questions?

These types of factor can all impact how FFC debt may trade shortly after the announcement and how it might trade longer-term.

It is unlikely that, in any given transaction, analysts will get all their questions answered and receive all the information they would like. Therefore, assumptions and decisions must be made based on imperfect information.

It would not be uncommon for FFC to decide to fully integrate GFC into its operations and to fully fund the transaction with new term bank debt and a new bond. The GFC bank debt would be retired, and the company would hope that the investors in the old bank line would roll into the new bank deal. The banks might be willing to increase the leverage at the senior secured level to 3×. This would allow $340 million of the acquisition funding to come from the bank line; the balance would need to be funded in the bond market. The new bank line would replace the existing FFC term loan and retire the GFC bank lines. There would likely also be an increase in the rate on the bank debt. Exhibit 21.1 shows how a sources-and-uses table might look for this transaction. It contains a line item for expenses related to the transaction.

Exhibit 21.1: Sample Sources-and-Uses Table for the GFC Acquisition in $000,000s

Sources		Uses	
New senior secured loan	1,140	Retire GFC bank lines	100
New senior notes	150	Retire old FFC bank lines	800
Total sources	1,290	Buy GFC equity	380
		Fees	10
		Total uses	1,290

The bank debt gets a takeout and a chance to roll into a new, higher-coupon, loan facility with a similar risk profile, so it is fairly positive for the bank debt.

If it is assumed that FFC management has a good track record with acquisitions, that this acquisition is in line with its overall strategy, that the bond covenants allow the transaction, and the company doesn't have to offer any consent payments to the bondholders, it might appear relatively neutral for the bondholders. However, it is not. Notice that the existing bondholders have senior subordinated notes and that the new notes are senior. The existing notes are getting hit with the brunt of the increase in leverage and are getting primed. Wherever the market decides to price the new notes, the existing notes will assuredly trade behind them. Although the transaction is not transformative enough and the increase in leverage is not large enough to cause a major sell-off in the existing senior subordinated notes of FFC, they will likely trade down. At the same time, management has sent a message that they are willing to prime existing note holders in future transactions if the covenants permit. Analysts should check how much more room for senior debt the covenants allow.

Scenario: The Issuer Gets Bought

The preceding case was analyzed from the perspective of the buyer of a company. The example in this section looks at the perspective of the company being bought. The sale of a company can have many twists. In most cases, bank debt gets refinanced, but this can sometimes eliminate an attractive holding from the bank market. The possible outcomes for the bonds are more varied.

The biggest factors are who the buyer is and how that buyer is structuring the acquisition. If a company is being sold to a stronger credit, this should be a positive for the existing bonds. If a company is being sold to a credit of equal quality or to a PE firm, it depends on whether the existing bonds need to be retired to complete the transaction. The buyers could leave the bonds outstanding and increase the leverage to pay for the transaction. The scenario described in this section looks at how the bonds of the company being acquired may act.

The other important factor is how the buyer is paying for the transaction. This is not always disclosed at the same time as the acquisition is announced. The acquirer could be planning to issue debt to pay for the acquisition, which would add leverage. The acquirer could be planning to use cash-on-hand, which would increase net leverage. The acquirer could be planning to issue equity to pay for the acquisition, which would be a big positive, and usually, deleveraging. The acquirer could use a stock-for-stock swap, which is similar to issuing equity but usually has less market risk. Finally, the acquirer could be using a combination of these funding paths.

When an announcement is made that a company is being acquired, the first thing an analyst should look at in the covenants is the change of control language in the bonds and loans. The analyst would want to see if the transaction would trigger this covenant and set a floor for what could happen to the bonds. However, because almost all change-of-control offers to repurchase the bonds occur at 101, this becomes a factor only if the bonds are trading at 101 or below. If the bonds are trading substantially over 101, the potential for some meaningful losses exists if the change-of-control tender price is the floor and actually ends up being used by investors.

In this case, we will assume that a German dialysis company, DeutscheDialysis (DD), is up for sale. After an auction, DD is being sold to an investment-grade company that is a health-care conglomerate, EuroMed (EM).

The first thing an analyst needs to discern is how EM will structure the acquisition. Some common ways this could be structured might include the following:

1. *DD as subsidiary*: Keeping DD as a separate wholly owned subsidiary means that DD will still be a separate credit. Although there is implied support from the stronger parent, the bonds of DD are likely to stay outstanding and trade at some yield higher than EM's bonds but lower than where they had been trading prior to the transaction. The analyst must try to analyze how much wider than EM's bonds the DD bonds should trade. This will be based on the reaffirmation of the underlying asset value due to the acquisition, the size of the new investment by EM, any synergistic cost savings that the combination may bring to DD, and the likelihood that EM will eventually refinance the existing bonds in an effort to get cheaper financing and perhaps better covenants.

2. *Retired/refinanced DD bonds*: EM may choose to either retire or refinance the existing DD bonds. Why might it do so?
   - First, EM might want to be able to lower the cost of financing costs, since it should have a lower borrowing cost than DD as it is investment-grade rated.
   - Second, EM might want to get rid of the covenants. Perhaps it wants to take more money out of DD than the restricted payments test allows.
   - Third, EM might not want separate reporting requirements that might be required in the covenants of the DD bonds.

3. *Refinanced bonds*: EM might look to refinance these old bonds or seek amendments from the investors. One analysis could be to see whether it is cost-effective to refinance the bonds, factoring in any call premiums or tender premiums that would need to be paid to retire the debt, and analyze whether some of the covenants are too onerous for EM to live with.

4. *Assumed bonds:* EM may also look to assume the bonds and make them part of the EM debt structure. This should cause the DD bonds to trade in line with the investment-grade EM debt and should be a big positive for bondholders.

What might be different if DD were sold to a PE firm in the auction?

One of the first questions should be how the PE firm will pay for the acquisition. Typically, the acquisition includes an equity component paid by the PE firm. This equity check does not add to the capital of DD. Instead, it goes directly to the shareholders, so it usually does not adjust any balance sheet or covenant terms. The second component of the acquisition funding is usually debt borrowings.

The PE firm often looks to see if it can keep the existing bonds in place so that it does not have to pay premiums to retire the debt. Any new borrowings to fund the acquisitions, if they were raised at the same corporate level or at a subsidiary of the existing DD bonds, would have to meet the debt incurrence tests of the old notes. If the money being raised were being used to effectively purchase company stock, it would need room under its restricted payments covenant tests and room in its basket to do this. One way around adding more leverage on the company and not having to work within the existing covenants is to form a new holding company that is not a party to the covenants of the subsidiaries.

Although the new holding company structure may not actually increase the leverage at the level where the old DD bonds reside, the new owners obviously still expect to be able to use the DD cash flows to service the new holding company bonds. Bondholders would want to analyze whether the DD credit now has to help service the new holding company bonds. Any buyers of the new holding company bonds would want to make sure that the holding company had access to enough cash flow that those bonds could be serviced. The buyers of the new notes would want to examine whether there is enough room under the restricted payments test to upstream this money to service the new bonds. This is obviously a concern for the existing DD bondholders, but it's an even bigger concern for the potential buyers of the new holding company bonds. DD bondholders will also want to check what senior and senior secured capacity there may be within the covenants. If there is capacity, it could allow debt to come in above the existing bonds and prime these notes.

An analyst has to look at the new structure and the levels of where the old DD bonds are trading and try to determine whether, in a given market environment, the new holding company financing could successfully be completed or whether the structure needs to be changed.

What if a company of relatively equal credit quality decides to buy DD? The same questions arise. How is the company paying for DD? If it is paying with stock, it is relatively neutral for the bondholders from a financial viewpoint, and the analyst must look at the strategic advantages of the combination. If the company is paying cash, it probably will have to leverage up. Then look at it on a combined basis, with assumptions about the new funding.

These two examples primarily dealt with the financial aspects of mergers and acquisitions. It is also important to consider the strategic aspects for the business of any merger or acquisition. An analyst will want to not only consider the merits of the acquisition that is being analyzed and how it fits with the company's strategy, but also if it indicates something about a shift in the industry or how the company is being managed.

Scenario: The Issuer Announces an IPO

When a company announces that it will raise financing through an equity offering, it is a significant event. Management is deciding that they are willing to dilute the ownership position of existing shareholders. In many cases the management are significant shareholders as well.

In this example, NewDisc is a computer memory company owned by a PE firm and it has announced it is going public. It has produced healthy growth for the past three years, ever since it was bought by the PE firm. It has lowered its leverage, as measured by a debt/adjusted EBITDA ratio from 6× at the time of the buyout to 4×. The company announces it will issue stock and go public in what is called an initial public offering (IPO).

How should a leveraged finance analyst react?

An IPO is usually a positive for a company's credit quality. This is due in part to the following factors:

- A meaningful amount of proceeds is often used for deleveraging. This may include some premium takeouts of the bonds.
- A public stock price helps solidify a valuation of the company.
- There is usually better information flow and therefore greater trading liquidity in the debt of a public company.

- If the company is acquisitive, a public stock often gives it another currency with which to buy assets other than by having to raise cash through debt issuance. Although shareholders may not always like the dilution from an acquisition paid for in stock, debt holders usually like it.

So, on the surface, everything looks good, and NewDisc's bonds should trade up. However, an analyst has to look at the details.

First, the IPO is probably being pursued so that the equity investors can get back some of their investment. It has to be examined how many shares the company is selling, in which case the proceeds go right back to the company (primary shares), versus how many shares are being sold by the PE firm, in which case the proceeds from the sale of stock go to the PE (secondary shares) and not to NewDisc.

The next item an analyst should look at is what the company plans to do with the proceeds it will receive. Sometimes, this information is in the initial document that is filed about the IPO. Other times, it takes a while for it to appear in the company filings. The leveraged finance analyst will want to look at how much deleveraging is expected to occur. The analyst should try to discern how and where that deleveraging is taking place, such as whether the company will look to retire bank debt or bonds, and which tranches.

An important factor for the bondholder, if NewDisc is planning to retire some of the bonds, is how it intends to do so. If the bonds are in their callable period, the company can simply call them. If they are not, the company could use the equity clawback (assuming this feature is in the bonds). Some bonds have a feature that allows 10% of the notes to be called annually with a 103 call. The company could utilize this feature, which is usually only in senior secured notes. Although this isn't typical in an IPO, the company could pursue a tender for bonds too. These features are discussed in the chapter on call prices.

Another valuable piece of information from the IPO may be how the company is being valued for the IPO and what multiple of EBITDA this equates to. This information is usually unavailable until near the actual marketing of the IPO, which may not occur for several months after the initial announcement.

The analyst must include in any model what the credit will look like pro forma for the IPO. What will the leverage be? What will the net FCF be? Does the document state if the company intends to pay dividends? Paying a dividend means that less money will likely go to debt service or deleveraging. An analyst also wants to see whether the IPO materially changes the flexibility under the covenants, particularly the restricted payments test and the debt incurrence test. Usually it does, as carve-outs in these covenants often include adjustments for proceeds raised from selling equity.

An analyst should look at the IPO filing for new information or insights into how the company operates. Frequently, these documents offer more information about the business than the typical annual and quarterly filings that the company provides, which can be helpful for analyzing other companies in the same industry as well.

It is also important to examine the overall stock market and get a sense of the type of valuation the company is using to see if the IPO is doable or if it will eventually be pulled. If the company's valuation expectations are unrealistic, the prices may end up disappointing market participants. If the IPO is pulled, the bonds and loans will likely trade down from their post-IPO announcement levels. This can happen even if the IPO is completed at what is viewed as a disappointingly low price.

If the IPO gets pulled, consideration should be given to whether the ownership of the company will try to do something else to get value for shareholders. The ownership and management were trying to accomplish something from the IPO, and just because that avenue was closed does not mean they will not look for another. Here are some possibilities:

- *Sell*: Will they look to sell the company? If so, what entities would be the natural buyers? Would a likely buyer be an investment-grade company that might improve the debt securities trading level, or could it be another PE firm that might look to releverage the company and hurt the trading levels of the debt securities?
- *Leveraged recap*: Could the ownership decide to do what is known as a leveraged recap (recapitalization)? This typically entails issuing new debt (usually bonds) and using this money to pay a dividend to the owners. This releverages the company and usually hurts the trading levels of the existing bonds and loans (assuming the loans do not require a refinancing).

- *Inaction*: The company's ownership may choose to do nothing and simply bide its time.

Scenario: The Issuer Is Facing a Maturity

In another scenario, a company is facing a debt maturity. Concern usually develops six to twelve months before the maturity. If the markets are healthy and the company has been doing well, this refinancing of a maturity is usually not a problem. New bonds or loans can be issued in the markets to retire the maturing debt. The coupons might be different on the new debt, but the refinancing is doable.

If the company is doing much worse than it had been in the past, or the markets are very bad, a pending maturity could be a major problem for the company. A new debt financing in the traditional markets could be unfeasible. The company will need to look for other funding or asset sales, find new equity investors, or try to negotiate a restructuring with banks and bondholders. It may be forced into bankruptcy.

If the company can access new financing, it may be required to pay a higher cost. An analyst needs to factor in market conditions and try to see what the company's options may be and what the credit might look like after such a higher-cost financing is completed. This is especially true if multiple tranches of debt are outstanding, meaning that one tranche is being refinanced while others remain outstanding. While addressing a near-term maturity for a company that is struggling or in difficult market conditions is a positive for a company, a higher cost of borrowing typically weakens a credit. When calculating the various options for a refinancing, the analysis must also see if the various scenarios that are being modeled can be done within the framework of the remaining debt's covenants.

In the scenario shown in Exhibit 21.2, the company is fairly leveraged and needs to refinance its bank debt. The new rate on the bank debt that the market demands is almost twice the prior rate. This does not change the leverage, but it clearly cuts the FCF dramatically and lowers the interest coverage ratio. The cost of capital can have a major impact on the company's credit quality, so that scenario analysis becomes very valuable in these cases These refinancings can have as large an impact on credit performance as an IPO or acquisition.

Exhibit 21.2: Simple Refinancing Scenario (in $000,000s Except for Ratios)

Debt Structure	Interest Rate	Operating Data	Pro Forma with Bank Rate of 6%
Senior secured bank loan	3%	1,000	1,000
Senior notes	8%	400	400
Senior subordinated notes	10%	250	250
Total debt		1,650	1,650
Total Interest Expense		87	117
FCF			
EBITDA		180	180
Interest expense		87	117
Capital expenditures		30	30
Cash taxes		0	0
Uses of working capital		3	3
Net FCF		60	30
Ratios			
EBITDA/interest expense		2.1×	1.5×
Debt/EBITDA		9.2×	9.2×
Net FCF/total debt		4%	2%

A Pragmatic Point on the Blended Price to Retire Debt

When a transaction occurs and it appears likely that the bonds in the structure will be retired, the analyst must assume that the company will choose the cheapest method to do this. Sometimes this may mean waiting for an upcoming call date to approach. If the bonds are not callable, it might involve a tender. Do not automatically assume the bonds should trade at the tender price. The company may look to utilize an annual 10% call if it is in the structure, and depending on the type of transaction, it may be able to use the equity clawback feature as well. The analyst should incorporate these factors and come up with a blended price to value the bonds. In the blended price (or weighted average), the analyst looks at the price at which bonds would be retired by each method and then multiplies this price by the percentage of the debt that can be retired from that method. These percentage weighted figures are then added up to equal the blended price. As shown in Exhibit 21.3, the blended price is meaningfully lower, in many cases, than the tender price would likely be.

Exhibit 21.3: Blended Price

Method of Buyback	% of Issue Retired	Price of Buyback
Tender price	55%	118.0
Equity clawback	35%	110.0
Annual debt call permitted	10%	103.0
Blended price		113.7

Closing Comment

There is no perfect way to prepare for all news events in the credit markets. As news items on a credit break, it is important to be able to analyze the most impactful aspects of the news. It is also important to recognize which information is lacking and try to develop the probability of likely outcomes with the combination of known and unknown information. Decisions will often have to be made with imperfect knowledge and those decisions can be refined as new information becomes available.

Chapter 22

Market Information: Relative Value Analysis

What's in this chapter:

- varied goals of relative value analysis
- financial ratios and relative value
- operational ratios and relative value

THERE ARE NUMEROUS steps in making an investment decision in leveraged finance. One decision is whether an analyst and investment team believe a credit will be able to meet its debt obligations. A second decision is whether the credit is likely to improve, decline, or stay the same over time. A third major decision is how to allocate capital to one investment versus another. Any investment vehicle has a limited amount of capital and decisions must be made as to where to allocate it. To choose between investments requires relative value analysis. This usually involves comparing the risks and the rewards of various investment options. Rarely a simple formula, it involves numerous factors: quantitative, qualitative, objective, and subjective.

Varied Goals of Relative Value Analysis

Although most investors in stocks or leveraged debt want to maximize their returns, there are different philosophies on how to achieve this. Just as there are macro or momentum investors, and growth or value investing in equities, there are also different investor types in the leveraged debt market. Examples include managers who emphasize bank debt or BB-rated bonds; those who are targeting a cash-plus return; or those who are mandated to mimic an index, or limit volatility. Others are more focused on total return and are less concerned with volatility. Still others need to match assets and liabilities. Some may favor credits with strong debt service and others favor those with particularly strong asset coverage. Many investment mandates set out formal rules about investment goals and formal restrictions on types of investment, even within the leveraged finance market (e.g., loan only, or only debt with at least a B- rating). Given the many types of investor in the market, with different strategies and goals, a bond or loan that may be attractive to one investor may be of no interest to another.

For all these different types of investor, it is usually helpful for analysts to lay out relative value comparisons using various financial and operational metrics and use them as a starting point for an investment decision. After that, other factors can be overlaid, such as subjective views on competitive position or the likelihood of upcoming positive or negative events, as well as structural and covenant analysis.

Financial Ratios and Relative Value

Relative value analysis can often compare potential investments, either in the same industry or across a broader spectrum. Relative value analysis is not just comparing the credit strength of different companies, but also comparing what return is likely upon investing in each company relative to the financial characteristics. The spread or yield is the most common proxy for the return.

This return from the yield comes over time. The investment must be held for a period of time to get the interest income. Part of the decision an investment team has to make is what they expect to happen to that investment during the holding period. If it is anticipated that it will improve and the prices will go up and the yield decline, the price appreciation can be factored into the return analysis when compared to other potential investments. Even if the analysis determines that there is a higher probability that the price will decline over the holding period, in some situations the interest income will be enough to make the investment attractive.

The analysis also has to examine risk as well as reward and determine which issuer, or issue, is a riskier investment, and if the investor is getting paid enough to take that additional risk. This risk-reward ratio has to be considered against the investment goals of a portfolio. For example, for a portfolio, is it worth giving up yield to be in an issue that may have less potential price volatility (e.g., duration) or greater operational stability? In relative value analysis, it is not just which credit is better, but a balancing of credit quality, structural issues, and return potential that together drive the decision on value.

Relative value analysis can start with taking market prices, yields, and spreads for various potential investments factors and comparing these value measures to assess credit quality in various ratios. This is often done within an industry group but could also be done across a credit rating category or other grouping. As a simplified example of how this might be done, Exhibit 22.1 looks at one industry: a hypothetical mobile telephone industry. It is assumed that this sector has five issuers.

The exhibit shows that, for relative value, it is important to not just compare companies, but actual securities. If a company has a senior note outstanding and a senior subordinated note outstanding, both need to be shown. Exhibit 22.1 shows two leverage ratios. One is the leverage through the specific debt issue (bond debt/EBITDA), and the other is the all-in leverage for the company (total debt/EBITDA). This is because when considering the asset protection, analysts can look at the level of leverage where the individual security is (e.g., the ranking, such as senior secured leverage or senior subordinated leverage), but they cannot ignore the amount of leverage that has to be serviced on the whole company to avoid a restructuring or distressed credit situation. Do the same analysis when comparing the bank debt to the bonds when they have different seniority rankings and look at the leverage through the loans but also the all-in debt leverage for the company.

Exhibit 22.1: Simplified Relative Value Sheet

		STW (bps)	Bond Debt/ EBITDA	Total Debt/ EBITDA	FCF/ Debt	TEV*/ EBITDA	STW/ (Bond Leverage)
Mobile Co.	8% senior notes	400	3.0×	5.0×	3.0%	6.0×	133
	10% senior-sub. notes	600	5.0×	5.0×	3.0%	6.0×	120
Cell Co.	7.5% senior notes	350	4.0×	5.0×	2.5%	6.2×	88
	9.5% senior-sub. notes	600	5.0×	5.5×	2.5%	6.3×	120
Phone Inc.	9% senior notes	300	3.5×	3.5×	5.0%	7.0×	86
Wireless Co.	8% senior notes	500	4.5×	4.5×	3.5%	5.8×	111
DataFone	9% senior notes	475	3.5×	7.0×	0.1%	7.1×	136
	9.5% senior-sub. notes	800	7.0×	7.0×	0.1%	7.1×	114

* Total enterprise value

Within Exhibit 22.1, the first column has the company name and a description of the debt instrument. These are followed by the STW, a few key financial metrics, and then a relative value measure. This takes the STW and divides it by the leverage at the bond level to show how many bps of spread an investor would get paid for each turn of leverage.

The last column is an example of the type of tool that can be created using measures of financial strength and potential returns. It is not a perfect answer but a step in the process. This column takes the STW of each bond and divides it by the leverage at the bond level. For example, the DataFone 9% senior notes look the cheapest (most attractive) by this measure, offering the widest spread per point of leverage. The DataFone 9.5% senior subordinated notes also offer the highest total spread. This may be because its all-in leverage (total debt/EBITDA) is higher than any of the other issues at 7×, and its FCF as a percentage of its debt at 0.1% is meaningfully lower than any of the other comparables. A minimal asset value cushion is implied by the equity market value at DataFone, primarily due to the high leverage. These factors add considerable risk to the DataFone senior notes.

It is also interesting to look at the intracapital relationships. For DataFone and Mobile Co., the senior subordinated notes offer less spread per point of leverage than the senior notes within each company's capital structure. However, for Cell Co., the relationship is inverted, and the senior notes offer less spread per point of leverage. Some of the reasons why this could occur include the fact that the Cell Co. senior notes might have particularly strong covenants or an unusual call feature that could make them more valuable. There is also the possibility that the Cell Co. senior notes are simply overvalued and trading too rich on a relative value basis. Finally, note that in Cell Co., the total debt/EBITDA ratio is higher than the bond level debt/EBITDA of the senior subordinated notes, indicating that there is additional debt outstanding, junior to this issue— perhaps a holding company convertible note or other instrument.

A more detailed relative value page might include the following:

- *Additional loan specifics*: More specific bond or bank loan data may be included, such as the issue size, a credit agency rating, and maybe the next call date and price.
- *Duration and maturity*: This analysis does not include any measure of duration or maturity, which can be a major factor for relative value comparison. Lower duration may indicate lower volatility, but also may indicate less potential upside if the underlying credit improves.
- *Additional market data*: This sheet is only showing one piece of market data: STW. A more detailed sheet could show the price, the YTW, current yield, and even historical price volatility. If the bonds are of varying maturities, the spread is often the more meaningful measure to compare than the yield.
- *Additional risk indications*: Bank debt issues and trading levels of credit default swaps (CDSs) could also be included as indications of how the market is viewing risk.
- *Additional financial ratios*: There are also a multitude of other financial ratios that could be helpful to compare to valuation measures. Most notably absent is the EBITDA/interest expense or EBITDA-capital expenditures/ EBITDA, but liquidity and operational ratios could also be valuable.

It is very important to include structural issues other than just priority ranking in the relative value decision process:

- *Non-priority ranking structural issues*: This can include factors such as any differences in call structures, trading liquidity, or whether it is a fixed coupon bond or a floating-rate loan.
- *Covenant differences*: Covenant differences can also impact relative value between investments.

Choosing the right credit can have just as critical an impact on investment performance as choosing the right part of the capital structure in which to invest.

There are other relative value tools that can be utilized:

- *Average index spreads/yields comparison*: One common tool is to compare a potential investment to the average spreads and yields of an index, or a subset of an index, perhaps by credit rating or duration bucket. This can help put the relative value of a potential investment in context with the market, a larger opportunity set than just industry-comparable credits.
- *Market valuations comparison*: The market valuations of the investment can also be compared to the average valuations of the portfolio in which it is being considered. This can show if an investment can increase or decrease the average yield or spread of the portfolio and also what it might do to the duration, maturity, and average coupon of the larger portfolio.

All these items help to put the relative value of the sector in the context of the universe of investment options.

Using Averages of Common Trading Relationships

It can be helpful to build out databases of average relative value relationships. This might include what the average difference in spread is between secured and unsecured debt or senior and subordinated debt or holding company and operating company debt. The same can be done for differences in a credit's debt of different maturities or duration. Not all companies have multiple tranches of debt, so the sample size of this data may be smaller than other data sets. An analyst has to be careful that other structural or credit nuances are not skewing the data.

Operational Ratios and Relative Value

Relative value analysis should not just include credit metrics, but also an understanding of operational performance of each company. The operational comparison shown in Exhibit 22.2 includes some information that could be meaningful for any industry, such as growth rates in revenue and EBITDA and EBITDA margins, but also industry-specific KPIs, such as growth in subscribers and the average revenue per unit (ARPU).

Exhibit 22.2: Simple Operational Comparison

	Latest Quarter Change in Revenue	Latest Quarter Change in EBITDA	Latest Quarter Change in Subscribers	EBITDA Margin	Monthly ARPU in $
Mobile Co.	12.0%	9.0%	7.0%	22.0%	56.00
Cell Co.	10.0%	10.5%	5.0%	20.5%	45.00
Phone Inc.	10.0%	9.5%	5.0%	22.0%	42.00
Wireless Co.	9.0%	8.5%	6.0%	23.0%	50.00
DataFone	7.5%	8.0%	4.3%	20.0%	39.00

There are a significant number of options to include in operational data. One area in particular can be longer-term operational trends and volatility of cash flow generation. It is often good to include on this sheet a dominant industry-leading comparable, even if it is not in the opportunity set of investments.

Anyone performing relative value analysis has to balance several items. This includes thoroughness versus timeliness. If the analysis takes too long, the market information on the potential investments becomes stale, and opportunities to buy and sell may have disappeared. With so many ratios and combinations and permutations of how financial and operational metrics can be mixed with valuation data, it is easy to prepare too many different ways to examine relative value data and make it difficult to reach conclusions. Therefore, an analyst has to learn to prioritize which data is most helpful and be careful not to get too anchored in examining just a few ratios, not recognizing that an industry or the markets are changing, and the relative value analysis needs to be refocused. With the last point in mind, it is good practice to periodically look at some nonstandard or different relative value ratios.

Exhibits 22.1 and 22.2 are based on fairly objective figures. There are also more subjective factors in an analysis. These can be helpful to lay out in tabular form as well. Management quality and strategy are important to consider, as is the potential for positive and negative events. For example, if a company is sold, would the likely acquirers strengthen or weaken the credit? Would the sale require a take-out of the bonds? Forward-looking estimates can be helpful to compare as well as backward-looking data.

Relative Value Scenarios for Debt

Using scenarios can be very valuable in determining relative value. If you are comparing investments opportunities in two different bonds and you have three scenarios for each one (e.g., base case, upside, and downside), you should estimate where each scenario would cause the bond to trade a year from now and what the total return would be to determine the best relative value. A probability should be applied to each outcome. These probabilities could be linked to your financial model scenarios and a probability-weighted total return can be calculated. Relatively minor structural issues, such as call prices, can make a meaningful difference in returns. Exhibit 22.3 presents a simple relative value return analysis. Note that the probabilities and the expected trading levels one year out both make a difference in the total return.

Exhibit 22.3: Relative Value Total Return Scenarios

	Current	Scenarios 1 Year Forward			
	Current	Base Case	Upside	Downside	Weighted
5.25% Five-Year Bond					
Probability		50%	30%	20%	
Price	101.00	101.80	104.60	99.11	
YTW	5.02%	4.75%	4.00%	5.50%	
Total Return		5.98%	8.60%	3.30%	6.23%
4.75% Four-Year Bond					
Probability		60%	20%	20%	
Price	100.00	100.60	102.80	98.60	
YTW	4.75%	4.50%	3.75%	5.25%	
Total Return		5.20%	7.50%	3.36%	5.29%

Closing Comment

Relative value is a vital part of the investment process in the credit markets. The data set, or universe, that gets chosen for relative analysis can bias the outcome, so it becomes very important to review the peer group that is being used and to be sure to use some broader measures of value, such as an index or a portfolio average. Establishing relative value between credits, and between individual investments within each credit, involves comparing objective and subjective factors. It is extremely useful not just to lay out the objective data, but also to include some of the key subjective issues that can make a difference. Whenever possible, the analysis should not just be based on historical data, but also utilize forward-looking estimates of where the credit and the debt might be a year ahead or longer.

Chapter 23

Investing Issues: Portfolio Management Interaction

What's in this chapter:

- portfolio types and styles
- trading liquidity and portfolios
- the basics of portfolio performance analysis

CREDIT ANALYSIS IS not done in isolation. It may be done in the context of an investment banking project or in an examination of risks on a broker-dealer trading desk. In many cases, credit analysis will be done as part of a decision on what goes into an investment portfolio. Understanding how the analysis, the relative value recommendations, and the decision-making process interact with the concept of portfolio management can improve credit analysis and make it more goal directed. It can also give insight into how the leveraged finance market works.

Portfolio Types and Styles

Any investment in the leveraged finance market is often a relatively small allocation of a very diversified pool of investment money that may have equities, government bonds, municipal bonds, and investment-grade debt investments alongside public and private leveraged finance investments. The ultimate capital for these portfolios may come from insurance companies, pension plans and other retirement savings programs, endowments, and individuals' savings. The individuals who manage these programs will decide how much they want to allocate to the leveraged debt markets and will also usually decide how they want the money managed.

The assets allocated to leveraged finance debt may be managed in-house by these organizations or they may allocate the money to unaffiliated money managers. The money could go into commingled funds where the assets are combined with the money of other investors. These could be in the form of mutual funds, ETFs, or a separate, limited-partnership-type of private structure. If the amount they are allocating to a money manager is large enough, it may be in a separately managed account.

The money could be in a dedicated asset class—for example, the allocation could be just for US dollar leveraged loans—or it could be a broad, corporate, fixed-income mandate where the manager decides how much is allocated to each asset class and in which currencies. More flexible mandates, such as hedge funds, may make periodic opportunistic investments in the leveraged debt markets, even though they do not have an allocation dedicated to the asset class. Understanding the type of money that is being invested in the marketplace can help an analyst understand some of the supply and demand dynamics in the market and also understand there will be different investing strategies, making up a diversified universe of buyers and sellers with different goals.

Usually, money allocated to the leveraged finance asset classes is put under the management of specialists who construct these investments to achieve client goals, or the stated goals of the commingled pool of money. Portfolio strategies can vary significantly. Some passive strategies just want to get exposure to one part of the leveraged debt markets and closely mimic some mandated index. Other strategies may be focused on maximizing interest income and minimizing realized losses. There can also be strategies that are willing to take more risk and are focused on total returns, and those that may want to minimize volatility. Analysts will do better at their job if they understand the strategic style of the portfolio or portfolios that they are working with. One investment idea may work well for one style, but not another.

One of the common concepts in portfolio construction is diversification. Portfolios can create diversification in many ways, including by geographic region, currency, rating category or levels of risk, duration, and industry. Portfolio managers in credit markets will often manage their diversity and exposures across a number of these categories simultaneously. Within the leveraged finance markets, industry diversity is a factor of considerable focus. Diversification helps guard against a sudden turn of fortune in one industry or another. This will lead portfolio managers to often think of an investment as a percentage of the portfolio, and they will analyze what the weighting should be in the portfolio. This will typically lead portfolio managers and credit analysts to set up ranking systems of recommendations.

As portfolio managers think about the construction of the overall portfolio, they may also look to add or sell certain investments with certain characteristics and may look for relative value recommendations with selected characteristics, such as short duration or higher-yielding recommendations. Analysts should compare their recommendations to comparable credits and indexes, and also to the statistics of the portfolio for which they are recommending the investment.

Trading Liquidity and Portfolios

The leveraged finance markets have historically not been as liquid from a trading perspective as some other capital markets, such as government bond and equity markets. In some cases, bonds and loans may not have any trading liquidity for a month or more. This can create several issues for credit analysis and portfolio management. One issue is the quality of pricing data: an investment may look very attractive, based on a given price, but a purchase of that investment cannot actually be executed at that price in the markets. Another issue can be a mismatch of liquidity. A portfolio, such as a mutual fund, may see daily flows of cash in and out of it. However, many of the investments in the fund's opportunity set may not have daily trading liquidity. For this reason, the liquidity of the investment will impact its attractiveness as a portfolio component. Some investors actually prefer illiquid issues because their prices tend to change less often, giving the impression of less volatility and therefore less implied risk. This can prove to be cold comfort if the credit starts to deteriorate and the portfolio looks for a bid and is suddenly down sharply from where it had previously been priced.

There are many factors that can impact the liquidity of an investment. Issue and issuer size are often a factor in trading liquidity. Information flow is also a factor—a company with public financials will often have better liquidity than one with private financials. If a credit has many comparables, it will often have greater liquidity as well, because relative value can more easily be determined than the debt of an issuer in a unique one-off business line. Credit quality can also impact liquidity. Stronger credits and issues with less volatility (e.g., short duration) tend to have better trading liquidity than those of weaker quality.

Analyst recommendations that are very hard to execute can prove to be less valuable to portfolio managers even if they look good on paper. Portfolio managers also are cognizant of overtrading a portfolio. So, quick buy-and-sell recommendations for minute changes can prove less valuable in a less liquid market. There is a cost for each transaction as there is a spread between the bid (price to sell) and offer (price to buy) prices in the market. An experienced analyst usually factors this into any recommendations.

Basics of Portfolio Performance Analysis

Understanding the basic concepts of how a portfolio's success is judged can give analysts insight into what types of investment might work best for a portfolio. There are numerous tools for analyzing performance, including detailed formulas for attribution of returns. Some basics are outlined below. Allocators of capital will look at various analysis tools to judge not just returns, but how much risk is being taken to achieve those returns, and they will compare these results to peer groups and benchmarks.

One measure of risk and return is to analyze a portfolio's return divided by the return of a broad market index in periods of positive and negative returns, referred to as upside capture and downside capture. As an example, if the benchmark index is down –5%, and the portfolio is down only –4%, it has achieved 80% downside capture. Comparing upside and downside capture will give those who allocated money to the portfolio a sense of how much risk they are getting for their returns.

In risk-versus-reward analysis, volatility of returns is often viewed as risk. One of the common and long-standing tools that uses this concept to measure risk versus reward is the Sharpe ratio.[20] There are three components to the ratio:

1. the return on the portfolio = RP
2. the return on a risk-free asset, usually a government bond = RF
3. the standard deviation of the portfolios returns over this risk-free rate, which is a measure of the volatility of the portfolio's returns = VP

Volatility is viewed as a measure of risk. The Sharpe ratio formula below is effectively showing the excess return per unit of risk:

$$\text{Sharpe Ratio} = (RP\text{-}FR)/\ VP$$

This type of ratio is commonly used to compare the risk-reward of different asset classes and different portfolios competing in the same asset class. As with many portfolio analysis tools, it was originally developed for the equity market. The ratio has many shortcomings, especially when applied to the leveraged debt markets. Some of the shortcomings are: 1) the formula treats both upside and downside volatility equally as a risk; 2) with interest income such an important part of the return in leveraged finance, volatility can get distorted when comparing asset classes; 3) the risk from volatility may be short lived; and 4) in a market where some securities only trade once a month, volatility measures may be misleading. Despite the shortcomings, measuring returns relative to the risk by means of volatility is common in portfolio analysis. Many similar analysis tools can be studied—such as the Sortino ratio, which uses the volatility of downside returns as a measure of risk.

---

20 This ratio is named after its developer, William F. Sharpe.

Indexes and Benchmarks

Portfolios are typically measured against other portfolios with similar strategies but also are measured against a benchmark, which could be a government rate plus a certain percent, such as a three-year German government bond rate plus 4% return. More commonly, the benchmark is an index designed by a third party. These indexes are used to compare and analyze a portfolio's performance. Many portfolio managers will focus primarily on issues that are in the assigned benchmark as their opportunity set. Other managers will actively look to add out-of-benchmark investments. If working with a portfolio measured by a benchmark, it is always helpful to understand what is included and excluded in the benchmark and have access to data about the benchmark. Benchmarks change over time and will even change their inclusion rules. Portfolio performance ratios, such as the Sharpe or Sortino ratio, are typically run in comparison to a portfolio's benchmark.

Portfolios often have specific rules about what they can and cannot buy. These could be based on ratings or a socially responsible restriction. It is also typical to have concentration restrictions, such as permitting no more than 5% of the debt of one issuer. Many regulated entities, such as insurance companies, may place restrictions on taking gains and losses for various reasons. These are all factors that analysts should be aware of as they analyze and interact with portfolio managers.

Closing Comment

The more analysts, traders, salespeople, and capital markets personnel understand how portfolios are designed and managed, the more insight they can have into relative value and how the markets act. This knowledge can help analysts tailor and manage their recommendations to meet the portfolio's needs and make the investment process more efficient. Even if analysts are not working directly with a portfolio, an understanding of how portfolios operate can be very helpful in developing a better view of the workings of the leveraged debt markets. When working with a portfolio management team, how each individual investment impacts the holistic characteristics of the portfolio must be considered.

Chapter 24

Investing Issues: Collateralized Loan Obligations

What's in this chapter:

- CLO basics
- CLO structures
- how CLOs impact an analyst's job

CLOS ARE AN important part of the leveraged finance market. These structures make up a huge buying base in the leveraged loan markets. They have very specific structural aspects that impact how the investment portfolio is managed, and there are numerous rules that govern them. It is important for analysts to understand these structured credit products and the differences in their management versus that of other types of investment in a portfolio.

CLO Basics

CLOs are specially formed investment entities created for the purpose of owning a basket of corporate leveraged loans. To fund these purchases, a CLO issues debt in the form of bonds to investors. That debt makes up the liabilities of the CLO and the loans that it owns are the assets. The loans are the collateral that backs the value of the debt tranches that the CLO issues. Buyers of CLO debt are attracted to the asset class for a number of reasons: 1) CLOs allow the acquisition of a higher-rated debt instrument while getting exposure to the leveraged loan asset class; 2) they can typically achieve a higher yield than debt instruments with similar credit ratings; and 3) they provide a means of getting diversified loan exposure by purchasing just one security.

The debt of a CLO is issued in several tranches, with the senior-most tranche rated AAA. The senior-most tranche gets such a high rating because of all of the excess value in the assets of the CLO. For example, if the assets and the liabilities of the CLO are worth $100 million and the AAA bond tranche of the CLO is 60% of the CLO's liabilities, it is over-collateralized by $40 million, so there are excess assets to support the debt by 40%. The AA rated debt issued by the CLO will still have excess collateral, but it will be somewhat less, thus the lower rating. The junior-most tranche is effectively the equity and receives any residual value after all of the other tranches are properly paid. This is not that different from many other asset-backed/securitized financing vehicles, such as mortgage-backed securities (MBSs).

CLOs fall into a category of investments called structured credit and also asset-backed securities (ABSs). CLOs are widely used, but there are other structures that may have different rules and structures but still invest in assets of the leveraged finance market. These could include collateralized debt obligations (CDOs) and collateralized bond obligations (CBOs). The basics of these products are similar to CLOs. The structured credit market is constantly evolving, adding nuance to existing structures and creating creating new structures.

As CLOs are both buyers and sellers of debt, credit analysis can be used to analyze whether a loan is a good fit for the CLO to buy. Analysts can also be used to analyze the debt that is issued by a CLO by analyzing the quality of the underlying investments (the assets) within that CLO relative to those of other CLO tranches.

Analysts examining investments in CLO tranches will use programs to stress-test the underlying collateral and the recoveries on the collateral in various default scenarios. The level of default loss rates can be critical to the success of a CLO and how CLO tranches trade. It will not just be the default rate but also the type of recovery expected on any defaulted loans. CLOs have structures that can help protect the most senior tranches of their debt should defaults or other risks spike in the market.

An extended period of very low default rates may lower default assumptions, and this could lead to a significant amount of CLO issuance coming to market and thus increasing demand for certain types of bank loan. But the reverse can also be true. Demand from investment-grade buyers for tranches of CLOs can be a factor in CLO formation, as the AAA tranches are usually the largest part of the capital raised by CLOs. Another key factor in CLO issuance is the spread at which they can be created. This refers to the difference in spread between the basket of leveraged loans and the spread that has to be paid out to the tranches of debt that are issued by the CLO. The CLO uses the income from the loans it owns to pay the interest on the debt it issued. The spread, or arbitrage, between what it gets paid and what it pays out is vital to the success of the CLO, particularly for the equity tranches. The size of this arbitrage will lead to increases or decreases in CLO formation. For example, if the spread demanded on AAA-rated CLO tranches widens too much relative to the rate on leveraged loans, it can be very difficult to attract equity investors and it can be difficult for new structures to work.

CLO Structures

CLO structures are typically actively managed. While there are static CLOs that do not actively manage the pool of collateral, the managed CLO structure is more common. In the managed structure, there is a collateral pool that changes as a manager decides to buy and sell assets during the life of the structure.

The debt tranches issued by the CLO will generally range from AAA to an unrated equity tranche. The coupons of each layer of debt issued by the CLO will go up as the ratings go down. In most structures the debt issued by the CLO will have floating-rate structures just as the majority of the underlying collateral does. This will help assure that cash flows from the assets used to pay the interest on the liabilities do not get mismatched if the interest rate environment changes.

The liabilities of a CLO could resemble the capital structure, as shown in Exhibit 24.1.

Exhibit 24.1: Hypothetical CLO Debt Structure

CLO Tranche Rating	% of Total CLO Capital
AAA	65%
AA	10%
A	7%
BBB	6%
BB	4%
Equity	9%

CLOs are not like mutual funds or a corporation; they have a defined life. The CLO structure typically starts when the CLO manager works with a provider that funds a warehouse to begin buying the assets that will be placed in the CLO. The provider of the funding expects to get paid back by the CLO when it sells its own tranches of debt and buys the collateral. The advantage of building up the assets in the warehouse is to better match the cash flows when the CLO's liabilities are placed, rather than scrambling in the market to try to buy all the collateral in one day. The CLO's life winds down as it goes into repayment and deleveraging mode, usually several years after the warehouse and the placement of the debt tranches issued by the CLO.

The typical phases of a CLO are as follows:

1. *Warehouse*: Assets are acquired over several months.
2. *Ramp-up*: The CLO closes on issuing all of its liabilities, receives cash, and purchases the warehoused assets and any additional shortfall.
3. *Reinvestment*: The manager can actively trade the asset holdings.
4. *Noncall*: Just as with other debt instruments, the CLO equity holders may want to call or refinance the liabilities because they believe they can get more attractive terms and there is a period when this is not permitted.
5. *Repayment*: The manager uses proceeds from repayment of the assets to pay down the CLO tranches in order of seniority, with excess proceeds going to the equity. Typically, after a period of time, the manager cannot reinvest or trade the assets and the CLO is static and in wind-down.

There are numerous aspects of the CLO structure that are covenanted in the debt instruments and they include the structure of the portfolio. These covenants are likely to require borrower diversification by industry and issuer. As a rule, they also define the types of asset they can buy, which are usually dominated by senior secured floating-rate loans. A significant number of tests are run on the collateral and the cash flows, and if those tests are violated, managers are required to try to cure them. All of these diversification rules and maintenance tests are also monitored by the credit rating agencies that rate the debt issued by the CLO. If the debt issued by the CLOs is downgraded, it will likely hurt the price of that debt and may hurt the manager's ability to create new CLOs. Some of the more important tests include the following:

1. *Weighted average rating factor (WARF)*: This is used to compare the average credit rating of a portfolio weighted for the size of each holding. Higher-rated investments get a lower score, but as the score increases for lower-rated holdings, the scale is not linear. A lower WARF implies a higher credit quality, as measured by the major rating agencies. Of course, the ratings agencies control both the ratings of the collateral and the CLO's liabilities.

2. *Overcollateralization test (O/C)*: The value of the collateral (the assets) needs to exceed the value of the debt that is issued by the CLO. The test measures the underlying collateral value at par versus each tranche of debt, including all classes senior to the tranche being examined. The test usually requires defaulted collateral be excluded and can also exclude from the collateral (haircut) loans with very low ratings (e.g., CCC ratings). This can make managers very sensitive to rating downgrades at the bottom of the credit rating spectrum.

3. *Interest coverage test (I/C)*: This examines whether the collateral pool generates enough interest income to service the payments on the debt tranches. It is similar to the collateralization test in that it is run for each tranche and usually has minimum acceptable levels stipulated in the documents.

When tests are not met, the manager has to try to cure them. Typically, the remedy is to cut off payments to the lowest tranches (e.g., equity, then single Bs, and so on) and use the excess cash flow that is generated to retire the most senior tranches of the CLO's debt structure until the violation is cured. This self-preservation mechanism can be a valuable tool during spikes in default or rating downgrade cycles.

How CLO Structures Impact an Analyst's Job

The structure of the CLO can make the goal of credit analysis different from that of other types of portfolios. The critical factors for the investments in a CLO portfolio are that the cash flows for the investment are not impaired and that the credit will not default or be rated so low it will not count as collateral. The CLO manager is less concerned about how a loan in the portfolio will trade and be marked to market. This is because the CLO is focused on the cash flow and meeting its maintenance tests. The maintenance tests are based on credit ratings and par value. Therefore, CLO portfolio managers are more likely than non-CLO managers to hold onto a position, even if they expect significant short-term downward price pressure, as long as it will not become insolvent or drop to the lowest credit ratings.

Because of this structure, where the collateral (e.g., loans) that the CLO owns gets treated as a par instrument for test purposes, CLO managers will sometimes try to build par during the reinvestment period of the CLO. In looking to build par, a manager may sell a loan that is trading at par or even slightly above and then look to acquire lower-priced assets that still get valued at par for collateralization tests and other risk measurements. Another reason CLO managers may be reluctant to sell assets if they have traded down to a discount is that the sale of assets at discounts can hurt the results of these tests.

Closing Comment

In undertaking credit analysis in the leveraged debt markets, it is important to understand the concepts behind CLO structures. If credit work is being done to support CLO portfolios or to help analyze investments in CLO-issued debt, it is important to understand how it is being used and realize that the market price vagaries are not as important to CLOs as they are to many other types of portfolio. Even if the credit work that is being undertaken is not directly involved with CLO structures, they are a large and important part of the market and can impact relative value, and supply and demand in the loan market, and affect companies' access to capital.

Chapter 25

Investing Issues: New Issuance

What's in this chapter:

- new-issue process
- pro forma adjustments
- supply and demand dynamics in the new-issue market

DEBT INSTRUMENTS HAVE maturities and lenders must be repaid. Companies that issue debt usually do not completely repay their debt obligations out of FCF, but do so by using cash raised by issuing new debt: a refinancing. This creates a natural flow of debt retirements and new issuance of debt in the credit markets. In the leveraged debt markets, companies are often in transition, which may trigger the need for additional issuance of debt to fund acquisitions or expansion. There are also first-time issuers that will raise debt in these markets. Perhaps a new leveraged buyout is being financed or a company that has always used smaller regional banks is expanding and has chosen the leveraged debt market as a source to raise money for additional funding. New issuance is a major part of the investment process in the leveraged debt credit markets, and understanding what drives the new-issue market can help an analyst understand a credit's refinancing options.

New-Issue Process

A large number of people involved in the leveraged debt markets spend a significant amount of time on structuring, pricing, placing, analyzing, and investing in and trading new issues. This includes company management, the sell-side investment bankers, lawyers, accountants, capital markets teams, and analysts, who may spend several weeks or even months working with the company and doing due diligence to assess the validity of its business and prospects. This team also is responsible for the preparation of documents for potential investors to review, which entails providing accurate information and meeting the detailed rules and limitations required by law. This team also usually prepares an informational presentation for management to give to investors, typically called a road show. More seasoned issuers may simply do a brief conference call for investors. Often when a new issue for a bond or loan is coming to market, analysts can get more detailed information about the industry and the company, as well as more access to management than they would from a quarterly conference call and press release.

The rules for bond offering documents tend to be more limiting than those for bank offering documents. In the documents for a bond offering, all of the information has to be public. In the loan market, investors can choose to go private on the bank side and can get projections, or they can stay public. Going private can limit the ability to trade the debt instruments.

The bank offering book (bond prospectus) has some items that investors should always read through:

- *Reason for transaction*: The use of the proceeds and the details of the reason for the transaction should be studied. Even if the investors like the credit, they may not want to fund a transaction they disapprove of.
- *Risks*: There is also a risks section that should be read. An analyst can decide which risks to focus on, which are of minimal concern, and which are priced into the transaction.
- *Structure and terms*: There is usually a structure and terms section, which should always be read. It should include covenants and transactions with affiliates, because they may give insight into the interaction among the company, management, and ownership.

- *Reason for new financings (sources and uses)*: While done for numerous reasons, new financings are often related to a merger or acquisition. A common item to look at in these transactions is the price that was paid for the asset. This price can be compared to other transactions and/or public equity multiples.
- *Proxy statement*: If the acquisition was of a public company, the company being bought typically has to file a proxy statement for shareholders to assess if the price was fair and how they want to vote on the transaction. This document can offer insights as well. Most notably, it often gives the price levels of other bids for the company, which can give an analyst comfort (or discomfort) that the winning bid was reasonable and that other bidders were willing to pay for the asset.

When a new issue is announced, the expected size of the offering is disclosed along with the use of proceeds and the tenor (tenor measures the time to maturity – at issuance, they are the same). Expected credit ratings are also released. Fairly soon after that, the offering documents are available, and the company will make itself available to investors. This is usually followed by the investment bank representing the company giving indicated price guidance. The price guidance is usually given in a yield or a spread. If the debt is going to be offered at an OID, that will be stated too.

At the same time, analysts and portfolio managers will be analyzing the new issue with the potential buyers and looking at the relative value to determine the price at which the investment would look attractive. They may also discuss any terms of the transaction they would like changed. Then begins a give and take between the potential buyers of the offering and the underwriters that are getting paid to place the debt for the company.

There are a significant number of rules governing the information that can be shared and rules designed to prevent collusion. There are times when the offering is just a single tranche of debt, such as an offering of a ten-year maturity bond. There are other times when multiple tranches of both bonds and loans may be offered and sometimes in multiple currencies. The underwriting investment bank will try to juggle demand across the various pieces of debt to get the best structure at the best price for the issuer.

Pro Forma Adjustments

Frequently new-issue transactions include pro forma results, especially if an acquisition is involved. These results may include a section on adjustments to EBITDA. It is important to look at the adjustments and the footnotes that accompany them. Although the debt offering documents may be allowed to show a number of adjustments to reach adjusted EBITDA, investors might be uncomfortable with including all these factors in their analysis. They might not want to give credit for certain items that are added back in the new-issue-adjusted EBITDA. These might include management fees paid to PE firms, planned cost savings, and cash costs related to restructuring. Analysts may choose different items to add back, or not, depending on what they are focused on. Acceptable add-backs may be different depending on whether the primary focus is on cash and liquidity or solely on operational trends.

Exhibit 25.1 shows how adjustments and add-backs might appear in a new-issue offering document. In this case there is a significant swing in EBITDA from negative reported EBITDA to a positive adjusted EBITDA.

Exhibit 25.1: Adjusted EBITDA in $000,000s

EBITDA	(90.6)
Management compensation one-time payments	(42.3)
Stock compensation expenses	2.1
Deferred revenue adjustments	159.6
Sponsor management fees	20.0
Implemented cost savings	50.0
Restructuring/reorganization professional fees	9.5
Internal restructuring cost	26.0
Total pro forma adjusted EBITDA	**134.6**

Supply and Demand Dynamics in the New-Issue Market

When the new-issue market is highly active, the number of new issues that are being offered to the investment community in loans and bonds can be daunting. When the market is strong and there is great new-issue demand, a new issue may get priced at a yield very comparable to its peer group or other bonds it has outstanding. Usually, new issues come with a slight discount to market levels of existing comparable debt to entice buyers and be able to place that large an amount of debt in the marketplace at one time. In addition to adjustments to the coupon and the offering price, the new issue will sometimes have other differentiated features to attract buyers. When the market is not as strong, there is a bigger new-issue discount in the pricing of the financing relative to existing bonds, because the price at which a company can sell $500 million of a bond may logically be lower than the price at which the company could sell $1 million of a bond.

In a period when the market has been strong for some time, more issuers may be drawn to try to raise money when funding is cheap. This can start to pressure the market as supply and demand rebalance. It is not just pricing of the yield that can change, depending on the supply and demand balance, but covenants and other terms may also shift, depending on market conditions. In markets that favor the buyers, when new issues may be more difficult to get placed, the buyers can often demand more stringent and debt-holder-friendly covenants in new financings. When demand outstrips supply, issuers can often get looser covenants.

In the loan market, new financing is often offered at an original issue discount, meaning that it is priced below 100% of face value. This discount pricing structure can offer a bit more protection to the loan investors, as they do not have much call protection. It can also be helpful for CLO structures, which are frequently big buyers of loans in the institutional loan market, as their structure can benefit from buying loans at a discount.

Closing Comment

Credits in the leveraged finance market are often in a state of perpetual change, and the marketplace is constantly changing as well. New issuance is a large part of life in the leveraged finance market and, over time, can change the characteristics of the market and the peer groups available for relative value analysis. The process of studying and analyzing new issues can give an analyst more insight into a company's operation and more access to information.

Chapter 26

Investing Issues: Preparing a Credit Snapshot

What's in this chapter:

- prioritization
- the basics of a credit snapshot
- trends
- example of a snapshot

ECAUSE MARKET PRICES can move rapidly, and news events can happen very fast, requests for a quick credit analysis after such an event are quite common. It is therefore best to have an analysis template in place for this credit snapshot. Each situation will require some unique aspects in the structure of the snapshot, depending on the events driving the request, but there should also be some commonality in what should be prepared. A consistent format for these snapshots can make it easier for the investment team to review the information

Prioritization

To prepare a credit snapshot, there should be a clear understanding of why it is being requested and what the goal of the project is. This should help to narrow the amount of work needed to be done. Common reasons for such a quick summary may include a sudden offering of new debt or breaking news on a company.

When the reason for the project is understood, it is easier to triage the situation. (*Triage* is a medical term referring to the process of determining which patients should be prioritized for treatment.) In these situations, the prioritization of work can be critical to arriving at a rapid response. The priorities of the snapshot will vary. Is there interest in looking at a credit because the bonds just dropped twenty points in the market? Or is a quick snapshot on a company being requested because it just announced it is making a large acquisition? Whatever the reasons, two basic credit questions will need to be addressed: 1) can the credit service its debt obligations and 2) is there enough asset value to pay off the debt if necessary? Typically the analysis will try to determine if the news improves or weakens a company's ability to address these two issues.

The Basics of a Credit Snapshot

Basic company information should be the first step and should include what the company does. Then comes the reason for the snapshot. This section should include whatever is notable about the company's competitive position within its industry. It should also include whether the company is private or public, and whether there is any meaningful ownership of the company. If the company has a major fatal flaw or outstanding strength, it can be helpful to include that information in this section. It is best to use bullet points and worry less about sentence structure.

One of the quickest ways to assess a company's ability to pay its debt and its leverage is to look at the statement of cash flow from operations and examine the cash flow from operations for the trailing twelve months. This accounting figure of free cash generation can rapidly be compared to the interest expense, capital expenditures, and the short-term liabilities where debt due in less than a year is listed. Then, the total debt outstanding, net of cash on hand, should be provided. These six financial statement items can give a very quick assessment of the credit and guide an analyst to the next step. If the company's finances appear challenged, a review of available borrowings might be required. If this is not the case, there should be time to look at the capitalization and business trend analysis.

The next more detailed data to gather is usually from the balance sheet: debt structure and maturity schedule. When doing this, liquidity sources should be laid out as well, which usually means cash and any available borrowing facilities. Just because a revolving loan agreement or other short-term borrowing facility shows it has availability does not always mean that it can be drawn. Limits on drawing revolving facilities can be in the covenants of the other debt instruments but are more likely to be in the actual revolver agreement. Sometimes short-term borrowings have a borrowing base, meaning the company can borrow up to a certain amount of receivables or inventory.

The absolute minimum that is needed on the debt capitalization is total debt, cash, and any upcoming maturities. If time permits, and the company's equity is publicly traded, it is helpful to include the market value of the company and the value to EBITDA ratio.

The next step should be to begin building the adjusted EBITDA calculation for the latest twelve-month period (often abbreviated as LTM). Then run some of the most basic ratios using EBITDA. These would include debt-to-EBITDA and EBITDA – capital expenditures/interest expense.

Pricing data on the debt securities must also be included in any snapshot, including, at a minimum, price, YTW, and STW.

This data would be the bare minimum that an analyst would want to pull from financial statements and should indicate whether the company is facing a liquidity crisis or is in sound financial condition.

Templates

Analysts often have templates for preparing credit snapshots. Because analysts tend to focus on a few industry sectors rather than being generalists, they can build and maintain a list of debt and equity comparables that can be quickly used in a snapshot. The template may also have some meaningful KPIs common to an industry.

Trends

The next step in building a snapshot will often be to get a sense of operational trends. The quickest way is to look at revenue trends from the income statement over the last three to five years. Then do the same with either cash flow from operations or EBITDA over the same time frame and the respective operational margins. If time permits, changes in debt and capital spending can be plotted in as well.

If the stock of the company is public, it can be helpful to see if there have been large stock movements in the past year—and if so, check for news stories around that time. A review of the last earnings release can also be insightful.

From that point onward, there are many directions in which the analysis can go, including the following:

- ownership and any changes to the ownership
- divisional performance and trends in operating expenses
- upcoming potential events, such as step-downs in maintenance covenants
- how competitors are performing

Pro Forma

When the request for a credit snapshot is driven by the announcement of an event, it is good to prepare a very quick pro forma analysis of the event: an estimate of what the company will look like after the event. Many times, not all of the information about the event will be available. For example, the company may have announced a major acquisition but not explained how it will be funded, or the company may be selling an asset but does not yet know the price. In all of these cases, the analyst will have to make assumptions based on the information available. If time permits, running a few different scenarios can prove to be helpful in the pro forma analysis as well.

Example of a Snapshot

Exhibit 26.1 shows what a simple snapshot of a credit can look like. The first section is a descriptive section. It includes, in the Recent News section, the reason for the snapshot request: an acquisition was announced, and the bond prices dropped. The second box is the very easy take on the credit quality of the company, using the cash flow from operations from the financial statements. The third box includes more detailed information. This section includes both cash flow and balance sheet information, as well as some trend analysis. The capitalization section includes market pricing information on the debt securities.

Since the company in this example has publicly traded stock, there is a section to analyze the market value of the company. Notice this analysis does not use the most recent stock price but a three-month average to give a longer-term view of how the market views value. The total enterprise value takes the equity market value and adds the total debt.

The final section of this snapshot offers a very simple view of how the announced acquisition may impact the credit. In this example, it is assumed that the acquisition will be financed with debt at an average cost of 6% for the company. Software Co. was leveraged 4.3× prior to the acquisition. Since the company is paying \$3.5 billion for the acquisition and the acquired company has \$400 million of EBITDA, the company is paying 8.75× EBITDA (8.75=3500/400) for NewSoftware Co. The assumption is that this will be paid with debt, which results in this transaction increasing the leverage of the company to 5×. So, it is understandable that the bonds traded down. However, with an equity valuation of about 8.4×, there still appears reasonable asset protection for the debt and adequate liquidity as seen in the FCF/debt ratio. To examine the acquisition further, an analyst would have to look at the growth potential and potential cost savings of the acquisition.

Exhibit 26.1: Simple Credit Snapshot after an Acquisition Announcement

Company Name: SOFTWARE CO.

Data in $000,000s (unless noted)

Business description:	Designs employee management software; uses subscription model
Business positives:	Large installed customer base, recurring revenue, minimal capital spend
Fatal flaw (biggest risk):	Several new competitors, few new wins; concern over obsolescence
Ownership:	Public; founder and CEO owns 15%, pays dividends, has retired debt
Recent News:	Bonds dropped ~ 5 points since company announced acquisition

Latest 12 Months Data:	12/31/XX		
CFFO*	1,500	Debt/CFFO + interest	3.3×
Total debt	6,200	CFFO + interest/interest	5.0×
Interest expense	372	CFFO − capital expenditures	1,400
Capital expenditures	100	Debt due in one year − cash on hand	100
Debt due in one year	300	CFFO/net det due in one year	5.0×
Cash on hand	200		

Latest 12 Months Data Ended:			Current		
	12/31/XX	12/31/XX	12/31/XX	Equity Market Value:	
Revenue	6,375	6,325	6,250	Shares (in millions)	500
Growth		−0.8%	−1.2%	Avg. stock price over 3 months	$12.00
EBITDA	1,530	1,486	1,453	Equity market value	6,000
Growth		−2.9%	−2.2%	Total enterprise value	12,200
Margin	24.0%	23.5%	23.3%	TEV/EBITDA	8.4×
Interest expenses	438	397	372	Debt Amortization:	
				Year 1	300
Capital expenditures	110	105	100	Year 2	200
Simple FCF	983	985	981	Year 3	200
				Year 4	3,700
Total debt	7,000	6,400	6,200	Year 5	2,500
EBITDA-cap. exps/interest exps.	3.2×	3.5×	3.6×		
Debt/EBITDA	4.6×	4.3×	4.3×		
Simple FCF/ debt	14.%	15.4%	16%		

Debt capitalization	Recent Pricing				
		Price	YTW	STW	OAD
L + 450 senior secured term loan	2,200	98.00	5.50%	450	
6% senior notes	2,500	97.00	6.25%	540	4.6
7% senior-subordinate notes	1,500	94.00	9.00%	700	3.8

Pro Forma for Acquisition of NewSoftware Co.

Price for NewSoftware Co.	3,500		
EBITDA of NewSoftware Co.	400		
	Software Co.	New Software Acquisition	Pro Forma Software Co.
EBITDA	1,453	400	1,853
Debt	6,200	3,050	9,250
Est. interest expense	372	183	555
		(~6%)	
Debt/EBITDA	4.3×		5.0×
EBITDA/interest	3.9×		3.3×

* Cash Flow From Operations

Closing Comment

Creating snapshots can be very helpful not only when news is breaking, but also when learning how to analyze a new industry, or as a way to monitor credits that might be actively followed but are on a watch list. Technology can be used to pull selected data from various sources to rapidly populate this type of snapshot.

Chapter 27

Investing Issues: The Investment Decision Process

What's in this chapter:

- varied approaches to investment decisions
- a sample investment decision process
- investment traps

ANALYSIS FOR ITS own sake is not terribly useful; analysis should be undertaken with a goal in mind. That goal usually involves a decision. In leveraged finance, the goal of analysis is usually to make a decision about a debt instrument. Often the decision is to buy, sell, or hold—but it can also be whether to go ahead with a debt or equity financing or how to structure and price a new issue. Since numerous decisions likely have to be made to improve efficiency, it is best to have a process in place for decision making. It can be an informal one that involves a personal mental checklist or a more formalized one involving a team. Participants in the leveraged debt markets have a variety of resources and different strategies, so the investment process will vary from company to company.

Varied Approaches to Investment Decisions

The level of risk tolerance that an investor is willing to take makes a major difference in the prioritization of topics within a decision process. Risk typically takes a few forms: interim price volatility risk over a given investment horizon; principal and interest income loss due to a default; or an earlier debt retirement, which can cause a mismatch of assets and liabilities.

These risks have to be weighed relative to potential returns. This risk-reward relationship is what analysts are constantly trying to divine when making buy, sell, and hold recommendations. Each risk-reward decision also has to be weighed against other investment options. When a decision is made to invest in one debt instrument versus another, there is always the risk that great potential returns are being passed up. This is often called opportunity cost. Investment decisions need to be made in the context of other opportunities. Ranking/rating systems can help make these decisions easier to manage and will typically include a combination of objective and subjective inputs, which should have unique designs to fit different investment styles.

A variety of investment styles can be successful and styles that have consistently succeeded over time have similarities. Successful strategies have a defined investment style and a process for decision making. Usually, over long periods of time, they are consistent and tend not to react to each market whim or sudden change in market mentality. This does not mean that these strategies are not adaptive. They are forward-looking enough to be periodically reconsidered and to evolve with major changes in the global or market environments, but they do this through a process and with analysis to back up the decisions.

Portfolios will often include investments with diverse performance characteristics. The goal is often to blend these varied factors to create an overall investment solution at the portfolio level. For example, many portfolios will want a balance of low volatility, lower risk investments and those that are likely to have higher market risk and, ideally, higher return. Depending on the investment team's market outlook, they may shift the portfolio's weighting between these types of investment. A decision process may need to not just measure the risk-reward of an investment versus an opportunity set but also, often, include a view as to which portfolio basket an investment might fit in.

A Sample Investment Decision Process

There are many effective styles of organizing an investment process. The following sections describe some core ideas.

Big-Picture Items

- *Macroeconomics*: A sense of the macroeconomic environment is necessary in reaching a decision. This does not mean trying to be a global economist as well as a credit analyst,[21] but putting the investment in the context of key themes of an expanding or contracting economy, or an environment of rising or declining interest rates.
- *Trends*: The macro environment should also include thematic and strategic trends in corporate finance. For example, is one industry suddenly in vogue for PE firms to buy in leveraged buyouts? Is the IPO market particularly strong as a source of deleveraging? Is a new securitized financing vehicle being widely used? These types of theme often come in waves and are important to consider.
- *Supply, demand, and momentum*: Big-picture technical questions can be helpful too. These generally involve supply and demand: how much cash is uninvested and in the hands of portfolio managers versus how many new financings will be coming to market. Demand for leveraged loans and bonds can also be influenced by the relative attractiveness of these assets versus other investments such as asset-backed securities or equities. This addresses the bigger question of market momentum too.
- *Risk*: In the investment markets, does it feel like a risk-on market where investors are taking on more risky investments; or perhaps it is risk-off, or risk neutral?

The Company and Industry

- What business lines is the company involved in?
- What are the stated goals or aspirations of the company, if any?
- Is the business in a notable part of its life cycle?

---

21 Good macro strategists and economists tend to seek out details on business and investment trends from industry analysts and not just look at macro factors.

- What industry dynamics are most influencing the company, such as price cutting or acquisition activity at the company or in the industry?
- Is the company overdependent on one customer or a government program?
- What is the competitive landscape for the company?
- What operating trends are occurring at the company, based on financial statements and any specific industry KPIs?
- Review any trends in stock market activity in the company or industry and M&A.
- Are there any specific comments on ownership/management style or perhaps operational successes or failures?

Credit Fundamentals

- Review key financial statements metrics and historical changes.
- Review cash flow and liquidity.
- Go over balance sheet details and compare to asset value.
- Review the company's structural issues and be clear which entities support the company's debt.
- Review sources of liquidity other than cash flow from operations.
- Review and analyze asset values and the implied equity value cushion for the debt.
- Summarize the overall credit quality, with a focus on liquidity and asset protection, and find out what the risk of default is.

Event Analysis

- Are any liquidity events likely to occur in the near future (over at least three years)?
- Is a refinancing likely?
- Are there maintenance covenants that might be violated?
- What is the probability that the company will be sold or acquire something?
- Is there a possibility of an IPO, dividend, or stock buyback?
- Is there a new plant or product launch, or a patent expiry, on the horizon?

For all these possibilities, a probability should be assigned. If the probability is high, it is worth conducting a scenario analysis as to what pro forma credit metrics would look like with and without the event over a given time horizon.

Structure and Security Analysis

- What are the key structural issues with the investment's ranking? This should not just involve the investment that is being discussed, but all the pieces of the debt capitalization and how they might impact or restrict the investment.
- Review key covenants and highlight any that stand out.
- Also review technical issues: How large is the security? Is it actively traded? Will it be a private placement or a publicly registered issue?
- Is it likely that the maturity, covenants, or structure of other debt in the capital structure will impact the bond or loan that is being examined?
- Review any unusual structural issues, such as off-market call prices or unique aspects in the coupon.

Relative Value and Return

- Review financial metrics and operating metrics relative to comparable credits. This should include the business trajectory and stability.
- Review specific debt characteristics of the peer group such as ranking, pricing, yields, spreads, and duration. This sheet should include similar data for any relevant indices or benchmarks.
- Review the likely return on investment. This should include an upside-downside return horizon analysis that can estimate where the investment might be valued at the end of the time horizon. A one-year time horizon is a good starting place.

It is not uncommon to establish a list that includes many of these items listed above and develop a credit scoring system where each item is given a score based on a scale (e.g., 0–10). The score could weigh some items more than others, or it could be even-weighted. The key is to try to make the scoring system consistent throughout the industry and across all industries. The score can be compared to the relative value metrics on the potential investment. Any scoring should be done before entering into the decision process. A simple ranking and summary list might include the following:

1. Credit: financial liquidity score
2. Credit: asset value protection score
3. Credit: operational trend score

4. Credit: event score (5 is neutral; below 5 is a negative event)
5. Debt instrument: trading liquidity
6. Debt instrument: structure
7. Debt instrument: relative value
8. Investment category relative to sector: ___more defensive _____neutral ____higher risk

The Decision

- Do the potential returns look attractive relative to the risks?
- Does the security fit with the general strategy of the investment portfolio? Where do its characteristics differ from the portfolio's averages?
- If this investment is bought, should something else be sold to balance exposures?
- Are there other ways to invest in this company that are more attractive— that is, are there other debt issues, equities, options, or converts that should be considered instead?
- Has this process triggered other investment ideas worth reviewing?
- Is the recommendation a buy, sell, or hold, and how heavily weighted should the investment be within a portfolio?

Every credit that is being invested in should be reviewed quarterly, or whenever earnings or news items are released. It is also important to design certain triggers that cause an immediate credit review. Some examples of triggers are a meaningful movement in the underlying equity or comparable equities (maybe 15% or more); a meaningful move in the debt prices of this credit or a peer; or some key target KPI or financial metric is missed. Additionally, if an event was listed as part of the investment thesis and it passes, such as an asset sale by year end, this should trigger a review of the investment as well.

Often analysts and portfolio managers may want to categorize the investments. In the ranking list, above the final item, categorize the type of investment by a risk tier. This could be a category tag. Category tags can include basic data such as debt ranking, or more specifically, something that has a high level of event risk, or exposure to currency volatility. All of these can be used in a database and can be queried if needed.

Personal Process

Even if a firm does not have a clearly defined structure for the decision process, analysts should have their own checklist for walking through key items and reaching a conclusion about a credit investment. Analysts may want to have their own decision-process format—one when time is short and a longer process when they have more time. Even if the credit work is being done for a purpose other than making an investment decision, using a checklist to reach the appropriate conclusions can allow for repeatable success.

Some Investment Traps

While trying to reach an investment decision based on analysis, it can be easy to fall into certain traps during the decision process. Any process that is put in place to help the decision process should be designed to avoid some of the common mistakes.

The decision process can become too controlled by market prices. If the prices are high, it is a good credit and if low, it is a bad credit. While the market should not be ignored, it does not mean it is always right. Some common traps caused by market pricing include the following:

- *Yield*: A common trap is to think that yield can make up for poor credit quality. Notice in the investment decision process that the discussions about credit quality and price, yield, and relative value are separate. A common trap is being lured into an investment in a credit that cannot fundamentally survive, but the low price and high yield make it attractive. Maybe someone suggested that the investment could be exited before it became too bad, but that is likely when others are selling too.
- *Low price*: On the opposite side of the equation, a low price on a company in disfavor should not color the fundamental credit decision (although it should be a warning sign to do more cautious analysis). Just because the market has decided a credit is in disfavor does not always mean it is right.
- *Complacency*: A high-priced investment that has had a history of stable market prices can also create complacency. Just because an issuer has been

a market leader for a long time does not mean that things cannot change. If an investment has a tendency to have a relatively high price and stable market performance, it can lure investors into complacency over a credit and keep them from properly assessing the risks.

- *Assets bias*: Some traps make investors miss opportunities, such as being overly biased toward one type of company, perhaps technology, or manufacturing. As an example, some investors may have a bias to have hard (physical) assets in a company to make it a compelling investment. Ultimately, the value of that hard asset is based on the cash flow it can produce for the company that owns it. The value of hard assets can be overweighted in making the investment decision and lead to misleading conclusions. For example, suppose the market has an overabundance of digital printing machines. Would it be better for a bank loan to be secured by these hard assets or by a valuable patent that can produce significant cash flow for a consumer products company? When looking at asset value, a prudent investor should consider which is more sellable and valuable relative to the amount of debt on a company.

- *Overdependence on ratios and metrics*: Depending too much on financial ratios and metrics in choosing an investment is another common trap. This is especially true in the age of data extraction and computerized spreadsheets. It is too easy to spit out a model that highlights bonds and loans with attractive relative value based on financial metrics and yields. This type of data query does not analyze structural issues of the individual security, potential positive and negative event risk, or the strategies that management wants to undertake with the company assets. Using relative value data queries can be a valuable way to search for opportunities, but this data shouldn't be the sole basis of a decision. Data extraction can also make analysts complacent in their model building and not add forward-looking thought into modeling, but simply rely on extrapolation.

There are many investment and decision biases that practitioners in the investment world should be aware of. There is a fascinating field of behavioral economics that, among other things, explores biases in investing. It is valuable to step back from the analysis and consider what personal or institutional biases are driving investment decisions. Below is just a sampling of some types of biases that can impact investment decision-making:

- *Anchoring bias*: An initial piece of information biases other decisions so that all other information received after the initial information is underweighted or ignored relative to the anchor.
- *Confirmation bias*: The decision-making process is diverted and exploited to reaffirm some previous decision that has been made or to prove some predetermined opinion.
- *Selection bias*: The decision-making process is biased because of the data that is used to derive that decision. In many cases this is caused by subjectivity in the selection of a peer group or a process that skews the data that is actually shown to the decision makers.
- *Availability bias*: What people have experienced before or what they can most easily comprehend drives their decisions.
- *Recency bias*: A decision-making process overweights the most recent piece of information received and underweights or ignores historical data.

Closing Comment

Be cautious about the lemming effect. This happens when it appears that all market participants have the same investment thesis or want to invest in the same type of company. In the flurry to invest in the next available hot item, analytical mistakes are often made, and investment decision rules are pushed aside. This is where a disciplined strategy for decision making can often pay off in the long run. The words of General George S. Patton Jr. highlight the risk of just following the current trend rather than following a disciplined process: "If everyone is thinking alike, someone isn't thinking."

Chapter 28

Data Science and Credit Analysis

What's in this chapter:

- queries and databases
- regression
- probability and decision trees
- issues for data science and credit markets

DATA SCIENCE COMBINES statistical and scientific analysis with computer science. The use of statistical data and other quantitative tools for investing dates back at least to the 1950s. At that time, scholarly work in the area, often referred to as modern portfolio theory, was developed. The revolution in computing power has increased and expanded the use of these techniques in the investment world. Quantitative and statistical techniques in investment analysis encompass a vast area, and only a few brief concepts are discussed in this chapter. Data science can be descriptive or predictive. Descriptive techniques tend to analyze what happened in the past, such as portfolio performance attribution. Descriptive types of data can often be used to develop probabilities that can be applied to scenario analysis. Predictive techniques are used to try to make a statement about what might happen in the future. Regression analysis is a very common technique in predictive analytics.

Queries and Databases

Computers can help to rapidly populate cells in spreadsheets by transmitting data straight from financial documents into an analyst's models and then highlighting where there are significant changes. Data science techniques can also use algorithms to do advanced word searches in company documents and highlight key words or changes in language from one quarter to the next. Data science tools can also be incredibly valuable in doing searches and rankings for relative value analysis. Many of these tasks involve queries and databases.

Credit analysis builds a plethora of data. The value of all this data can be enhanced if it is prepared in a usable format and stored in the right systems in such a way that it can be easily accessed. Not only should the analytical algorithms be easy to use, but it is important that the investment teams that are reacting to rapidly moving markets have easy access to them too.

A good database and query technology can allow an analyst, portfolio manager, or investment banker to input criteria for a data search and generate a list of options. For example, an investment banking analyst may want to generate a list of companies in an industry. The analyst may want them ranked by revenue growth and then by weakest EBITDA margins. The goal might be to find companies that would be attractive acquisitions for a more efficient operator. An analyst working for a portfolio manager may want to search for companies that have seen the biggest improvement in leverage ratios over the last three years. Good query systems should be able to generate lists that meet a number of prioritized selection criteria and simultaneously supply rankings for certain criteria as well. They can be valuable tools for relative value screens and analysis. Analysts and portfolio managers may also want to set certain automated queries. For example, these may be regularly generated reports that highlight changes in equity market values or if a key credit ratio has changed by more than a certain amount.

Corporate credit markets have numerous characteristics for both the companies that issue the debt and the actual debt instruments. All of these items need to be captured to make a database and query system valuable. Analysts need to be aware of how critical it is to design data fields correctly and enter the right data when building data science systems. Analysts have to try to be forward-thinking about what types of field might be of interest now and in the future when they collaborate with the data science team.

The quality of the data and the design of databases is important for all aspects of data science. If designed correctly, they can allow query systems to be linked with performance analytics and scenario analysis.

Regression

Regression is a basic statistics technique that can be used to examine the strength of the relationship between two variables (e.g., leverage and YTW). Regression can also be used as a predictive tool. Simple regression shows how one data point (the dependent variable) will likely react in relation to change in another data point (the independent variable). This technique is based on how the two datasets have acted in the past. Ordinary least squares is the technique used to run regression analysis.

The simple form of linear regression produces a linear equation that can be used to create a line on a graph, sometimes called a fitted line. The equation and the line can, theoretically, be used to predict the dependent variable that would occur for each value of the independent variable. As an example, the line could produce a theoretical prediction of how much the yield on a bond would move if its leverage ratio moved from 3.5× to 2.5×. More advanced regression models can use multiple variables.

Combining regression techniques with computing power can be a very valuable tool to analyze data and generate some predictive models. Systems can run regressions on any number of combinations of variables to look for the most meaningful relationships and even which relationships are the strongest in different market and economic conditions.

Correlation is an output generated from regression. It is a measure of the strength of the relationship between the variables in the regression. If the relationship is particularly weak, there are techniques that can be used to improve the relationship between the variables, such as using exponents or logarithms to adjust the datasets into a stronger prediction.

Exhibit 28.1 shows a graph for a hypothetical dataset of bonds where the leverage ratio and the YTW were regressed against each other. In this example, the YTW is the dependent variable and the leverage ratio is the independent variable. The outcome that the regression predicts is represented by the squares along the fitted line. The diamonds show the actual results from the data, so the diamond on the upper far right represents a bond with approximately 5.5× leverage and a yield of 6.75%. Theoretically, a leverage ratio could be picked, and a line drawn until it hits the predicted line and then a perpendicular line to the Y axis, and it would predict where a bond should trade from the Y axis. This technique can be used as relative value tool as well. If the diamond is below the predictive line, it implies that the yield on the bond is too low relative to its leverage and the price of the bonds should move down so that the yield is more in line with the predicted yield. The difference between the actual datapoint and the predicted data point is called a residual. Most regression programs will print out the actual residual values. In this case, the residuals could be used to predict how rich or cheap a bond was based on its leverage.

The closer the dots cluster around the predicted line, the stronger the quality of the relationship between the two variables and the greater the implication that the independent variable is a strong predictor of the dependent variable. Exhibit 28.1 shows strong evidence of dependence on the independent variable.

Exhibit 28.1: A Sample of a Regression Output

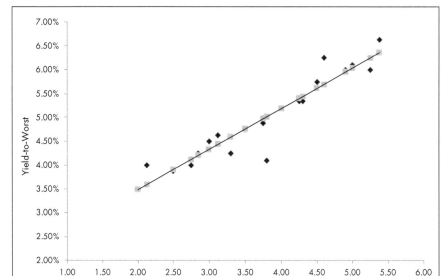

Probability and Decision Trees

Scenario analysis can be a large part of decision making, especially when analyzing the potential outcomes of an event, such as merger and acquisition activity, or when doing total return analysis. Scenario analysis is used by investors, investment bankers, and corporate financial officers. Once an analyst starts to lay out various scenarios and outcomes, the next logical step is to apply probabilities to each case, and perhaps, probability-weight the outcome. Probability is used all the time in decision making, though often it is done informally and intuitively. Probability is also the basis of many data science techniques.

One easy way to explore probabilities and scenarios is to lay out the possible outcomes in a decision tree. Decision trees are a form of flow chart, and each step in the decision process is a node. There are different types of nodes, including those that involve making a decision—these are often the root node or starting point from which branches extend to other nodes. Many of the other nodes will have uncertain outcomes and are often called chance nodes. When there are no more options and a conclusion for one decision branch, or path, is reached, there is an end node.

If the situation being examined is similar to past situations, data and outcomes from these other case studies could be downloaded, and an analyst could develop some probability guidance based on past experiences. For example, if two PE firms are making competing bids to buy a company with publicly traded stock and bonds outstanding, an analyst may want to analyze the probability that the company has been bought, how the PE firm will likely finance the company (e.g., 20% equity, 60% subordinated debt, 20% secured debt), and what will happen to the existing bonds. A decision tree with probabilities for each outcome could be helpful in analysis. It could get fairly complex rather quickly, with numerous outcomes, including third-party bidders and all the varied financing options. If a database had details of the PE bids that had been made in the past, including the success of the bids, how they were financed, and how the previously existing bonds traded, an analyst could start to build probabilities for each outcome. Artificial intelligence algorithms have been designed to process probabilities for these types of problem, using decision trees. These algorithms can calculate the probabilities for these outcomes based on past data

Conditional probability, and specifically Bayesian probability, is the basis behind much of this logic used to develop predictive models that are based on multiple decision levels. Even in its simplest form, understanding conditional probability can help with decision making. When designing decision trees or simpler scenarios, conditional probability helps adjust probabilities as new information becomes available. Using the acquisition example above to outline conditional probability, assume a decision tree with probabilities for each outcome has been built with the goal of determining what the likely pro forma capitalization will be. When there are multiple bidders for the firm, each decision branch will end with a different buyer and the various likely capitalizations they will use for the acquisition, with a probability assigned to each outcome. Once it is clear that one of the PE firms will be buying the company, the probabilities for what the final capitalization will be all change because of this new condition.

Bayes's theorem helps show how to adjust the probability of an event as new data is received.

In this case, the goal is solving for the probability of event A occurring if event B has occurred.

The theorem needs three key pieces of data:

1. the probability of an event A occurring, designated by $P(A)$
2. the probability of a second event B occurring, designated by $P(B)$
3. the probability of event B occurring given that A has occurred. This is designated by $P(B|A)$. The vertical line stands for the word *given*, so in the formula below, P stands for *probability*, and $P(A|B)$ reads: *the probability of A given that B has occurred.*

$$P(A|B) = \{P(B|A) \times P(A)\}/P(B)$$

Issues for Data Science and Credit Markets

There are many aspects of credit markets that can add to the complexity of using data science. Each constituent in the market requires a significant amount of descriptive data, such as issuer entity, industry, currency, country of risk, coupon, ranking, maturity, credit rating, call prices, and any special call features. There is also significant market-related data that has to be fed into the database and calculated, including price, spread, yield, and duration, all of which need to include various scenarios. As an example, for yield, there needs to be data for current yield, YTW, YTM, and YTC. The list above is not complete and does not include covenant differences or public stock, or ownership data.

Having good data can also be vital to a database. Unfortunately, pricing data in the credit market adds a level of complexity to creating a good data series. Some debt instruments in the market trade regularly, but others may only trade once a week or once a month, which makes some pricing data more readily available than others. The lack of consistent pricing data can make statistical analysis more difficult and less accurate.

Another factor that adds to the complexity of using data science techniques is the transitional nature of many constituents in these markets, and that requires constant updates. The constituents in the market are constantly changing through new entrants, maturities, calls, upgrades, and downgrades from investment grade and defaults. Most statistical techniques are based on historical data. Therefore any data scientist has to be very cautious—when examining data on the fixed-income market—that the historical data is still relevant to the current market in which investment decisions are being made.

There are also numerous problems that develop in statistical analysis, regardless of which market is being analyzed. Any number of biases can creep into analysis either intentionally or unintentionally. Selection bias and the base rate fallacy are common examples. Other common problems can include designing the analysis poorly, bad data, or gaps in data sets, all of which can distort probabilities. These risks are magnified if the market being analyzed goes through rapid changes. It can be dangerous to blindly follow the results of data output without applying logic and thought. Improper use of even the simplest probability model can result in poor decision making.

Closing Comment

Regression and probability analysis can be incredibly valuable tools to enhance analysis and decision making. They can also improve modeling and forecasting techniques. Data science can enhance them and improve the ability to quickly analyze changes in data. Analysts should embrace these tools and not be worried about them. Credit analysis is more than crunching numbers; it is also about designing how those numbers should be crunched, how they should be analyzed, and how people will react to them. Data analysis is only as good as the data that is being used. In a market that changes so rapidly, always be wary of inputs that might be outdated.

The introduction of more quantitative tools increases the value of interaction with corporate management teams. This is a skill that algorithms still have not yet developed. An understanding of motivations and strategies at the companies that are being analyzed can be a material differentiator in analytical work, and the best insights come from interaction with management.

Closing Comments

WHEN I WAS a teenager and wanted to get my pilot's license, my father bought a small poster for my room. It was a black-and-white photo of a biplane crashed into a tree, with a mangled pilot hanging upside down from the cockpit. The caption read, "Flying is not inherently more dangerous than any other means of transportation. It is just less forgiving." This statement also could describe investing in the leveraged finance market relative to other securities markets.

The market is a valuable financing tool for a diverse universe of corporations around the globe. It has a history of constantly evolving and developing creative ways to meet the needs of these corporations. For these reasons, credit analysts need to try to stay abreast of new developments and structures in the marketplace. Remember not to become complacent and assume that just because something was done one way in one company, or in one bond indenture, the next one will be done the same way.

It is an exciting segment of finance to work in. The market includes companies that are taking risks and trying to grow. It is a market of innovative structures and change. In addition, it is exciting that headlines in the news and breaking stories impact how every day will go.

Because of the leverage on these companies, the thoroughness of the work is key. The higher leverage increases the risks and the rewards. Credit analysts constantly struggle to balance thoroughness and timeliness.

Cynicism can be a positive trait in credit analysis because an analyst must always look at downside possibilities. However, remember that in this market, which is so heavily impacted by events, both negative and positive events can occur for the debt holders.

The basis of credit analysis can seem very simple. There are just two major factors: liquidity and asset value. However, other factors make the analysis more complex. Business trends, event risks, and structural issues all make a huge difference in the outcome for investments in the leverage finance market. Credit analysts always have to be focused and understand that their work will ultimately be used to make a good decision, and they have to understand how that decision fits into the business goal of their enterprise.

Index

www.ingramcontent.com/pod-product-compliance
Ingram Content Group UK Ltd.
Pitfield, Milton Keynes, MK11 3LW, UK
UKHW020704260125
454095UK00004B/47